Contents

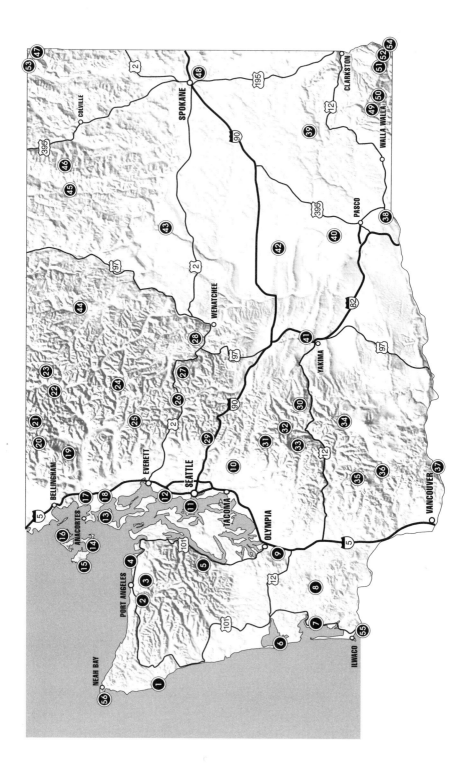

Hiking

WASHINGTON'S GEOLOGY

SCOTT BABCOCK
and
BOB CARSON

**PHOTOGRAPHY BY BOB CARSON
AND KATHLEEN ETHERINGTON**

THE
MOUNTAINEERS

I dedicate these hikes to my father, who first took me hiking; my mother, who paints landscapes; my favorite field assistants, Clare, Ben, Chris, and Henry; and my indispensable helpers, Karen and Patti. I also appreciate the support and companionship of Whitman students and colleagues; an Irish setter, Cinnabar; and an English springer spaniel, Breccia.

—Bob Carson

Published by
The Mountaineers
1001 SW Klickitat Way, Suite 201
Seattle, WA 98134

First printing, 2000

Published simultaneously in Great Britain by Cordee, 3a DeMontfort Street, Leicester, England, LE1 7HD

Manufactured in the United States of America

Managing Editor: Kathleen Cubley
Editor: Lannie MacAndrea
Designer: Ani Rucki
Mapmaker: Moore Creative Designs
All photographs by Bob Carson and Kathleen Etherington

Cover photographs: Background: *Columnar basalts in a cliff near Steamboat Rock State Park in the Grand Coulee.* Inset: *A linear section of the Tye River flowing along a fault zone at the Deception Falls Rest Area off Highway 2 near Stevens Pass.* (Photos by Kathleen Etherington)

Title page photo: *Years of swash and backswash by waves created the "skipping stones" along the shore at Rosario Beach.* (Photo by Kathleen Etherington)

Library of Congress Cataloging-in-Publication Data
Babcock, Scott, 1941–
 Hiking Washington's geology / Scott Babcock and Bob Carson.
  p.   cm.
 Includes bibliographical references and index.
 ISBN 0-89886-548-4
 1. Hiking – Washington (State) – Guidebooks. 2. Geology – Washington (State) – Guidebooks. 3. Washington (State) – Guidebooks. I. Carson, Robert J. II. Title.
 GV199.42.W2 B32 1999
 557.97 – dc21   99-050693
                                                          CIP

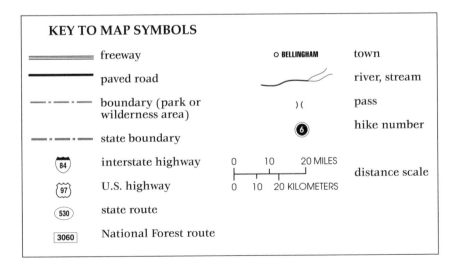

Introduction

Hiking Washington's Geology is written with the hope it will encourage you, the casual walker or serious hiker, to enjoy exploring Washington's geologic wonders and its panoramic landscapes.

The Geology 101 section provides basic information for understanding the rocks and landforms you will see. Additional resources may be found in the General References section. Bolded terms are defined in the Glossary.

These fifty-six hikes have been selected with the intent of covering all regions and as many rock types and landforms as possible. We hope we have included something for everyone. Some hikes are short, less than a mile, and some are 20 miles or more. A majority of the hikes are in mountains or along the shore since this is where geology can best be observed. There are several hikes close to urban areas; these can be easily accomplished in a day. Each hike is fully described, with one-way mileage given (unless a loop is specified), and is assigned a degree of difficulty.

Easy means a walk on well marked trails with no steep climbs or any scary cliffs.

Moderate hikes are a more serious undertaking. You should have a backpack with a water bottle and the Ten Essentials (see Gearing Up for Field Geology, page 9).

Strenuous hikes are for those experienced in backcountry travel who are willing and able to hike uphill and/or many miles on the trail. In addition to the essentials, you should have extra supplies with you.

Directions are provided for each hike. There are a few abbreviations on the route descriptions that you should know: I is for Interstate as in I-5. SR is for State Route, such as State Route 542 that leads from I-5 in Bellingham to the Chain of Lakes hike at Heather Meadows. We use FR for the US Forest Service Roads, US for US Highways, and CR for County Roads. CRiv. indicates river miles or location references on Hike 8.

With the few exceptions noted, all of the hikes are on public lands, so you won't need to worry about obtaining permission for access. Most of the trailheads on federal land, however, require trail park permits. In some cases a right-of-way has been granted through or adjacent to private land. Please respect property rights.

7

The fossils in these shales (from a quarry in Republic) show plants that grew in a Washington forest 50 million years ago.

We have only scratched the surface. If we had written 560 hikes, there would still be many fascinating places left for a sequel, and some of these may be in your own backyard. We hope that in completing these hikes you will develop the skill of reading the stories rocks tell about the history of the earth.

Gearing Up for Field Geology

The classic list of Ten Essentials for backcountry travel first appeared in *Mountaineering, Freedom of the Hills* (The Mountaineers Books), and included a map, a compass, a flashlight, extra food, extra clothing, sunglasses, first-aid supplies, a pocket knife, waterproof matches, and fire-starting material. Other lists of the ten essentials have included a canteen and water purification equipment, large garbage disposal bags that can serve as an emergency shelter or as waterproofing for your pack, a plastic trowel and toilet paper for waste disposal, a whistle or signaling mirror for emergency situations, a cellular phone for the same purpose, and at least $10 in cash. On many hikes you will also want to add sunscreen, insect repellent, rain gear, a hat, 10 feet of nylon cord, a small roll of duct tape, and an ensolite pad or a space blanket.

For observing geology, there could be yet another list of ten essentials, including topographic and geologic maps, a good pair of binoculars, a Global Positioning System (GPS) receiver, a hand lens, a camera and a photo scale, binoculars, a rock hammer and chisel, sample bags and marking pens, a field notebook, and a good reference book for rock and mineral identification.

To be useful for identifying geologic features, the topographic map should be at a scale of no greater than 1:24,000 (the U.S. Geological Survey, or USGS, 7.5-minute quadrangle series use this scale). Most of the geologic maps for Washington are at a scale of 1:100,000 or greater, but several 1:24,000 quadrangle maps are available, especially for the northeast part of the state (see Appendix A). Most topographic maps are available at outdoor-gear stores or at the library. Geologic maps are more difficult to find. The best sources are university libraries and the U.S. Geological Survey (see Appendix A).

GPS receivers have become a favorite new tool of geologists for establishing location, at least partly replacing the highly specialized Bruton compass. Using a GPS unit, you can find your location (plus or minus 100 feet) almost anywhere in Washington, except in deep woods, which can scatter the satellite signals. A GPS unit can also tell you how to get where you want to go, how to get back from where you have been, and how many more miles you have to hike to get where you are going.

One of the best ways to keep track of where you are on the trail is by using aerial photographs. You can obtain them from the U.S. Geological Survey, the EROS Data Center, the Washington Division of Geology and Earth Resources, or even county planning departments. Orthophotoquads are even better because they superimpose topographic lines on an aerial photo. These are available from the Washington State Division of Geology and Earth Resources (see Appendix A).

For identification of minerals and rock textures, a hand lens is essential. We recommend a triplet-type lens that provides several different degrees of magnification. To be useful for geologic purposes, the minimum magnification required is 8x.

A camera is necessary for recording information that is too complex to record in writing. Many geologists now carry a digital camera with a minimum 1024-pixel resolution. But a conventional camera can also be used to capture essential information that might otherwise go unrecorded. APS (Advanced Photo system) cameras are desirable because of their exceptionally small size combined with excellent image quality. In photos of geologic features, it is sometimes difficult to tell how large or small they are. To provide a size comparison, geologists include something, such as a ruler, a coin, or a rock hammer, in their photos.

In order to preserve exceptional outcrops for future generations of observers, hammering and rock collection should be kept to a minimum. You should also observe and obey signs prohibiting collection in parks and other areas you may be visiting. However, where the outcrop is abundant, and collection is permitted, it is legitimate to gather samples. A rock hammer and sometimes a chisel are the necessary tools for doing this job. If you do hammer rocks, be aware that rock chips can do a lot of damage—most geologists have at least one rock-shrapnel scar. Long sleeves and pants are recommended, and *always* wear eye protection when hammering rocks.

If you do collect rocks or minerals, you need to have something in which to put them. Geologists generally use heavy-duty cloth sample bags, but resealable bags also work well. Be sure to label both your sample and your sample bag with a permanent marker. A very effective way to label samples is to make a stripe on the rock with whiteout, and then label the sample with a permanent marking pen.

You will want to bring along a notebook to record your observations. Engineers and field geologists use waterproof notebooks (available at college bookstores or stationary stores). Look for Rite-in-the-Rain notebooks, which are manufactured in Tacoma and come in a variety of sizes. If you choose a regular notebook, be sure to keep it in a resealable plastic bag. You never know when you'll encounter wet weather—or a mud puddle.

A field guide is just as useful for identifying rocks and minerals as birds and flowers.

A final comment on what to wear—your feet are an essential consideration.

To minimize the impact of foot traffic, new conservation ethics call for running shoes rather than hiking boots. This is fine as long as you intend to stay strictly on a well-maintained trail. However, to see some of the geologic features described in this book, you may have to deviate from the trail, and sometimes hike a considerable distance cross-country. Under these circumstances, an ankle-high, lightweight boot with a scree-collar and lug soles would be more practical. The rest of your apparel is a matter of personal preference. Just remember the adage that there is no such thing as bad weather, only inappropriate clothing!

If the hike you're taking is on the Pacific Coast or along the shores of the inland waters, consult a tide guide so that you're on the beach or rocks at low tide. Be cautious of waves, and slippery rocks and logs along the shore and in the mountains.

Do bring curiosity and a willingness to take your time observing along the trail. If you discover any fascinating geologic features that we have missed, let us know via the email addresses listed at the back of the book.

Nature has almost healed the wound of a sign nailed to a tree growing along the Lime Kiln trail on San Juan Island.

Geology 101
What You Need to Know to Read the Rocks of Washington

To fully appreciate the remarkable geology displayed along Washington trails, it is useful to have some background information on the essentials of geologic time, mineral and rock identification, landscape development, and plate **tectonics.** This chapter is a brief summary of the most relevant concepts of an introductory geology course. More detailed information can be found in the books listed in Appendix A. You will find highlighted words in the Glossary at the end of the book.

GEOLOGIC TIME

One of the most difficult concepts for the human mind to comprehend is the immensity of geologic time. The basic method subdivides time into eons, eras, systems, and epochs as shown in figure 1, which also shows some of the most significant events in Washington's geologic history.

In order to visualize geologic time a comparison between the age of the earth and the elevation of Mount Baker might be helpful. The profound length of the Precambrian eon alone would be equivalent to 9100 of the 10,778 feet Mount Baker rises above sea level. Another perspective is this: if Mount Baker represents geologic time elapsed since the earth formed, a human lifespan of 100 years would be equivalent to less than one snowflake on the summit.

MAPPING

One of the primary roles of a geologist is to create maps showing where the rocks of a region are exposed. Rocks that have a similar age and origin are named for places where they are best exposed. The fundamental mappable unit of rock is called a formation. Distinctive rock layers within a formation are known as members. For example, the Chuckanut Formation seen on Hike 17 is named for nearby Chuckanut Mountain. The Chuckanut Formation includes **sandstones** and **conglomerates** of the Bellingham Bay Member. Two or more formations occurring together are called a group or even a supergroup, as in the Columbia River Basalt Group.

MINERALS

Although more than 4000 minerals have been identified, only about a dozen comprise nearly all of the rocks that you will ever see on the trails of Washington. The "top twelve" minerals are listed along with their diagnostic properties in figure 2. Feldspars are by far the most common, appearing in about half of all rocks exposed in Washington. Quartz is found in about 10 percent, followed by mica, amphibole/pyroxene, and clay at about 5 percent each. The rest range from uncommon to unusual.

FIGURE 1				
Time Scale and Geologic Events in Washington				
ERA	**PERIOD**	**EPOCH**	**TIME (MIL. YRS.)**	**EVENT**
Cenozoic	Quaternary	Holocene	.01 to present	Great earthquakes in western Washington
		Pleistocene	2 to .01	Glaciation in Puget Lowland
		Pliocene	5–2	Ringold Formation in Pasco Basin
	Tertiary	Miocene	23–5	Columbia River basalts
		Oligocene	38–23	Ohanapecosh Formation in South Cascades
		Eocene	54–38	Crescent basalts in Olympics
		Paleocene	65–54	
Mesozoic	Cretaceous		146–65	Terrane accretion in the North Cascades
	Jurassic		208–146	Terrane accretion in the Okanogan Highlands
	Triassic		245–208	Blue Mountains terranes form
Paleozoic	Permian		286–245	Knob Hill Group of Okanogan Highlands
	Carboniferous		360–286	Grass Mountain carbonates of northeast Washington
	Devonian		410–360	Chilliwack Group of North Cascades
	Silurian		440–410	Basalt Hill sediments of northeast Washington
	Ordovician		505–440	Ledbetter slates of northeast Washington
	Cambrian		544–505	Metaline Limestone of northeast Washington
Precambrian			4600–544	Quartzite at Steptoe Butte

FIGURE 2
Common Minerals in Washington

Feldspars	Rectangular shape. *Plagioclase:* white to gray. *Orthoclase:* pink.
Quartz	Rounded to hexagonal grains, clear to white, scratches glass.
Mica	Clear, brown, or black. Flakes or sheets.
Pyriboles	Brown, black, or dark green. *Amphibole:* in prisms or needles with diamond shape. *Pyroxene:* chunks with square shape.
Iron Oxides	Red, yellow, or orange coating on weathered rocks.
Clay	Tan, brown, or cream-colored masses. Easily scratched with fingernail.
Calcite	Clear to white or gray masses. Sometime appears in rhombs.
Epidote	Yellow-green crystals or veins.
Serpentine	Green to black masses and veins. Easily scratched with knife.
Olivine	Green masses or crystals weathering orange.
Pyrite	Brassy-yellow cubes.
Garnet	Dark red, equidimensional crystals.

IGNEOUS ROCKS

The common denominator of **igneous rocks** is that once they all were molten. **Volcanic** rocks (named for Vulcan, the Norse god of fire) crystallize at or near the surface of the earth. These can be simply classified according to color.

Good examples of light-colored **rhyolite** and **dacite** can be seen as **dikes** around Harts Pass (Hike 23) and as flows or ash layers along the Kennedy Hot Springs trail (Hike 24). Intermediate gray, green, brown, and reddish **andesites** form most of the major volcanoes of the Cascade Range, including Mount Baker (Hikes 19 and 20) and Mount Rainier (Hikes 31 and 32). Dark brown to black **basalts** are extruded as individual flows such as the Ape Caves basalt of Mount St. Helens (Hike 36), or as vast **lava** plateaus such as the Columbia River basalts at Palouse Falls (Hike 39) and Steamboat Rock (Hike 43).

If gas is abundant in the melt, a rock froth can be formed during eruption. This solidifies to make the **pumice** found along the Hummocks trail (Hike 35). Within volcanic vents, blocks of rock can be ripped off and included within the extruding lava; this produces the volcanic **breccia** found along the Chain of Lakes trail (Hike 20).

Melts that crystallize underground form **plutonic** rocks, named after the Roman god of the underworld, Pluto. Due to slower cooling rates, the mineral crystals are generally much larger than in volcanic rocks, although some lava flows contain large **phenocrysts** that formed when the lava was deep underground. Conspicuous phenocrysts in andesite are found in the vicinity of Table Mountain (Hike 20).

Columbia River basalt flows near Dayton

Granites and **granodiorites,** such as those making up Plummer Peak (Hike 33), are light-colored because they are composed dominantly of quartz and feldspar. Diorites are made of a roughly equal mix of light feldspar and dark mica or hornblende, as seen on the Kettle Crest trail (Hike 46). **Gabbro** is usually composed of dark feldspar and pyroxene. This rock type is uncommon, but can be found near the Copper Ridge lookout (Hike 21). **Ultramafics** are composed predominantly of olivine and pyroxene. These rocks are rare in most places, but the Twin Sisters Range seen from the Park Butte lookout on Hike 19 represents the largest exposure of its type in the world.

SEDIMENTARY ROCKS

The minerals in **sedimentary rocks** are the products of weathering and **erosion.** These **sediments** are called clastic if they are bits of preexisting rock, or chemical if they form by precipitation from a solution. Some sedimentary rocks also contain organic material from the remains of plants and animals.

Clastic rocks consist mainly of quartz, feldspar, and clay, which are the

Folded sedimentary rocks on the Olympic Peninsula

survivors of weathering by mechanical breakdown and chemical reactions. They are generally classified according to grain size, shape, and composition. For example, the clastic rocks of the Chuckanut Formation (Hike 17) are deposits of a stream system that flowed across Washington 50 million years ago. The clays of the floodplains formed shales, while the sand and pebbles of the stream channels formed sandstones and conglomerates.

If the pebble sized fragments are angular instead of rounded, as at Cape Flattery (Hike 56), the rock type is called a breccia. Chemical and organic sedimentary rocks are named primarily on the basis of composition. Thus the calcium **carbonate** rock that makes up Gardner Cave (Hike 53) is called a **limestone,** while the carbonized plant remains found in the vicinity of Flaming Geyser (Hike 10) are coal.

METAMORPHIC ROCKS

Metamorphic rocks have all changed form either by deformation or recrystallization, but without melting. There are three types of metamorphism: (1) dynamic, where the rocks have been stretched or broken by intense pressure; (2) thermal, where the rocks have been baked at temperatures above 200 degrees Celsius; and (3) regional, where the rocks have been changed by both heat and pressure.

Dynamic metamorphism occurs mainly in the vicinity of fault zones and typically produces mylonites, like those seen on the Ross Dam trail (Hike 22).

Gneiss in the North Cascades

Thermal metamorphism occurs around the margins of plutonic rocks such as the **granodiorite** of Denny Creek (Hike 29), where the heat of the granite has baked shales into a flinty rock called **hornfels.** Also, hot fluids have reacted with limestones to form spectacular **skarns.** Regional metamorphic rocks develop in the roots of mountain ranges where the heat and pressure are high enough to recrystallize the original minerals of igneous and sedimentary rocks to new metamorphic minerals.

Foliation, another change, occurs when minerals are squeezed into parallel alignment. As any stone mason knows, metamorphic rocks, like **schist** will split along planes of foliation, just as wood will split along the grain.

Deeper within a mountain range, as the temperature and pressure increase, the nature of the metamorphism changes. The initial stages of metamorphism produce the **argillites** and semi-schists seen along the Hurricane Hill trail (Hike 3). Deeper within the earth, a stronger foliation develops, forming slates of Slate Peak (Hike 23) that split into sheets like a blackboard. Still deeper yet, the foliation is crinkled into accordian-folds making phyllites, like those that crop out on the Bat Caves trail (Hike 18). In schists (Hike 27), the foliation is so extensive that visible mineral grains have grown, unlike slates and phyllites in which the mineral changes are microscopic. At even higher temperatures, chemical elements in the rock become so mobile that metamorphic minerals segregate into light and dark bands, forming a gneiss (Hike 22). In some regionally metamorphosed rocks, the heat is sufficient to cause thorough recrystallization, but the pressure is not high enough to form foliation. Examples are the quartzites of the Elk Creek trail (Hike 46).

PLATE TECTONICS

If you are sitting in a chair reading this book somewhere in Washington, you are taking a ride on the North American Plate, which is moving westerly at about the same speed as your fingernails grow. The plate movement is powered by huge currents that move through the mantle of the earth, slowly driving tectonic plates like blocks of ice in the Arctic Ocean. Plate velocities range from less than 1 to as much as 6 inches per year. This is far less than a snail's pace, but ultimately all of the rocks of Washington have been moved by this plate motion.

Mount Baker (Hikes 19 and 20), Glacier Peak (Hike 24), Mount Rainier (Hikes 31, 32, and 33), and Mount St. Helens (Hikes 35 and 36) are the most obvious consequence of plate tectonic processes. These big volcanoes formed as a result of **subduction:** the seafloor of the Juan de Fuca Plate moving easterly forced under the westerly moving North American Plate. Another rock type related to subduction is **melange** that consists of churned up marine sediments

Dome in crater of Mount St. Helens

along with bits and pieces of seafloor rock that have been scraped off the top of the Juan de Fuca Plate as it descends. Good outcrops of this rock are found at Third Beach (Hike 1) and Hurricane Hill (Hike 3).

Earthquakes are another outcome of subduction. This process is not smooth; the Juan de Fuca Plate jerks under the edge of North America once every 300 to 500 years or so. If it moves 30 feet or more, a magnitude 8 to 9 earthquake occurs and the landscape of the Pacific Northwest is instantly rearranged. Giant landslides like the one that created Crescent Lake (Hike 2) and the "ghost forests" along the Washington coast (Hike 7) provide evidence that great earthquakes of this magnitude have occurred within the past few thousand years. Fortunately, earthquakes of this magnitude are infrequent. Magnitude 6 to 7 earthquakes, however, can be expected every 35 years. The last one was in 1965, so the next one is about due.

In addition to the major plates (e.g., the North American Plate) there are numerous microplates (also known as **exotic terranes**) that range from tens to hundreds of miles in size. One example of a microplate is Baja California and California west of the San Andreas fault. This block of the earth has been detached from North America and is now moving northward on the Pacific Plate. If the present rate of motion continues, Los Angeles will be at the same latitude as Seattle in about 25 million years and will become part of southeast Alaska about 50 million years from now. The same northward progression of microplates has apparently been going on for at least the past 160 million years;

much of Washington is composed of a mosaic of microplates that originated to the south. Just how far south is the subject of heated debate. Some geologists think the transport distances on the "Great Northern Express" amount to a thousand miles or more. Others argue that the distance traveled could not have been more than a few hundred miles. Whatever the distance traveled, it is clear that 180 million years ago the only land area in Washington was in the extreme northeast corner of the state. Then Quesnellia was added, followed by the **terranes** of the North Cascades.

About 90 million years ago, Wrangellia slammed into the edge of North America creating widespread melting and metamorphism throughout the North Cascades and Okanogan Highlands. By 60 million years ago the shoreline was in the Puget Lowland. Some geologists believe that the process of microplate accretion continued and that the Olympics and Willapa Hills represent a series of oceanic islands (like Hawaii) that were swept by subduction onto the continental margin about 40 million years ago. However, recent evidence indicates that the sedimentary rocks and basalts of the Olympics originated in a great rift valley along the continental margin, like present-day East Africa.

LANDFORMS

A famous American geomorphologist, W.M. Davis, stated that landforms are the result of structure, process, and stage. In his time, at the turn of the century, structure referred to the starting materials, their composition, fracture density, resistance to degradation, attitude, etc. For example, quartzites are more resistant than shales; granites with closely spaced fractures are more erodible than massive granites. Attitude refers to the orientation of bedding (or fractures). For example, coastal landforms would vary, even with the same rock, depending on whether the strata are horizontal, gently or steeply inclined, and/or perpendicular or parallel to wave attack.

Process refers to the geomorphic agent operating at the earth's surface, and may even include internal processes. Agents include ice, water, and wind. Some geomorphologists divide processes into ten groups: volcanism, tectonism (bending and breaking, often accompanied by earthquakes), weathering and soil formation, mass wasting (landslides and related phenomena), running water, wind, glaciers, periglacial phenomena (dominated by freezing and thawing), karst (e.g., limestone cavern development), and waves.

Stage refers to time. Landforms evolve. The longer the period of time waves attack a coast at a particular point, the more potential there is for erosion and deposition. Sea cliffs may get higher, beaches may get wider.

A landform built by one process may be degraded by others. A **moraine** deposited during the Little Ice Age a few hundred years ago is likely to have steep slopes, a sharp crest, and little soil. A moraine deposited during the last continental glaciation 20,000 years ago has been subjected to weathering, creep, and erosion, so that it has gentler slopes, a rounded crest, and a well-developed soil. A moraine deposited during the previous glaciation 200,000 years ago may be so degraded that it is difficult to recognize.

It is important to realize that most landscapes are polygenetic; that is, different processes have operated separately or together at different rates and for different time periods. The following is a summary of the influence on landscapes by each of the processes.

VOLCANISM

Volcanic landforms are very much related to the explosivity of the **magma.** Basaltic magmas usually result in quiet eruptions because the magma is relatively fluid and not rich in gasses. Basaltic magma may be so fluid that it does not pile up near the vent and make a volcano. Instead, the magma travels some distance, making a thin lava flow. Many superimposed basaltic lava flows construct a basalt plateau. The earth's youngest basalt plateau is the Columbia Basin of the Pacific Northwest; it has only a few small volcanoes (Hike 51). If basaltic magma is a little more viscous, the lava flows do not travel far from the **vent,** and a gently sloped shield volcano (like those in Hawaii) is constructed. If the basaltic magma is a little more gaseous, small explosions pile up cinders and ash near the vent, building a **pyroclastic** cone (like those at Schreibers Meadow, Hike 19).

Pyroclastic debris

Rhyolitic and dacitic magmas generally are explosive because they are viscous and have a high gas content. Ash may be blown high into the atmosphere, transported downwind, and settle to the earth as an ash fall deposit as can be seen on Hike 19. Pyroclastics (a general term for ash, cinders, and pumice) may also sweep down the side of a volcano like a liquid and settle to rest as a pyroclastic flow deposit such as seen on Hike 24. If rhyolitic or dacitic magma happens to have a low gas content, the high viscosity of the lava flow prevents it from going far from the vent. A typical landform would be a volcanic dome such as the one in the Mount St. Helens crater.

Andestic magmas are typically intermediate in explosivity. If there is a high gas content, pyroclastics are generated. If there is a low gas content, the lava flow is shorter and thicker than most basalt flows. Most andesitic volcanoes produce both pyroclastics and lava flows; the combination creates a stratovolcano or composite cone like Mount Rainier (Hikes 31 and 32).

Some volcanoes erupt different magma compositions at different times. A good example is Mount St. Helens, which has erupted everything from a basalt flow (Hike 36) to dacitic pyroclastics (Hike 35).

TECTONISM

Plate tectonic activity results in differential movement of parts of the earth's crust at different scales and over different time periods. Over millions of years the large Colorado Plateau was uplifted 2 miles with relatively little internal deformation. The somewhat smaller Teton Range in Wyoming was uplifted as a fault block, with the adjacent Jackson Hole subsiding. The Pacific coast of Washington may drop 5 to 10 feet in seconds during great earthquakes. Tectonics not only move land up, down, and sideways (as on California's San Andreas fault), but tilt, bend, and break rocks.

The Tertiary strata in the vicinity of the Columbia River Gorge are tilted to the south. The Columbia River cut down through these strata, so the rocks on the north side of the gorge slide downhill toward the river. The result is a high frequency of huge landslides on the Washington side of the Columbia River Gorge (Hike 37).

Compression of a portion of the earth's crust is likely to lead to folding of the strata. A very impressive group of folds exists in south-central Washington (Hike 41). **Anticlines** (uparched strata) alternate with **synclines** (downwarped strata). The strata of the Yakima Fold Belt are basalt flows and sedimentary interbeds.

Tectonic forces may break rocks with the resulting faults steeply dipping (even vertical) to gently dipping (even horizontal in places). The sense of motion of the adjacent rock masses may be vertical, sideways, or oblique. Perhaps the most spectacular tectonic feature in the Pacific Northwest is the Olympic-

Wallowa **lineament.** Just north of Hike 38, this lineament has geomorphic evidence that the south block moved up, but slickenlines (scratches on the fault plane) indicate that the most recent fault motion was nearly horizontal.

WEATHERING AND SOIL FORMATION

Weathering is the reaction of rocks and sediments to the atmosphere, hydrosphere (water), and biosphere (living organisms). Weathering includes two groups of processes: physical disintegration and chemical decomposition, which usually work together and may be aided by organisms.

Physical weathering results in the breaking of rock into smaller pieces. This contributes to the effectiveness of chemical weathering because chemical reactions occur on surfaces, and smaller pieces have more surface area. Geologists have long debated whether or not temperature changes can break rocks. It is unlikely that daily temperature changes are effective, but the sudden heat of a forest fire can cause slabs to spall off rocks. Another type of physical weathering is the growth of crystals. Ocean waves splash onto coasts and seawater permeates the rocks; the salt crystals that grow during evaporation may pry out particles of rock. Ice is the most widespread crystal that grows and is the dominant force in the periglacial environment.

Chemical weathering is the reaction of minerals in rocks to the water and air near the earth's surface. Precipitation is naturally acidic because carbon dioxide dissolved in rain makes carbonic acid. Feldspars, the most common minerals, are altered to clay minerals. The red colors often seen between lava

Caliche (calcium carbonate) horizons in loess (wind-deposited silt), Palouse Hills

23

flows are due to oxidation of iron silicates to iron oxides and hydroxides.

Soils form at the earth's surface. Soils may be transported or residual. Transported soils include **alluvium** (the general term for stream deposits), **drift** (glacial deposits), **eolian** sediments (wind deposits), and volcanic ash. Residual soils are mainly due to chemical weathering of rocks. Of course, a transported soil may be altered by chemical weathering.

The six soil forming factors result in different soils. 1) Parent material: a residual soil developed on granite is different from one weathered from basalt. 2) Organisms: soils vary based on the biota present, especially microorganisms; the soil determines what organisms (such as crops) can grow, and the organisms (such as burrowing rodents) influence the characteristics of the soil. 3) Topography: soil is more susceptible to erosion on steep slopes; high areas are generally well drained; bottomlands may have waterlogged soils. 4) Climate: chemical weathering proceeds at a faster pace in warm moist climates; **caliche** (calcium carbonate) is common in the soils of arid eastern Washington. 5) Time: more time allows for more weathering; a thick residual soil generally takes hundreds of thousands of years to develop. 6) Humans: people add fertilizers and pesticides, irrigate arid lands, and may accelerate soil erosion.

MASS WASTING

Weathering prepares the way for **mass wasting** and erosion as it weakens rocks. Mass wasting is downslope movement of earth material in response to gravity without the aid of an agent like water, wind, or ice. Streams and glaciers flow downhill in response to gravity, but this is not mass wasting. Water in a hillside reduces internal friction and increases the likelihood of slope failure.

Mass wasting can be slow or fast; the material may fall, slide, or flow. On many slopes you'll see trees with curved trunks bending downhill in response to creep of soil or snow. The huge landslides in the Columbia River Gorge (Hike 37) are flowing, generally slowly and intermittently. Mount Rainier has been the site of many rapid mass wasting events including the Osceola Mudflow about 6000 years ago and the Little Tahoma rockfalls in 1963 (Hike 31). The entrance to many **lava tubes** (Hike 36) is through a window where the roof has collapsed (this is a type of rapid **subsidence**).

Colluvium is the general term for any material that has undergone mass wasting. The term landslide is a general one and refers to any type of mass wasting except creep or subsidence. The term mudslide, popular with the media, is usually a misnomer since mud generally flows rather then slides.

RUNNING WATER

When precipitation hits the ground, some evaporates, some percolates into the soil and rocks, and some runs across the surface. The surface water may begin as a sheet, but soon cuts a small channel (a gully that holds water only when it rains). The little channels connect into successively larger channels until there is a permanent stream. The stream flows even when it is not raining because the precipitation that infiltrated the surface became groundwater that slowly travels to the stream channel.

Most valleys are cut by streams. On the floors of most valleys there are floodplains of alluvium. Streams with gentle slopes and relatively fine-grained loads of sediment usually meander (Hike 8). A braided stream has a steeper slope and lots of coarse-grained alluvium (Hike 31). Where a tributary stream's gradient decreases as it enters a main valley, it is common for an **alluvial fan** to be deposited. Where a stream slows as it enters a lake or the sea, a delta is deposited.

Braided meltwater stream, White River on Mount Rainier

WIND

Wind is not very effective at erosion except in a few places like parts of the Sahara Desert. Wind transports silt-sized particles in suspension; wind deposits silt (**loess**) as a blanket. Loess is a common component of soil, and reaches a great thickness in the Palouse Hills of eastern Washington.

Wind transports sand-sized particles by saltation (bouncing) and by surface creep. The sand grains accumulate in dunes of various shapes and sizes. Dunes are found in deserts and along coasts; dune fields are scattered across eastern Washington (Hike 42).

GLACIERS

Glaciers, landforms in and of themselves, come in many sizes and shapes. The earth's largest glacier during the Pleistocene Ice Age stretched from eastern Greenland to western British Columbia. The southwest corner of this continental **ice sheet** invaded Washington from the northern Olympic Peninsula to the Okanogan Highlands. A much smaller mountain ice cap buried all but the highest Olympic summits. Today, only valley and **cirque** glaciers occupy the higher parts of the Olympics and Cascades.

A cirque is an armchair shaped depression on a mountain carved by a small equidimensional cirque glacier. These small glaciers may advance downhill, join, and fill a stream valley. The resulting valley glacier deepens, steepens, and straightens the former valley, turning it into a glacial trough (popularly called a U-shaped valley). A long lake in such a trough is simply a glacial trough lake; examples are Lake Washington in the Puget Lowland and Crescent Lake on the northern Olympic Peninsula.

A **fjord** is a glacial trough invaded by the sea; the best example is Eastsound

Ripples on sand dune

Blue Glacier on Mount Olympus

in the San Juan Islands. Some geologists consider Hood Canal and the arms of Puget Sound to be fjords.

Cirque glaciers eat away at mountains, turning them into three- or four-sided pyramids called **horns** (like the Matterhorn in the Alps, or Pinnacle Peak on Hike 33). An **arête** is a sharp ridge that has been eroded by cirque (and valley) glaciers on both sides. Glaciers may erode a low point, or **col,** on an arête, which may be a pass across the mountains.

A glacier erodes by plucking or quarrying rocks bounded by **joints** and/or bedding planes (particularly on downglacier slopes) and by abrading rocks with the tools (sediment) at its base (particularly on upglacier slopes). The abrasion leaves grooves, striations, and polish on the rock surfaces (Hike 14).

The general term for all glacial deposits is drift. Because glaciers are so viscous, they transport rocks of all sizes, and deposit them together in a material called till. In contrast, a river sorts sediments, flowing around and over boulders, depositing cobbles, pebbles, and sand in bars, and transporting silt and clay to a lake or the sea. The wind can move only sand and finer grains, but is excellent at sorting the sediment, transporting the finest sediment the farthest. Glacial meltwater leaves the largest boulders behind, deposits cobbles, pebbles, and some sand as a type of drift called **outwash,** and transports some sand plus silt and clay in suspension to a lake or the sea.

Some glacial landforms are composed of drift. Moraines are ridges of **till** deposited at the edge of a glacier (Hike 31). Outwash is deposited as an outwash plain downvalley of a glacier; this plain may later be incised by a stream to leave outwash terraces on the valley sides.

PERIGLACIAL LANDFORMS
The periglacial environment is one too dry for glaciers, but cold enough for freezing and thawing to be very effective at breaking rocks, accelerating

Glacial striations

creep, and sorting sediment. The increase in volume as water turns to ice in a crack may break rocks that then may fall from a cliff to form a **talus** below. Freezing and thawing of the soil (as well as processes like wetting and drying, warming and cooling) cause volume changes; this expansion and contraction causes the surface layer of a slope to creep downslope. Freezing and thawing also sorts sediment by heaving stones up out of finer sediment (only millimeters per freeze-thaw cycle, but the results may be significant after thousands of years).

The coldest periglacial environments are underlain by permafrost, or permanently frozen ground. Permafrost is widespread at high latitudes such as northern Alaska where repeated freezing and thawing result in periglacial landforms such as patterned ground. Permafrost was much more widespread during glacial periods. The stone-ringed silt mounds on the tops of some of the Yakima Hills are evidence of a former periglacial environment.

KARST

Karst landforms develop as water dissolves soluble rocks such as limestone. Worldwide, the most common karst landform is the sink, a depression a few

Patterned ground in the Yakima Hills

tens of feet to a few miles in diameter. The depressions are due to a solution of limestone near the surface, or below the surface so that collapse eventually occurs.

Caverns, widespread in parts of eastern and central United States, are better known than sinks. Caverns form as groundwater moves through soluble rocks, widening fractures into passages and then partly filling the passages with stalactites and stalagmites. The Pacific Northwest has few limestone caverns. Gardner Cave, one of the longest caves in Washington, has a slope length of a little more than 1000 feet (Hike 53).

WAVES

Waves are the dominant process along the coast of Washington and along the shores of inland waters including Puget Sound, large lakes, and reservoirs. Where coastal waves attack resistant rocks like basalt, there are sea cliffs with some sea caves and rare arches (Hike 56). Where coastal waves attack erodible rocks like mudstone, there are embayments with beaches. The main sources of beach sediment are bluffs eroded by waves and sediment moved to the coast by rivers. The waves move the sediment along the coast, in places forming long peninsulas like Dungeness Spit (Hike 4).

The drift of the Puget Lowland is relatively erodible. Waves along Hood Canal, Puget Sound, and elsewhere undermine the drift until landslides occur. The waves then erode the colluvium, transport it along the shore, and

Wave-cut cliffs, sea caves, and pocket beach on Olympic Peninsula

deposit the sand, pebbles, and cobbles as beaches. Some of the finer-grained sediment is moved into quieter places like bays, where there are mudflats exposed at low tide. Because the prevailing wind in Washington is from the southwest, the dominant direction that sediments are transported along the shores is to the north and east.

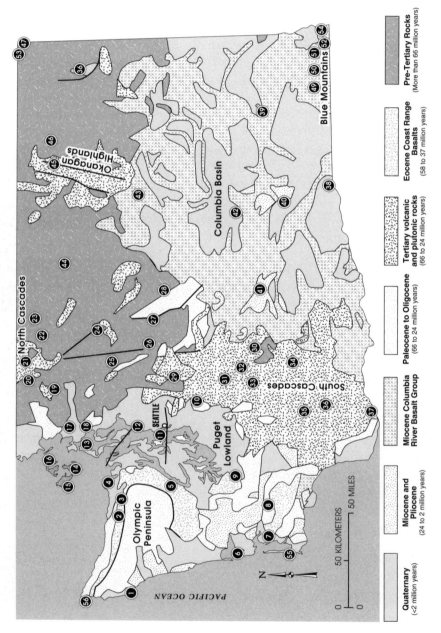

Chapter 1
COAST RANGES

Glaciated Olympic Mountains

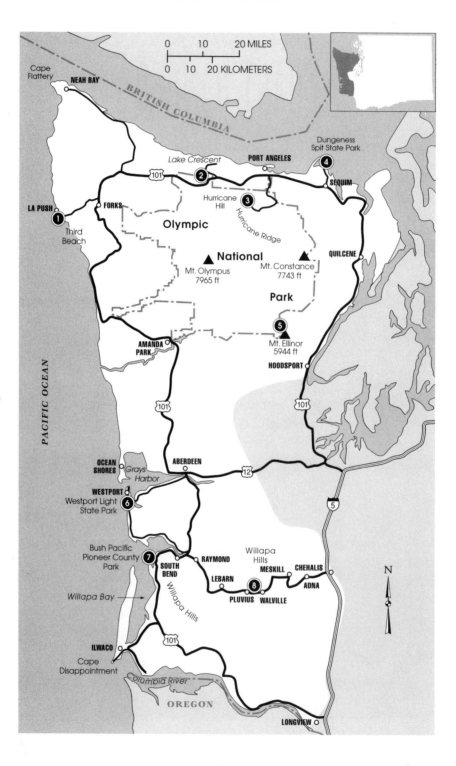

The Washington Coast Ranges include both the Olympic Peninsula on the north and the Willapa Hills on the south. The province is bounded by the Pacific Ocean to the west, the Strait of Juan de Fuca to the north (including the southernmost part of Vancouver Island across the strait), and the Puget Lowland to the east. The Oregon Coast Ranges to the south contain similar rocks and landforms.

Almost all bedrock of the Olympic Peninsula is of volcanic or sedimentary origin, and accumulated on the floor of the Pacific Ocean during the Tertiary period. The volcanic rocks are varieties of basalt. The sedimentary rocks are quite varied, from conglomerates to mudstones, with lots of sandstone and siltstone, and even a little limestone.

Two major tectonic domains can be recognized in the Coast Ranges. Originally, these were named the Core Rocks and the Peripheral Rocks (figure 3). Both domains contain rocks of Paleocene to Miocene age, but are of different composition and are everywhere separated by the Hurricane Ridge fault. The Core Rocks are also known as the Olympic Subduction Complex because they consist mainly of melange that has been scraped off the Juan de Fuca Plate

figure 3. Tectonic domains of the Olympic Peninsula

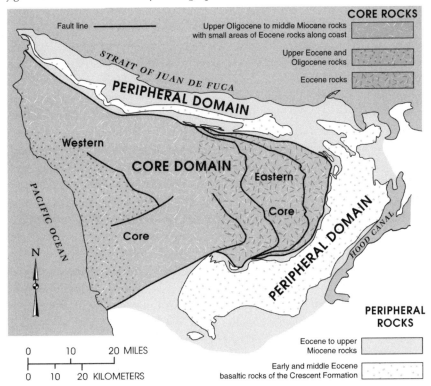

as it has moved beneath the North American Plate at the Cascadia subduction zone.

The subduction process that formed these melanges still continues, as indicated by evidence for recent downwarping of the Washington coast (Hike 7). Due to burial in the Cascadia subduction zone, the Core Rocks have been variably metamorphosed and deformed. However the intensity generally decreases from east to west. To the east, the sedimentary rocks have been metamorphosed to slate or phyllite, and the basalts to **greenstone.** Folding and faulting is intense in places. To the west, metamorphism is weak to nonexistent. At least two separate terranes have been defined within the Core (figure 4). The Ozette terrane is an Eocene melange and comprises most of the Olympic Mountains including Hurricane Hill (Hike 3). The Hoh terrane is younger (late Oligocene to Miocene) and is found mainly along the Olympic Coast between Third Beach (Hike 1) and Point Grenville. The Peripheral Rocks surround the Core Rocks like a giant horseshoe (figure 3). This package of rocks, also known as the Crescent terrane, is like a sandwich with sedimentary rocks as the bread and basalt as the filling. The basalt is thick, perhaps as much as 10 miles, and resistant, so mountains of basalt dominate the landscape of the northern, eastern, and southern Olympics including Mount Ellinor (Hike 5) and Hurricane Hill (Hike 3).

Much of the volcanic rock is pillow basalt formed on the seafloor (Hikes 2, 3, and 8). This huge stack of basalt must have originated either as a chain of seamounts like the Hawaiian Islands, or as great rifts in the earth like the East African rift valleys.

About 40 million years ago, it appears that the Crescent basalts were jammed underneath the southern edge of Vancouver Island forming a deep marine trough known as the Tofino-Fuca Basin. During late Eocene to Miocene time this was slowly filled with sediments eroded from adjacent land areas. Sandstones of the Aldwell Formation seen along the Spruce Railroad Trail (Hike 2) and the Lyre conglomerates of the Cape Flattery area (Hike 56) are good examples.

Most of the existing glaciers occupy small cirques high in the mountains. On Mount Olympus, the cirque glaciers have expanded downhill into valley glaciers as much as 3 miles long. During the glacial periods of the Pleistocene, the glaciers got longer and thicker and reached well beyond the front of the mountains, burying most of the Olympic Peninsula under a mountain ice cap. The maximum extent of ice originating in the Olympic Mountains (during the last glaciation) occurred about 18,000 years ago.

On the north and east sides of the peninsula, the Olympic ice merged with a larger glacier, the Cordilleran Ice Sheet. Specifically, lobes of the Cordilleran Ice Sheet, which originated in the many mountain ranges of British Columbia,

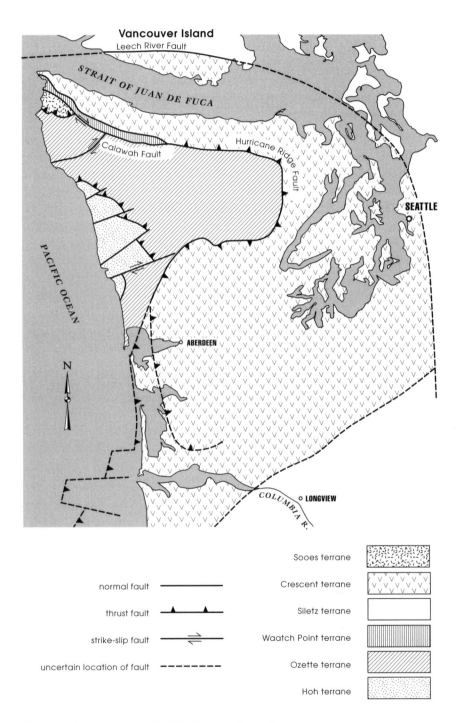

figure 4. Terrane map of the Washington Coast Ranges

extended westward out the Strait of Juan de Fuca, and southward to occupy the Puget Lowland. The Cordilleran Ice Sheet reached its maximum extent (during the last glaciation) about 14,000 years ago. By that time the Olympic ice had retreated significantly, so that the Cordilleran Ice Sheet transported granitic boulders from British Columbia into Olympic valleys. The granites can be seen along the shore at Dungeness Spit (Hike 4).

As the Pleistocene gave way to the Holocene about 10,000 years ago, most of the world's ice melted, and sea level rose about 400 feet, filling Puget Sound and Grays Harbor. This has caused extensive erosion along the outer coast of the Coast Ranges, as indicated by the steep sea cliffs of Third Beach (Hike 1) and the problematic jetty area at Westport (Hike 6).

Hike 1

THIRD BEACH

A walk along a wild portion of the northern Olympic Coast to view the mixed up rocks of a subduction zone.

DISTANCE ■ 3 miles

ELEVATION ■ 250 feet to sea level

DIFFICULTY ■ Moderate

TOPOGRAPHIC MAPS ■ USGS Toleak Point; Custom Correct South Olympic Coast; Green Trails La Push

GEOLOGIC MAP ■ DGER GM-24 Washington Coast

KEY REFERENCES ■ Orange and others (1993); Rau (1980)

About the Landscape: The rocks exposed along Third Beach are part of the Hoh rock assemblage, mostly sediments deposited on the seafloor, carried down a subduction zone, and then thrust back up to the surface. During this process, the rocks were literally shredded into a highly deformed rock type called melange, a French word meaning mixed. The melange includes a conglomerate that was part of a river delta, and sandstones, shales, and **cherts** that were marine sedimentary rocks and basalts of the seafloor itself. Apparently there was abundant organic material carried down into the subduction zone. This organic material has been converted to petroleum, which forms the brownish seeps seen along the beach.

Trail Guide: Turn off US 101, 1 mile north of Forks, and follow the La Push road to the well-marked trailhead 11.3 miles from the junction. There is an excellent trail to the beach, but the route south to Taylor Point involves some scrambling up the bluff and climbing on sand ladders.

The melange begins when you descend the coastal bluffs to the shoreline

These rocks of the Hoh melange were mangled as they were stuffed down and thrust back out of a subduction zone along the Washington coast.

after a pleasant walk through a mature spruce forest, replete with nurse logs and blowdowns which indicate the high velocity wind storms that sometimes hit this coast. Start your beach walk by heading north. Numerous slumps and debris falls indicate that the slope is very unstable. Take some time at one of the cliff exposures to see the Hoh melange, consisting of broken blocks of durable sandstone and chert floating in a twisted matrix of a clay-rich rock called argillite. These rocks have a fascinating history. They started life as marine sediments deposited on the Juan de Fuca Plate, then were jammed down the Cascadia subduction zone as deep as 15 miles. They are back at the surface now, regurgitated as more and more sediments were stuffed in behind them, a sort of geologic binge and purge.

At low tide you can see fingerlike seeps of goo coming out of the melange. These seeps contain petroleum that somehow accumulated in the subduction zone.

There are rusting remnants of equipment used to drill an exploratory oil well in the early 1900s in the woods at the north end of the beach that are worth checking out if you have time for a little side exploration.

The beach ends at Teahwit Head, which is impassable, so turn around and head back south toward Taylor Head. Most of the boulders on the beach are sandstone, siltstone, and chert, but here and there are hard green blocks of spilite, basalt from the seafloor altered by the circulation of hot fluids and by metamorphism in the subduction zone. All of these blocks have been left behind as the erodible part of the melange was washed away by wave action.

Notice the waterfall as you look south toward Taylor Head and the **sea stacks** of the Giant Graveyard. Shoreline erosion has been much more rapid than stream downcutting, so the valley is left hanging above the beach with the resultant waterfall.

Near the waterfall, the boulders on the beach are dominated by conglomerate, which has fallen from the layered cliffs above. A major fault zone has jammed these rocks from the Hoh Sedimentary Sequence into the melange.

The conglomerate boulders mark the point of return for casual hikers. From now on, the trail is challenging. From the beach, scramble up the bluffs, where you will find a series of sand ladders that will take you progressively up, over, and around Taylor Point. While sand ladders are not for anyone suffering from fear of heights, they will lead you to some very interesting geology.

Looking south, as you come out of the woods after ascending the sand ladders, you can observe some of the recent deposits of the Olympic Coast. The uppermost buff-colored layers are loess, fine sand, and silt deposited by the wind after the glaciers melted away. Underneath the loess are thin beds of silt and sand with lots of carbonized branches and logs; probably interglacial floodplain deposits. Below this are the conglomerates and massive sandstones of the Hoh melange.

As you descend to the beach at Scotts Bluff, the Hoh melange appears again, indicating you have crossed the boundary of the Taylor Point fault block. Notice that the bedrock forms a wave cut terrace now nearly 150 feet above sea level. This means there has been substantial uplift of the Olympic coast in the last 8000 years. It is estimated that more than two miles of shoreline erosion has occurred during this time, and it is obvious that rapid erosion continues today.

There is a fabulous hike along some of the most spectacular coastal terrain in the world if you care to continue south another 14 miles to the next road access point at Oil City on the Hoh River. But from a geologic viewpoint you have been there and done that; the rest of the rocks are similar to what you've seen.

Hike 2

SPRUCE RAILROAD TRAIL

A walk through the woods along the shore of Lake Crescent reveals deposits of an ancient seafloor.

DISTANCE ■ 1.5 miles

ELEVATION ■ 600 feet to 450 feet (lake level)

DIFFICULTY ■ Easy

TOPOGRAPHIC MAPS ■ USGS Lake Crescent. Custom Correct Lake Crescent

GEOLOGIC MAP ■ USGS Misc. Inv. Map I-994

KEY REFERENCES ■ Babcock and others (1992); Suczek and others (1994)

PRECAUTIONS ■ Poison oak grows along some parts of this trail.

About the Landscape: The sedimentary rocks that were deposited in the Tofino-Fuca Basin formed when the basalts of the Crescent Formation were thrust under Vancouver Island about 40 million years ago. The rocks exposed along the shoreline of Lake Crescent are **turbidites** of the Aldwell Formation. These were formed from submarine landslides that tumbled off the shoreline into the depths of the Tofino-Fuca Basin. You can also see the same kind of pillowed submarine basalts as those exposed on Hurricane Hill (Hike 3) and evidence of a gigantic prehistoric landslide.

Trail Guide: About 16 miles west of Port Angeles, take East Beach Road off US 101 to the sign for the Log Cabin Resort and the Spruce Railroad Trail. The trailhead is at the parking lot at the end of the road.

The first 0.7 mile of the hike is through the woods crossing some springs that flow across the trail. About 0.1 mile beyond the springs, look for a side trail on the left heading down to Harrigan Point on Lake Crescent. If you get down on your hands and knees and look very carefully at the Harrigan Point rocks, you will see a pattern called a Bouma Sequence. The sequence starts with a layer of sand or pebbles, the first elements to settle out of the sediment that was suspended in water from the submarine landslide. Above this, you will see progressively finer grained sediments, culminating with a layer of clay on top. Close inspection will reveal that some of the layers have been offset by faulting. The unique aspect of this faulting is that it apparently occurred as the sediments were being deposited. These are called syndepositional growth faults. The evidence for this is that the amount of offset decreases as you follow the layers upward from the shore toward the lake. The older layers have been moved more than the younger layers. This is one of the best places in the world to observe this geologic phenomenon.

After you've experienced the marvel of growth faulting, look east toward

Turbidites in the Aldwell Formation were formed by a series of submarine avalanches in the Tofino-Fuca Basin.

the lumpy topography at the head of the lake. This is the debris from a huge landslide that roared down Storm King Mountain in prehistoric time damming the drainage and creating Lake Crescent. Quite possibly the landslide was triggered by one of the magnitude 8 + earthquakes in western Washington during the last few thousand years.

Head back through the woods to the main trail and continue another 0.1 mile to a talus slope formed from bits and pieces of turbidite that have eroded from the cliffs above. If you scramble up to the cliffs you can see how the originally horizontal layers are twisted and broken by folds, faults, and joints. Geologists have spent a long time looking at these outcrops and are still puzzled by them.

Just past the talus slope there is a side trail leading upward to the remnants of an old tunnel on the Spruce Railroad. Here the turbidites have been bent upward to an angle of about 70 degrees. The oval forms you see in these rocks are concretions, parts of the rock more resistant to erosion because they have been glued together by a natural cement composed of calcium carbonate.

From the tunnel, continue up and over an incline to the bridge at Devils Point. The rocks here are mega-breccias, huge (20 to 30 feet across), angular blocks of rock produced by a submarine avalanche.

If you continue another half mile beyond Devils Point you can see the seafloor upon which the avalanche at Devils Point was deposited. This outcrop consists of big blobs of lava that geologists call pillow basalt. Pillows form only when lava is erupted beneath water, so we know these are submarine basalts.

From here you can continue another 2 miles through scattered outcrops of Crescent basalt to Camp David and Fairholm or return to the trailhead.

Hike 3

HURRICANE HILL

Hike through alpine meadows and forests of the high Olympics to view rocks that originated on the seafloor, were thrust more than 10 miles underground, and now are more than 1 mile above sea level.

DISTANCE ▓ 1.5 miles

ELEVATION ▓ 5060 feet to 5760 feet

DIFFICULTY ▓ Moderate

TOPOGRAPHIC MAP ▓ USGS Hurricane Hill. Custom Correct Hurricane Ridge

GEOLOGIC MAP ▓ USGS Misc. Inv. Map I-994

KEY REFERENCES ▓ Babcock and others (1992); Tabor (1987)

About the Landscape: Back at the beginning of the Eocene epoch, about 50 million years ago, the Olympic Mountains did not exist. Instead, there were a series of deltas being built out into a sea with active volcanic islands ultimately forming the rocks of the Crescent Formation. By about 40 million years ago, these volcanoes were extinct, most had sunk or eroded beneath the sea, but sediments from adjacent land areas continued to be deposited. These are called the Peripheral Rocks.

Imagine a jam on a conveyor belt where all of the packages being carried get shoved underneath each other and then pushed back up to the top as more and more packages move onto the belt. The conveyor is the seafloor off the Washington coast that has jammed itself under the margin of North America. The marine sediments on top and the seafloor beneath have been subducted and then shoved up along the continental margin for the last 50 million years to become the Core Rocks of the Olympics. The Peripheral Rocks and the Crescent Formation that surround the Core have also been warped upward in the shape of a horseshoe open to the west.

Trail Guide: Drive from Port Angeles to the very end of the Hurricane Ridge Road. The trailhead is at the north end of the parking lot. This trail goes through forest and alpine meadows with panoramic views of the Olympics, Vancouver Island, and the Strait of Juan de Fuca. The first mile is paved and wheelchair accessible. The last 0.5 mile is partially paved and a steep climb over some ground that is rough in places.

The first rock outcrops are only about 0.1 mile from the trailhead. These

41

are turbidites, consisting of thin layers of shale and sandstone that were originally deposited by immense submarine avalanches that rumbled off the continental margin into a subduction zone just off the Washington coast. Like the Hoh melange (Hike 1) these sediments were pushed 10 to 15 miles deep into the subduction trench, driven back out, and warped upward to form most of the peaks seen from Hurricane Ridge. Going into and out of the trench, the rocks were twisted into folds and broken into long pencil-like fragments that can be seen here and there along the trail. The sandstone and shale have been slightly metamorphosed into argillite and semi-schist, but metamorphic textures are not apparent.

Just beyond the junction with the Little River Trail there is a thick sandstone cut by numerous white veins of quartz. These formed when the rock was fractured by earthquakes deep underground, allowing hot fluids to circulate through cracks in the earth. When the hot fluids cooled they precipitated the crystals of quartz seen in the veins.

The trail continues through the woods for about 0.5 mile with no outcrops,

The crest of Hurricane Hill is composed of pillow basalts of the Crescent Formation that originated as extrusions of basalt underwater.

then breaks out into spectacular subalpine meadows. A few scattered outcrops of sandstone and shale are found along the trail, but the cliffs ahead are composed of knobby outcrops of basalt. You might guess this is the seafloor upon which these rocks were deposited, but this is actually the Hurricane Ridge fault, that runs just in front of the cliffs. So there is a terrane boundary between the Crescent Formation basalts and the sedimentary rocks of the Olympic Core. Unfortunately, the terrane boundary is so shattered and broken that no outcrops along the trail show what it looks like.

The summit of Hurricane Hill provides a good look at the pillow basalts found in the submarine portion of the islands that make up the Crescent volcanics. These lavas are pock-marked with gas bubbles, many of which have been filled with white crystals of calcite or zeolite.

From the summit of Hurricane Hill there is a panorama of Olympic Peninsula geology. Looking toward the south, the Bailey Range and Mount Olympus rise as much as 7000 feet above the deep gorge of the Elwha River. The Elwha's U shape is characteristic of an origin by the erosive action of valley glaciers—glaciers that probably started retreating from the Olympics more than 18,000 years ago. All of these peaks and valleys are composed of Core Rocks. Numerous landslide scars indicate that these slopes are very unstable.

Looking to the north across the Strait of Juan de Fuca, you can see the southern end of Vancouver Island, which is composed of Crescent Formation and Peripheral sedimentary rocks.

If you are fortunate enough to take this hike in late July or August, you will enjoy the profusion of wildflowers as well as the geology.

Hike

4 DUNGENESS SPIT

*An easy walk along the world's largest natural **spit**.*

DISTANCE ■ 1 to 5 miles depending upon length of beach walk

ELEVATION ■ 75 feet to sea level

DIFFICULTY ■ Easy

TOPOGRAPHIC MAP ■ USGS Dungeness

GEOLOGICAL MAP ■ DGER 79-17 Dungeness

KEY REFERENCES ■ Othberg and Palmer (1979); Schwartz and others (1987)

About the Landscape: Since the end of the last glaciation, about 10,000 years ago, sediments derived from the erosion of sea cliffs and streamflow have been carried by currents along the shoreline of the Strait of Juan de Fuca. At the mouth of Dungeness Bay the sediments have accumulated as an immense complex of sand and gravel spits. Spits are among the most dynamic of land-forms as they constantly change shape according to conditions of wave energy, sediment supply, and sea level.

Trail Guide: Just west of Sequim, turn north of US 101 onto Kitchen Dick Road. Drive 3 miles to the Dungeness Recreation area. Follow the access road to the parking area at the end.

From the parking area the trail goes a little less than 0.5 mile through a forest of cedar, madrona, alder, and grand fir before coming to a spectacular overlook where you can see the entire 5-mile length of the spit to the New Dungeness Lighthouse, a National Historic Site. The 80- to 100-foot cliff along the shoreline to the west is clearly a major source of material for the spit. These sand and gravel deposits are **cross-bedded,** so they must represent deltas of glacial outwash. You can walk along the narrow beach at the base of the cliffs, but the big blocks of fallen debris indicate erosion here is still a little too active for comfort. A much better idea is to walk eastward along the outer margin of the spit (note that most of the inner margin of Dungeness Spit and Graveyard Spit are closed to public access to protect wildlife).

The first thing to notice on the spit is the shape and composition of the pebbles. Lots of different rock types can be found: granites, greenstones, quartzites, cherts, and various volcanics. Durability is what these rocks have in common. Most have been eroded from glacial deposits and all have been bashed by innumerable years of wave action. The more susceptible rocks have been ground into sand, silt, and clay, or even dissolved. Many of the pebbles have been flattened into "skipping stones" by the swash and back swash of waves. Others are not flat because they have only recently been eroded from the sea cliffs. The most recently eroded rocks must be the sandstone cobbles that probably won't last for more than a few decades.

The reason spits are commonly shaped like a pointing finger is that they are deposited by currents that flow along shorelines. This is called longshore drift. The direction of drift follows the prevailing wind, sometimes reversing direction on a seasonal basis. The finger of the spit points in the direction of net longshore drift, the direction that dominates over a period of years or even centuries. Here and there along the beachfront are indicators of net longshore drift. For example, logs oriented perpendicular to the shoreline trap sand on the updrift side like little dams. Along Dungeness Spit all of the sand and gravel has piled up on the west side of the logs, so the sand must be moving mostly toward the east.

About 4 miles along, Graveyard Spit forms a branch pointing toward the shoreline. It is fed by sediments that go around the end of the main spit and come back the other way. Eventually it will join up with Cline Spit, which is fed by the Dungeness River, and Dungeness Harbor will turn into a closed lagoon.

Dungeness Spit, which extends more than five miles, consists of sediments deposited by longshore currents that flow from west to east along the Strait of Juan de Fuca.

If you are interested, continue another mile to the New Dungeness Lighthouse for their daily tour; otherwise, retrace your steps to the trailhead.

Hike 5 MOUNT ELLINOR

Panorama of the Olympic Peninsula, the Puget Lowland, and the Cascade Range

DISTANCE ■ 3 miles from the lower trailhead; 1.6 miles from the upper trailhead.

ELEVATION ■ Lower trailhead, 2666 feet; upper trailhead, 3500 feet; summit, 5944 feet

DIFFICULTY ■ Strenuous

TOPOGRAPHIC MAPS ■ Mount Skokomish (1990), Mount Washington (1985)

GEOLOGIC MAP ■ USGS Misc. Inv. Map I-994

KEY REFERENCES ■ Tabor (1975)

PRECAUTIONS ■ Do not attempt this route without an ice axe and mountaineering skills if there is much snow visible on the south side of Mount Ellinor. There have been injuries and deaths on Olympic snowfields in the summer.

About the Landscape: Mount Ellinor, at the southeastern corner of the Olympic Mountains, affords the opportunity to view much of western Washington, and to study most of the geologic phenomena of the Olympic Peninsula:

Mounts Ellinor and Washington across the glacial trough of Hood Canal

Tertiary volcanic and sedimentary rocks, and Quaternary glaciation by both the Cordilleran Ice Sheet and Olympic alpine ice. On a clear day from the 5944-foot summit of Mount Ellinor, you will see a breathtaking panorama (especially appreciated after the steep ascent): from west to north, the Olympic Mountains, including Mount Olympus; from northeast to southeast, the Cascades, including the volcanoes Mount Baker, Glacier Peak, Mount Rainier, Mount Adams, and Mount St. Helens; to the southeast, the southern Puget Lowland and southern Hood Canal; and to the south and southwest, the southeastern Olympic Peninsula and Lake Cushman. The trail (812) is short, steep, and popular: in 1997 volunteer trail crews estimated that 10,000 to 15,000 people use this trail every year.

Trail Guide: There are two routes to get to the foot of the Mount Ellinor-Mount Washington massif from US 101 along the west shore of Hood Canal. You will need a permit to park at either trailhead for Mount Ellinor; the nearest place to obtain a trail park pass is the US Forest Service district office at the start of SR 119 in Hoodsport.

The first route is from Hoodsport; set the trip odometer at mile 0.0 here. Drive west on SR 119 toward Lake Cushman. In the vicinity of Lake Cushman State Park (entrance at mile 7.1) there are occasional views north to Mounts Ellinor and Washington. At mile 9.3 turn right on FR 24. Turn left on FR 2419 at mile 10.9.

The other route to this hike is from the mouth of Jorsted Creek, located near milepost 321 on US 101 between Eldon and Lilliwaup. Drive west up the valley of Jorsted Creek along FR 24. The junction with FR 2419 is in about 7.5 miles.

From either Hoodsport or the mouth of Jorsted Creek, you are now at the beginning of FR 2419 (reset odometer to mile 0). Go northerly into the drainage basin of Big Creek. At mile 1.2 roadcuts of pillow basalts begin. These are lava flows that erupted on the seafloor in the Eocene; note the basalt blobs that are the size and shape of pillows. At mile 4.7 is the lower trailhead. Park here (trail park pass required) or continue toward the upper trailhead. At mile 6.3 turn left (southwest) on FR 2419-014. The upper trailhead is at the end of the road (mile 7.3), and a trail park pass is required to park.

The lower trail: The gentle lower trail is about 1.5 miles long; the entire route is through an open virgin forest with large trees. Most of the trail is along or just north of the crest of an east-west ridge. One gains the ridge just west of the lower trailhead, where there is a roadcut of fractured Eocene pillow basalt. The ridge is a huge bedrock-cored moraine. The lateral moraine was deposited along the northeast side of the valley glacier that occupied the valley of Lake Cushman.

In about 0.5 mile is a view of a clearcut to the north. Just above the trail are outcrops of the Eocene basalt that cores the ridge. Note that many of the trees are curved (convex downhill) just above ground level. Creep of soil and/or snow tilted the trees downhill; the trunks curved as the trees regained a vertical position.

The trail leaves the westerly course along the morainal ridge in about a mile and turns northerly toward the upper trail. Just before this turn, where the trail is right on the ridge, look down to the southwest toward Lake Cushman (elevation 735 feet). The ridge is asymmetric, with a very steep southern slope and a gentle northern slope. Imagine standing here during the last glaciation. You would be much higher than the Puget Lobe of the Cordilleran Ice Sheet on the lowland to the southeast, but you would be standing right at the edge of the valley glacier along the North Fork Skokomish River. You are looking down about 3000 feet to Lake Cushman, where once there was 3000 feet of ice!

From this point to the junction with the upper trail there is little basalt bedrock exposed, but one can see a few large boulders left behind by the retreating valley glacier.

The upper trail: This steep trail begins on a northwest-southeast oriented ridge, a lateral moraine built on the northeast side of what was once a huge valley glacier along the North Fork Skokomish River. This ice began near the center of the Olympic Mountains, then advanced south from the headwaters of the North Fork. The valley glacier was fed by dozens of cirque glaciers on Mounts Duckabush, Stone, and Skokomish, and on Sawtooth Ridge. During the last glaciation this ice extended south beyond Lake Cushman; during an ear-lier glaciation it reached all the way to Hood Canal. When the moraine on this upper trail was built, the valley glacier was about 3000 feet thick.

Between here and the headwaters of the North Fork Skokomish River are volcanic, sedimentary, and low-grade metamorphic rocks. The ice deepened, steepened, and straightened the former stream valley, forming the U shape of a glacial trough. The glacier eroded the different types of bedrock, trans-porting sediment south, and depositing it in and on the moraine. Note the variety of volcanic (basalt), sedimentary (sandstone), and metamorphic rocks along the trail; the ice-transported boulders are up to 20 feet in diameter.

At about 0.3 mile is the junction of the lower and upper trails. Continue up along the moraine, which soon merges with the steep slope. The first bed-rock is greenstone, formed when basalt is metamorphosed. Some of the dark iron-bearing minerals are altered to the green minerals chlorite and epidote. The greenstone contains amygdules of secondary minerals that fill the origi-nal **vesicles** (gas-bubble cavities) in the bedrock. There are also secondary quartz veins in the greenstone.

In a little more than 1 mile you reach tree line. The forest gradually gives way to cliffs, rockfall deposits, and taluses. Glaciation left a steep slope sub-ject to mass wasting (downhill movement of earth materals by gravity). In places there are huge rocks that fell from the cliffs above; elsewhere there are taluses, steep slopes of smaller rocks that fell from the cliffs and are creeping downhill.

The bedrock cliffs near timberline are weakly metamorphosed sedimen-tary rocks. Dominant here are purplish thinly-bedded argillites which, when originally deposited on the ocean floor, were sands and muds. The basalts and greenstones below are within the Crescent Formation; the argillites here are called the Blue Mountain unit (the names come from Crescent Lake and Blue Mountain in the northern Olympics). The contrast between the massive **amygdaloidal** greenstones and the purplish, thinly-bedded argillites is par-ticularly notable in the large blocks of the rockfall deposits. Look closely at some of the greenstone blocks and you'll find small green crystals of epidote.

The presence of **slickensides** and slickenlines are notable. Slickensides are where movement of rocks on either side of a fault has smoothed and scratched and ground up rocks along the contact. Slickenlines are scratches that indi-cate the relative direction of movement between the two rocks.

The trail ascends a large talus and alpine meadow to reach the south ridge of Mount Ellinor. Just below the large talus/meadow the trail crosses bedrock polished and grooved by a cirque glacier that existed on the southeast side of Mount Ellinor. The glacier joined with ice from two cirques on the southeast side of Mount Washington; the ice descended the valley of Big Creek.

Glaciers erode bedrock by different mechanisms. On the upglacier side of bedrock, the ice smooths and scratches, with the result dependent on the size of rock particles in the base of the ice. Finer sediment polishes and striates (scratches) bedrock, whereas larger, harder rocks erode grooves; here the grooves are small. On the downglacier side of a bedrock obstacle, the ice plucks and quarries blocks of rock.

Follow the trail up the south ridge of Mount Ellinor toward the summit. Just before the top, the trail loops eastward. The ridge and summit are composed of argillite; note, particularly near the top, that some of the thin beds are folded and faulted.

On a clear day, the view from the summit is spectacular. Due west are the peaks of Copper Mountain. To the northwest is Sawtooth Ridge, and beyond, glacier-clad Mount Olympus. To the north, across a small lake, is Mount Pershing. To the northeast a serrate ridge extends to Mount Washington. All of the nearby peaks experienced intense alpine glaciation. The sharp pyramid-shaped peaks are horns (like Europe's Matterhorn). The knife-edged ridges connecting the horns are arêtes. More rounded mountains and ridges were eroded by cirque glaciers to make horns and arêtes.

Cirque glaciers fed valley glaciers, which carved glacial troughs that we can see on different scales. Due north is a small lake on the floor of a small glacial trough carved by the valley glacier along Jefferson Creek. Due south is a medium-sized glacial trough holding, with the help of a dam on the North Fork Skokomish River, Lake Cushman. To the east is Hood Canal, its bottom more than 1000 feet below the general surface of the Puget Lowland.

As the Puget Lobe of the Cordilleran Ice Sheet advanced south from Canada, it encountered preexisting valleys of north-flowing streams. The ice deepened the stream valleys to well below sea level. When the Puget Lobe retreated and sea level rose, the glacial troughs became fjords, with Hood Canal being the best example.

Across the Puget Lowland are the Cascades with their prominent volcanoes. To the northeast (almost behind the Brothers) is Mount Baker, close to Canada. South from Mount Baker are the other big glacier-covered volcanoes, Glacier Peak, Mount Rainier, and Mount Adams. Just west of Mount Adams lies the shattered stump of Mount St. Helens.

Imagine being here about 16,000 years ago: it was probably colder, even in summer; no trees were in sight.

A few hundred feet below you, three or four cirque glaciers surround the peak (a permanent snowfield still lies against the headwall of the cirque to the northwest, at the head of Jefferson Creek). The cirque glaciers feed valley glaciers; the ice along the North Fork Skokomish River is slowly retreating, perhaps its terminus lies near the south end of Lake Cushman. To the southeast, the Puget Lobe is advancing south along what is Hood Canal. In front (south) of the ice terminus is a large lake about 200 feet above sea level. The lake exists because the north-flowing streams have been blocked by the ice. Meltwater from the valley glacier along the North Fork Skokomish River runs south into the lake in front of the Puget Lobe. The lake overflows to the south, building a delta (at Shelton) into a slightly lower lake along the arms of southwestern Puget Sound. The lower lake overflows to the south (near Olympia) and a giant meltwater river extends from there to a lower Pacific Ocean west of Grays Harbor.

Hike

6 WESTPORT DUNE TRAIL

Walk along the crest of a sand dune to view the dynamics of a rapidly changing shoreline.

DISTANCE ■ 1.5 miles

ELEVATION ■ 30 feet to sea level

DIFFICULTY ■ Easy

TOPOGRAPHIC MAP ■ USGS Westport and Point Brown

GEOLOGIC MAP ■ DGER 87-8 Chehalis-Westport

KEY REFERENCES ■ Gelfenbaum and others (1997); Logan (1987)

About the Landscape: This beach walk is very different than Hike 7, which is along an eroding marine terrace. The sand supply here is sufficiently abundant so that over the past one hundred years or more, the shoreline has been advancing outward into the sea. The main source of sand is sediments from the Columbia River that have been swept northward by longshore currents. Because this is an accreting coast, the landforms are constantly changing. At present there is a ridge and valley topography formed by the dunes, but a hundred years ago, the dunes existed as sand islands surrounded by the sea. Fifty years ago the main dune extended continuously along the shoreline, and there were a series of freshwater lakes in the back dune area. Now, the back dune area has completely filled in with sediment and the dunes are being stabilized by grass and shore pines. If the sand supply is not interrupted, the dune field will continue to grow outward creating a series of shore-parallel ridges.

At Westhaven, on the north end of the trail, the pattern of accretion ends, due to a jetty built in 1896 to help keep the entrance to Grays Harbor open. In the vicinity of the jetty there is extensive erosion because this structure interferes with the natural pattern of currents.

Trail Guide: Follow SR 105 to the Westport Light Road about a mile south of the town of Westport. Turn left and drive to the trailhead at a parking lot at the end of the road. This hike is 3 miles round trip and nearly level. The trail is paved from the Westport Light Road access to Westhaven, so it is suitable for bicycles or wheelchairs. The return trip can be made along the beachfront if the tide is low.

From the parking area, climb about 30 feet up onto the crest of the main dune ridge. You can see the ridge and valley topography that is characteristic of accreting shorelines from here. Looking eastward toward the Westport Lighthouse, it is apparent that the lagoons that existed here in the past still persist in the form of a series of saltwater marshes. From the paved main trail, there are several side trails out to the beach. If you take one of these trails or return along the shoreline, look for evidence showing the direction of sand movement along the coastline. This is called net longshore drift. One common indicator is a buildup of sand on the upstream side of obstructions such as logs projecting out into the water. Another indication is a general increase in the width of the beachfront going downdrift.

Driftwood logs cover a jetty built by the Army Corps of Engineers to protect the harbor at Westport.

Continue northward on the main trail, reading, about every 0.3 of a mile, interpretive signs that describe the natural and human history of this area. The trail ends in another parking area at Westhaven, but to see shoreline geology in action, walk out to the South Jetty, which is a line of huge riprap blocks, perpendicular to the shoreline, that extends out to sea. The beach is much wider here. You might guess this is because the jetty is serving as a dam which traps sediment as it travels northward. However, there is also evidence of active erosion in the steep bank that is clearly being undercut by wave erosion. In fact, during the winter of 1993, wave action breached an area just south of the jetty resulting in extensive damage at Westhaven. As a temporary measure, the breach was filled with 750,000 cubic yards of dredged material. A permanent solution to the problem is still being studied.

Hike 7 — BAY CENTER GHOST FOREST

A hike through a Geo-Mystery. When did all these trees along the Washington coast die, and why?

DISTANCE ■ 1 mile

ELEVATION ■ 20 feet to sea level

DIFFICULTY ■ Easy

TOPOGRAPHIC MAP ■ USGS Bay Center

GEOLOGIC MAP ■ DGER 87-8 Chehalis-Westport

KEY REFERENCES ■ Atwater and Hemphill-Haley (1997)

About the Landscape: The big question for emergency service planners in the Pacific Northwest is: what is the maximum magnitude earthquake that can occur? The biggest historic earthquake in Washington was probably a magnitude 7.2 with an epicenter somewhere in the North Cascades. But geologists digging through the muck and mire on the Washington coast have discovered evidence that magnitude 8 or even 9 earthquakes have shaken our habitat repeatedly during the past 3000 years. Dead trees indicate a sudden sinking of the coastline that occurs in conjunction with major earthquakes. By looking at tree ring patterns and by carbon-14 dating, geologists have established that the last major episode of coastal sinking was approximately 300 years ago and that the area affected from northern California to British Columbia indicates a magnitude of 8 or 9.

Coincidentally, historical records indicate a major **tsunami** hit the coast of Japan on January 27, 1700. The Pacific Northwest is the only feasible source area for an earthquake to generate this particular major seismic sea wave

52

Stumps of a sunken forest stick up through intertidal muds at Bay Center.

(tsunami). We know, therefore, when the last great earthquake occurred; the big question is, how often do they occur? The best answer from the information currently available is about every 300 to 500 years.

Trail Guide: Drive 16.8 miles south of South Bend on US 101 and turn east onto Bay Center Road. At 3 miles from the turnoff, cross the bridge into Bay Center and follow 2nd Street north to Bush Pioneer Park. Take the park road into the camping area to a sign that says, "Footpath to Beach and Viewpoints." The footpath begins on a forested terrace and continues to the beachfront. A low tide is required to walk across mudflats to outcrops along the beach. The sediments along the shore are fairly sandy so this is not as mucky as it sounds.

Begin the hike in Bush Pioneer Park at the northern end of the campsite loop from the "Footpath to Beach and Viewpoints" sign. Follow the footpath, going right at the first two junctions and left at the third. Cross a primitive walkway of boards and logs to the beachfront. Hopefully you have arrived at low tide, so you will see a broad sandy tide flat located between two headlands. The tidelands are embedded with snags that are the remnants of trees, probably

53

willows that were once part of a coastal bog. These trees were killed when this segment subsided during a great earthquake and then was buried by sand from a tsunami. Geologists call this a ghost forest; it is a major piece of evidence for earthquakes of magnitude 8 or greater in the Pacific Northwest. Another indication of the tectonic forces that have affected this area is that until a few thousand years ago Bush Pioneer Park was underwater. When you walk across the tide flats, look at the coastal cliffs. These are composed of marine muds that were originally deposited in a basin just off the shoreline. During one of the great earthquakes, this basin was uplifted to become part of the land as a marine terrace. If you look closely at these cliffs, you can find layers of peat that were originally part of bogs along the coast. Additionally, there are out-crops of cross-bedded sand and gravel that formed where stream deltas were built out into the bay.

All along the shoreline, sea cliffs, toppled trees, and fallen blocks of cliff material indicate erosion is presently a dominant process. Erosion is a seri-ous problem along most parts of the southern Washington coast; in some places the rates of erosion are as much as several thousand feet per century.

If you want to see an even more spectacular example of a ghost forest, drive 1.4 miles south of the bridge on Bay Center Road to find huge snags of cedar trees that died during one of the recent great Pacific Northwest earthquakes.

Hike

8

WILLAPA HILLS

An old railroad grade along the Chehalis River with exposures of sedimentary and volcanic rocks that tell the geologic history of the Willapa Hills.

DISTANCE ■ 22.5 miles

ELEVATIONS ■ Start, 560 feet; end, 200 feet

DIFFICULTY ■ Easy

TOPOGRAPHIC MAPS ■ USGS (west to east): Pe Ell, Doty, Rainbow Falls, Boistfort, Curtis, Adna; 1:62,500 maps for historical purposes (west to east): Pe Ell, Adna

GEOLOGIC MAP ■ USGS Misc. Inv. Series I-1832 Willapa Hills Trail State Park

KEY REFERENCES ■ Wells (1989)

PRECAUTIONS ■ Railroad bridges without decking or handrails are dangerous, especially in the rain and wind.

About the Landscape: The Willapa Hills are a portion of the Coast Ranges bordered by the Pacific Ocean on the west, the Columbia River to the south, the Chehalis River on the north, and a lowland including portions of the Chehalis and Cowlitz Rivers to the east. There are no significant north-south routes across the Willapa Hills, and only one east-west route. SR 6 winds up the Willapa River from Raymond to the drainage divide at Pluvius, and down Rock Creek and the Chehalis River to the city of Chehalis. (The Chehalis River isn't quite sure where it's going; it rises in the southern Willapa Hills, flows north to near Rainbow Falls, then east to Chehalis, then northwest between the Willapa Hills and the Black Hills, and finally west to Grays Harbor and the Pacific Ocean.)

A railroad built in 1891 and 1892 by the United Railroads of Washington later became part of the Northern Pacific Railroad, and finally, part of Burlington Northern. The last train rode these rails in September 1993. Purchase of the right-of-way by the Washington State Parks and Recreation Commission was completed in December 1993.

There are other old railroad lines along parts of this route: the Chicago, Milwaukee, St. Paul, and Pacific Railroad stretched from Raymond 6 miles up the Willapa River, then up Mill Creek, over a divide, and down Elk Creek to rejoin this route between Doty and Dryad on the Chehalis River. On the south side of the Chehalis River from river mile 88 (the mouth of the South Fork Chehalis River) to river mile 75 (west edge of the city of Chehalis) ran the Chehalis Western; this railroad turned up the South Fork.

Rainbow Falls of the Chehalis River is on Columbia River basalt.

The Burlington Northern right-of-way, now the Willapa Hills Trail State Park, is part of the rails-to-trails endeavor in the United States. Washington State Parks is in the process of installing signs, trailheads, rest areas, and camping facilities along the route; the intent is to have camping facilities about every 12 to 15 miles along the trail. The thirty-six bridges along the route will get decking and hand rails. The trail will be suitable for hikers, horses, and wide-tire bicycles.

Between South Bend and Chehalis there are a great variety of Tertiary sedimentary and volcanic rocks. These include both marine and continental rocks, meaning that some of the sediments and volcanics were emplaced on the seafloor, whereas others are the result of sedimentation and volcanism on the land. Figure 5 shows the stratigraphy of this portion of the Willapa Hills. As you hike this trail, you'll see exposures of most but probably not all of these units. Streamcuts, railroadcuts, quarries, and borrow pits along or close to the trail are good places to look for exposures.

FIGURE 5

Stratigraphy along the Willapa Hills Trail

CENOZOIC	Quaternary	Holocene	alluvium: silt, sand, and gravel
		Pleistocene	terrace sediments
			old outwash: sand and gravel
	Tertiary	Miocene	Montesano Formation: marine sandstone (with mudstone, siltstone, and conglomerate)
			Mashel–Wilkes Formations: continental sedimentary rocks
			Grande Ronde Basalt
			Astoria Formation: marine sandstone (with siltstone)
		Oligocene through upper Eocene	Lincoln Creek Formation: marine siltstone and sandstone
		Eocene	Cowlitz Formation: basaltic tuff / marine siltstone, claystone, shale, and sandstone / nearshore sedimentary rocks, including coal
			marine siltstone and sandstone
			Crescent Basalt

The lower to middle Eocene Crescent Formation, mostly submarine basalt flows and breccia, forms the basement of the Willapa Hills. On the Crescent

Formation mostly marine sediments were deposited. In the middle Miocene, about 16 million years ago, lava flows (the Grande Ronde Basalt) arrived from the vicinity of today's Blue Mountains, hundreds of miles to the east of the Willapa Hills. In the middle to upper Miocene both marine and continental sediments were deposited; this ended widespread sedimentation in the Willapa Hills.

No Pliocene sediments are recognized in this area. Along the eastern part of this hike there are ancient (probably hundreds of thousands of years old) outwash sands and gravels deposited by meltwater from glaciers in the Cascade Range. Along the western part of the trail are terrace sediments, probably from the last interglacial high stand of sea level (about 125,000 years ago). All along the valley floors is modern stream alluvium.

Except near Willapa Bay, the entire landscape is the result of stream erosion and deposition coupled with weathering and mass wasting of the Tertiary rocks. Streams have cut the valleys; larger streams have constructed floodplains, and smaller streams have deposited alluvial fans at the edges of the valley floors. Landslides in this area are common due to weak sedimentary rocks, steep slopes, and high precipitation.

The high rainfall makes for rapid growth of vegetation. The land use is almost entirely private tree farms. There is little if any virgin or old growth forest left in the Willapa Hills. Towns are tiny and farms are few; timber is king. For information on current conditions, contact Washington State Parks and Recreation Commission, 7150 Cleanwater Lane, Olympia, WA 98504, (360) 902-8500; and Rainbow Falls State Park, 4008 SR 6, Chehalis, WA 98532.

Trail Guide: The Willapa Hills Trail can be hiked in whole or in part because it is always within a mile of SR 6 (unfortunately, the trail and the highway are adjacent to each other for some of the route). It can be hiked in either direction; west to east is preferable if you want most of the wind, rain, and sun at your back. Also, overall, you'll be walking from older rocks to younger sediments, going through tens of millions of years of geologic time. The entire Willapa Hills Trail is more than 56 miles long. Our geologic hike starts at a major trailhead at Walville and goes east through Pe Ell, the only big community (population about 600) between Raymond and Chehalis. It ends at Adna, where there is a minor trailhead.

The west end of the Willapa Hills Trail is in the city of South Bend, where the Willapa River empties into Willapa Bay. South Bend is on US 101 about halfway between Aberdeen, at the head of Grays Harbor, where the Chehalis River meets the Pacific Ocean, and Astoria, Oregon, at the mouth of the Columbia River.

From South Bend the trail goes east 4 miles to Raymond, at the intersection of US 101 and SR 6. To get to the start of our hike, drive east (up the Willapa

River) along SR 6. The major trailhead is at Walville, about 4 miles east of the divide between the Willapa River and Chehalis River drainage basins.

The east end of the Willapa Hills Trail is at the west edge of the Chehalis city limits. Chehalis is on I-5 about an hour south of Olympia, and 2 hours north of Portland, Oregon. To get to the end of our hike, drive west (up the Chehalis River) along SR 6, about 5 miles to the minor trailhead at Adna.

The Willapa Hills Trail is going to be established a few miles at a time. As of early 1999, the portion between South Bend and Raymond was mostly complete. Plans for the summer of 1999 were to improve the portion of the route from Pe Ell northeast to at least Rainbow Falls State Park (a significant portion of this hike). The planned order for development of the rest of the trail is Rainbow Falls to Adna, Chehalis to Adna, fish hatchery (west of Lebam) to Raymond, and hatchery to Pe Ell.

As of 1999, a major trailhead was planned at Walville. The trail along the old railroad grade, SR 6, and Rock Creek are all located in the bottom of a narrow valley. There is a roadcut in an Eocene basalt flow immediately to the east of where Rock Creek and the trail pass beneath the highway. Nearby quarries expose pillow basalt with amygdules (filled vesicles) of zeolite minerals. In places there are pyrite (iron sulfide) crystals, and pyrolusite (manganese oxide) dendrites on fractures.

The trail crosses Rock Creek on its way to McCormick. Another 0.5 mile east, on the north side of a very narrow portion of the valley, is a basalt quarry in the Eocene Pe Ell volcanics, a member of the Cowlitz Formation.

Soon the trail enters a wide valley floored by Pe Ell Prairie (a major trailhead is at Pe Ell). Just south of the mouth of Rock Creek there is a bridge over the Chehalis River (CRiv. mile 107). We'll use river miles for location references on this hike (indicated by "CRiv."). By trail it's less than 20 miles to Adna from here, but Adna is at CRiv. mile 81, 26 meandering miles downstream.

Why is this wide valley called Pe Ell Prairie? There may have been a grassland here when Pe Ell was originally settled. With all the rain, you'd expect a forest. Maybe the water table gets high enough in the spring to kill trees, or perhaps the alluvial sediments deposited by the Chehalis River and its tributaries are so permeable that seedlings die from lack of water during the occasional long dry, hot summer. There is also the possibility that Native Americans used fire to make and/or maintain a prairie here.

North of Pe Ell Prairie (CRiv. mile 101), the Chehalis River cuts through a ridge of Miocene Grande Ronde Basalt. The north-dipping basalt overlies the Miocene Astoria Formation and the Eocene-Oligocene Lincoln Creek Formation, both marine sedimentary rocks. There are no exposures right by the trail, but there is weathered sandstone in the roadcut to the east, and a small basalt quarry just to the north. Unlike the Eocene basalts to the west, which

Eocene pillow basalt near Rock Creek

probably were erupted from nearby submarine vents, the Miocene basalts here erupted near the southeast corner of Washington and traveled hundreds of miles westward.

From Doty (CRiv. mile 100) to Meskill (CRiv. mile 94) the Chehalis River and trail wend eastward in a wide valley. There is a campground and major trailhead at Rainbow Falls just south of CRiv. mile 97. Rainbow Falls is supported by resistant Miocene Grande Ronde Basalt. On the south side of the valley immediately east and west of the state park are young landslides.

At Meskill (minor trailhead), the Chehalis River takes a semicircular route south (the radius of the circle is 2 miles) around Ceres Hill. Just to the south of Meskill, on each side of the river, you can see quarries in the Grande Ronde Basalt. The quarry just east of the trail is huge and exhibits basalt with columnar joints.

At Ceres (CRiv. mile 91), there is a minor trailhead with a hike/bike only campground planned. Ceres Hill is a sandwich of Miocene strata: Astoria Formation at the bottom, Grande Ronde Basalt in the middle, and continental sedimentary rocks at the top. A huge roadcut of weathered sandstone (Astoria Formation) is visible high to the northeast just before the trail crosses the road at Ceres. There's no need to hike up the road to inspect it because a large railroadcut exposes the massive sandstone 0.5 mile before the bridge over the

Chehalis River at CRiv. mile 86. There are exposures of basalt above each of these sandstone cuts. South of Ceres Hill, the main stem of the Chehalis River meanders quite a bit before being joined by its South Fork and entering a narrow valley.

This narrow valley southeast of Ceres Hill has sandstone of the Astoria Formation to the northwest and Grande Ronde Basalt to the southeast. The basalt is exposed in a quarry on the east side of the railroad tracks of the Chehalis Western, which lie immediately east of the trail right after the bridge over the Chehalis River (CRiv. mile 86).

Once again the Chehalis River enters a wide valley, which extends downstream from Millburn to the cities of Chehalis and Centralia and beyond. There are many oxbow lakes where river meanders were cut off. The oxbows slowly fill with sediment to become arcuate meander scars upon the flood plain. The meander scars are particularly prominent south of the trail at CRiv. mile 80, right after the next (and last) bridge over the Chehalis River. You might be interested in contrasting the flood plain meanders and oxbows of the Chehalis River with the incised meanders and cutoffs of the Grande Ronde River (Hike 52).

Our hike ends at the minor trailhead at Adna (CRiv. mile 81). To the north of Adna is pre-Fraser outwash (sand and gravel deposited by meltwater long before the last glaciation). The gravels are weathered red and contain mostly rotten clasts; they are exposed just to the north, in the ditch between the road and the school. During the last (Fraser) glaciation, ice flowing south down the Puget Lowland from Canada terminated about 9 miles north of here.

Chapter 2
PUGET LOWLAND AND THE SAN JUAN ISLANDS

Cascade Lake on Orcas Island

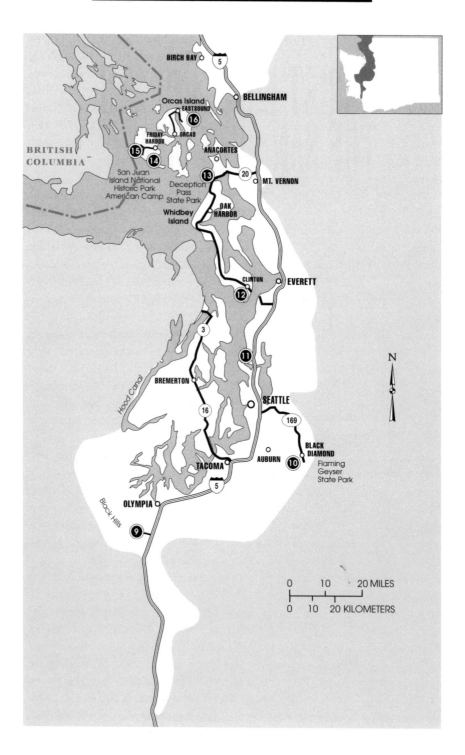

The Puget Lowland is part of a long trough stretching from the Willamette Valley in western Oregon and the Chehalis Valley in southwestern Washington to the Strait of Georgia between Vancouver Island and the British Columbia mainland. This trough has the Cascade Range to the east, and the Coast Ranges to the west. Weather permitting, a hike in the Puget Lowland almost always allows a glimpse of a Cascade volcano like Mount Rainier (elevation 14,411 feet) or Mount Baker (10,778 feet) and a view of the Olympic Mountains, especially the higher eastern peaks like Mount Constance (7743 feet) or the Brothers (6866 feet).

There is quite a bit of relief within and at the edges of the Puget Lowland. On the west, it is only a few miles from the 6000 feet and higher peaks of the eastern Olympics to more than 600 feet below sea level at the bottom of Hood Canal. Mount Constitution in the San Juan Islands rises 2409 feet above sea level (Hike 16). Bedrock is exposed elsewhere in the Puget Lowland in places like Deception Pass at the north end of Whidbey Island (Hike 13) and the Black Hills west of Olympia. The bedrock portions of the Puget Lowland are almost entirely of three types: (1) exotic terranes of mostly Mesozoic rocks (as in the San Juan Islands), (2) basalts, and (3) clastic sedimentary rocks (coal-bearing in the southeastern Puget Lowland). The forces of plate tectonics moved many of the various rocks (or sediments) from the Pacific Ocean islands or seafloor to their current locations in western Washington, and created the long basin of the Puget Lowland by pushing up mountain ranges to the east and west. These same forces occasionally rock western Washington with an earthquake (magnitude 7 in 1949 and another at 6.5 in 1965).

However, the Puget Lowland is dominated by drift (glacial deposits), and other sediments deposited by **lahars** (mudflows from Cascade volcanoes) and streams. In places, these sediments are more than 2000 feet thick. Much of the land of the Puget Lowland is about 600 feet above sea level. This is a drift plain with a layer of Vashon till at or just below the surface. The till was deposited by the last big glacier to occupy this area, a glacier that was responsible for much of the topography of the Puget Lowland.

Glaciers of different sizes arrived in the Puget Lowland repeatedly beginning early in the Pleistocene epoch. The oldest drift has reversed magnetism, meaning that it was deposited more than 780,000 years ago (the last time the earth's magnetic field reversed), and is associated with the Lake Tapps Tephra, a layer of volcanic ash erupted from the vicinity of Mount Baker more than 1 million years ago. During each of the many glaciations of the Pleistocene Ice Age, ice entered the Puget Lowland from British Columbia, from the Olympic Mountains, and from the Cascade Range. The ice from British Columbia was part of the Cordilleran Ice Sheet, a glacier complex that stretched from southern Alaska to northern Washington, Idaho, and Montana. This is the same ice complex responsible for the Missoula floods and for glaciation of the Okanogan Highlands. Additionally, small glaciers descended from the eastern Olympic valleys, and down from the western valleys of the Cascade Range.

Let's look at the last glaciation of the Puget Lowland, which began perhaps 25,000 years ago and ended about 10,000 years ago. Glaciers had been growing in the mountains of British Columbia and western Washington since about 100,000 years ago, when the climate gradually became cooler and more moist. The first glaciers to reach the edges of the Puget Sound region were valley glaciers originating in the nearby Cascade and Olympic Mountains. A glacier from the vicinity of Mount Rainier advanced northwesterly and occupied the southeastern Puget Lowland about 20,000 years ago. At about the same time, valley glaciers descended eastward from the Olympics toward Hood Canal. Meanwhile, a large portion of the huge Cordilleran Ice Sheet was advancing southward along the Strait of Georgia, where, about 20,000 years ago, it crossed from British Columbia into Washington. By the time this ice reached its maximum position, about 15,000 years ago, the Olympic and Cascade valley glaciers had already retreated back into the mountains.

Near the San Juan Islands and the southeast end of Vancouver Island, the portion of the Cordilleran Ice Sheet in the Strait of Georgia split into two lobes: the Juan de Fuca Lobe traveled west between the Olympic Peninsula and Vancouver Island; the Puget Lobe advanced south to beyond Olympia and Shelton. Meltwater from the Puget Lobe flowed southwesterly around both sides of the Black Hills into the Chehalis River, then west through a valley now including Grays Harbor and out into a lower Pacific Ocean. At the peak of the last glaciation about 20,000 years ago, the world's oceans were about 400 feet below present.

Before the last glaciation, a river system drained north through the Puget Lowland. As soon as the Puget Lobe of the Cordilleran Ice Sheet extended south to the latitude of Port Townsend on the northeastern Olympic Peninsula, the north-flowing river system was blocked. A large lake formed in the southern Puget Lowland which drained south into the Chehalis River and west into the Pacific Ocean. Fine-grained sediments (muds and sands) accumulated in this lake.

The Puget Lobe continued to advance south. Immediately in front of the glacier, meltwater deposited outwash (sand and gravel). The ice then overran the lake sediments and outwash. Till, an unstratified (without layers), unsorted (a range of grain sizes—in this case from mud to boulders) sediment, was deposited directly by the ice. Till deposited at the base of ice can be as hard as concrete. The Puget Lobe was more than 0.5 mile thick near Seattle and about 1 mile thick near Port Townsend.

In addition to depositing till, the Puget Lobe greatly affected the landscape of the Puget Lowland. In places the till forms drumlins, elongated hills, stretching from Bellingham to Seattle (Mercer Island and Capitol Hill are examples). The ice overtopped all preexisting high places in the Puget Lowland (for example, it buried and rounded the hills west of Bremerton). On a smaller scale, it grooved and striated the bedrock (Cattle Point on San Juan Island, Hike 14). Perhaps the most pronounced action of the Puget Lobe was the creation of the long, narrow, and deep arms of Puget Sound. Where river valleys were present, the glacier was thicker and had the capability to erode deeply: the preexisting river system became Lake Washington, Lake Whatcom, Hood Canal, and the many arms of Puget Sound (as stated before, the maximum depth of Hood Canal is more than 600 feet). These deep valleys may have been carved partly by meltwater streams flowing underneath the ice sheet.

About 15,000 years ago, the Cordilleran Ice Sheet beat a hasty retreat toward British Columbia. As the ice retreated from the southern Puget Lowland, the proglacial (in front of a glacier) lake reformed. This lake emptied once the ice margin had retreated north of Port Townsend. With the world's glaciers melting, sea level was rising. The Cordilleran Ice Sheet floated as a thick ice shelf in the northern Puget Lowland. The tidewater ice shelf calved icebergs just as coastal glaciers in Alaska continue to do today. Marine organisms were smothered with sediment and bombarded with ice-rafted stones. The mixture of marine fossils, mud, and stones is called **glaciomarine drift** and is exposed in places throughout the Puget Lowland (a good example can be seen at Double Bluff, Hike 12). The reason glaciomarine drift is exposed above sea level is that although sea level has been rising for 20,000 years, the Puget Lowland underwent isostatic rebound. The weight of a mile thickness of ice had pushed the earth's crust down. With the ice melted and the weight gone, the crust rebounded, just as a ship rises as its cargo is unloaded.

The advance and retreat of glaciers in western Washington occurred about every 100,000 years during the Pleistocene Ice Age. The Cascade and Olympic valley glaciers made it, respectively, to the eastern and western edges of the Puget Lowland. At least once, glaciers from the southeast Olympic Mountains extended east of present day Hood Canal. Sometimes the Cordilleran Ice Sheet advanced only as far as the northern Puget Lowland, but at least once, the Puget Lobe advanced so far south that its meltwater flowed south down the lower Cowlitz and Columbia Rivers on its way to the sea.

During the Ice Age there were alternating glaciations and interglaciations. During interglaciations, fluvial (river), deltaic, and marine sediments accumulated in the lower parts of the Puget Lowland. The climate during the last interglaciation, about 125,000 years ago, was much like that of today. The last glacial/interglacial transition occurred about 10,000 years ago, with the Cordilleran Ice Sheet completely retreating from the Puget Lowland back into British

Columbia. The peak of warmth and dryness of the present interglaciation was about 5000 years ago. If global warming by humans does not prevent it, another glaciation may begin in a few thousand years.

The glacial history seen in the Puget Lowland is also well displayed in the San Juan Islands. Spectacular examples of glacial erosion can be found at Cattle Point (Hike 14). Other evidence for glaciation is seen at Rosario Beach (Hike 13) and Mount Constitution (Hike 16).

The difference between most of the Puget Lowland and the San Juan Islands is that in the latter there are abundant exposures of preglacial bedrock that are as much as 400 million years in age. Geologists have discovered that these islands are a stack of miniterranes that were pushed one over another as the microcontinent of Wrangellia was being accreted to North America about 90 million years ago. One hypothesis is that much of this accretion happened in the vicinity of the Mexican Baja, and since then the bedrock of all the San Juan Islands has been transported more than a thousand miles northward. The counterhypothesis is that none of these terranes moved northward more than a few hundred miles. Only time and more research will resolve this controversy.

Presently, at least six terranes have been mapped in the San Juan Islands. We will see five on our hikes. The Decatur and Lopez terranes are well displayed in the vicinity of Rosario Beach and Deception Pass (Hike 13). At Cattle Point, the Lopez, San Juan, Deadman Bay, and Garrison terranes can be examined in detail. The Deadman Bay and Garrison terranes can also be observed at Lime Kiln Point (Hike 15) and at Mount Constitution (Hike 16).

Hike 9

MIMA MOUNDS

Gophers? Glaciers? Earthquakes? Where did these bumps come from? Stroll through one of the most controversial topographic features on Earth to formulate your own theory.

DISTANCE ■ 0.5 to 2 miles

ELEVATION ■ 240 feet

DIFFICULTY ■ Easy

TOPOGRAPHIC MAP ■ USGS Rochester

GEOLOGIC MAP ■ DGER 87-11 Centralia

KEY REFERENCES ■ Washburn (1988); Berg (1990); Nelson (1997)

About the Landscape: Unlike most of western Washington, the Puget Lowland south of Olympia has been a treeless prairie since prehistoric time. This is partly due to lightning-induced fires, but is mainly a consequence of the unique soils that developed from a thick sheet of outwash sand and gravel de-

Scientists can't agree on the origin of these enigmatic mounds. Gophers, freeze-thaw action, and earthquakes have all been proposed as the cause.

posited during the last stages of the Fraser Glaciation, 11,000 to 14,000 years ago. Near the town of Rochester, the prairie is covered with thousands of mounds: Mima Mounds. Similar mounded terrain is found in many other places, including the Basin and Range and the Central Valley of California, where they are variously referred to as "hog wallows," "pimpled plains," or "gopher mounds." When first studied by the Wilkes Expedition in 1841, it was concluded that the mounds were constructed by "the savage labour of some bygone race." However, most geologists believe they developed either by alternate freezing and thawing of soils and/or by meltwater erosion during the waning stages of glaciation.

Another radical geologic theory, with no confirming evidence, is that the mounds were shaken into existence by seismic waves during past great earthquakes. Biologists agree that the mounds might have initially formed by geological processes, but they argue that pocket gopher colonies were essential to maintaining the shape and spacing. Geologists counter that no gophers presently live in the mounds, nor have any remains of these animals been found. However, gopher colonies do exist in the vicinity, and the mounds contain abundant remains of a beetle species that is almost always associated with these rodents. As yet, there is no definitive evidence, so explore the mounds looking for that critical piece of evidence that might resolve the controversy.

Trail Guide: Take Exit 95 from I-5 and drive 3.5 miles west on SR 121 through the village of Little Rock to a T junction. Turn right on Waddell Creek Road. Drive 0.8 mile to a sign for Mima Mounds Natural Area. Turn left and continue 0.4 mile to the Nature Trail parking area. The Nature Trail (about 0.5 mile) is paved and wheelchair accessible.

Follow the asphalt path from the parking lot past a bronze plaque proclaiming the Mima Mounds to be a "Registered Natural Landmark." Your first view upon emerging from the forest onto the prairie is a stark concrete building that could be a structural engineer's version of a mushroom. This is the interpretive center which contains a wealth of information on the history and scientific interpretation of the area. Ignore all of this for now and climb up the stairs to the top of the Mima Mushroom to gaze out across the dimpled sea of mounds. They seem to be nearly identical, popping up for miles across the rolling landscape.

At the southern end of the paved nature trail there is an elevated viewing platform. From there you can examine the stuff of which the mounds are made: a dark, organic-rich soil containing abundant pebbles of chert and various plutonic rock types. The pebble composition fits the hypothesis that the prairie is underlain by glacial outwash, but the organic material must have been added later. Next, check out the size and shape of the mounds. They are all circular, about 4 to 6 feet high and 15 to 50 feet across, looking a bit like a megaversion of a gopher dwelling, but there are no visible burrows and no other sign of these rodents. This place certainly doesn't look anything like a typical glacial outwash plain, which would be nearly flat with numerous meltwater channels incised.

The preferred seasons for this walk would be during the spring or summer when the mounds are covered by successive waves of wildflowers—camas followed by bluebells, sunflowers, and daisies. From the paved path, you can wander southward a couple of miles on trails that meander through the mounds. Once you have seen enough, return to the interpretive center to read the technical explanations. Did you discover anything not mentioned? Somehow the mounds seem more suitable as a mystery.

Hike 10 | FLAMING GEYSER

Geysers of methane gas and springs with carbon dioxide bubbles are the focus of this unusual hike in the Green River Gorge area.

DISTANCE ■ 0.5 mile

ELEVATION ■ 225 feet to 300 feet

DIFFICULTY ■ Easy

TOPOGRAPHIC MAP ■ USGS GQ-407 Black Diamond

GEOLOGIC MAP ■ USGS GQ-407 Black Diamond

KEY REFERENCES ■ Mullineaux (1970)

About the Landscape: During the middle to late part of the Eocene epoch (about 43 to 36 million years ago), neither the Olympic Mountains nor the Cascade Range existed. The outer coast of Washington was close to Seattle and

The Flaming Geyser

Tacoma. Along this continental margin were immense floodplains and river deltas delivering sediments to downdropping basins formed by faults that were somewhat similar to the present day East African rift valleys. The rocks formed from these sediments, called the Puget Group, are mostly sandstone and shale with some conglomerates. But because vegetation was so abundant, there are also thick beds of coal, which were extensively mined from 1883 to 1940 and gave the town of Black Diamond its name.

After the sedimentary rocks were formed, they were crunched and crumpled into folds that look like waves on a sea surface. Some of these rock waves were also broken and moved vertically by faults. The organic-rich sediments deposited in deltas, bent by folds, and cut by faults are an ideal place to seek petroleum and natural gas. Nothing of commercial value has been found in the numerous wells that have been drilled.

Some of the coal has been heated to the extent that it has been converted to natural gas. In 1911 when Eugene Lawson drilled a well to a depth of 1403 feet looking for coal seams, he found mostly methane gas. This was ignited to form the Flaming Geyser, which was once so impressive it was featured in *Ripley's Believe It or Not*.

Trail Guide: Take SR 169, 1 mile south from Black Diamond and turn west on Green Valley Road. Drive 2.7 miles, turn south and follow Flaming Geyser Road 0.3 mile to a junction where you turn right and proceed another 0.8 mile to a parking area at the south end of the park. The trail to Flaming Geyser is barrier free.

To begin the hike, head east on a path at the end of the Flaming Geyser access road. Follow Bubbling Geyser Loop to the world famous Flaming Geyser, which is now not a geyser at all. Flaming Geyser is an emanation of gas that exists as a pathetic reminder of its former glory. In a shallow pit, a small flame flickers a foot or so high, far short of an account written in 1927 describing violent bursts of flame 10 to 15 feet high and 3 to 4 feet wide. The big bursts are probably why this place was described as a geyser. Even though the flame has diminished, it is still impressive that enough methane is generated to burn continuously for almost ninety years.

From the Flaming Geyser, continue on the trail to the Bubbling Geyser. There are several outcrops of Puget Group shale exposed that are steeply inclined because they have been bent into folds. At about 0.25 mile, the Bubbling Geyser can be seen on the right side of a bridge. Instead of methane, this gas is carbon dioxide, so no flame is possible, but you can see more clearly how the gas bubbles out of the springs. Note the gray slick substance around the springs. This is mostly clay formed by chemical reactions between the spring water and the rocks through which it flows.

From here you can return to the parking lot or follow a sign marked "Trails" up to a ridge above the stream valley where you can find Vashon till deposited by the Puget Lobe of the Cordilleran Ice Sheet.

DISCOVERY PARK

This hike along shoreline bluffs, in a gem of a big city park, reveals major changes in the climate and in the sea level of the Puget Lowland over approximately the past 20 thousand years.

DISTANCE ■ 2 mile loop

ELEVATION ■ Sea level to 150 feet

DIFFICULTY ■ Easy to strenuous

TOPOGRAPHIC MAP ■ USGS Seattle North

GEOLOGIC MAP ■ USGS 91-147 Seattle

KEY REFERENCES ■ Galster and others (1994); Mullineaux and others (1965); Yount and others (1993)

About the Landscape: The sea cliffs at Discovery Park are composed of layers of sediment that tell a story of amazing changes at this site before, during, and after the most recent glaciation. The oldest layer is composed of clay, silt, and sand deposited by streams flowing across a floodplain during the "Olympia non-glacial stage." This period of relatively warm climate was probably just a little cooler than that during the past 8000 years in the Puget Lowland. Radiocarbon dates of 22,400 and 18,400 years ago indicate that these sediments were being deposited at the same time that the Cordilleran Ice Sheet was building up in British Columbia and beginning to flow south across the border.

The next layer up is the Lawton Clay, which can be recognized by its distinctive gray color. This was probably deposited in an immense lake that was formed when the advancing Puget Lobe blocked rivers flowing northward and out the Strait of Juan de Fuca. Remember that Puget Sound did not exist then.

The uppermost layer is the Esperance Sand deposited by meltwater streams flowing south from the Puget Lobe as it moved toward Seattle. This sand and silt is called outwash by geologists. Radiocarbon ages indicate the Lawton Clay and Esperance Sand were deposited between 18,000 and 15,500 years ago. Elsewhere in the park, Vashon till overlies the Esperance Sand. The glacier that deposited this till was at least 3000 feet thick over the Seattle area at its maximum! Later, meltwater streams deposited more sand and silt as the ice sheet melted away.

Unfortunately, all of these sediment layers have very little resistance to movement, so wherever nature has created steep slopes, the sediments tend to obediently respond to the force of gravity and come tumbling down.

Trail Guide: The trails in Discovery Park are well marked, well maintained, and sometimes fairly crowded with both walkers and joggers. The climb to the

The instability of these cliffs at Fort Lawton is indicated by the "drunken forest" of trees tilted by earth movement.

top of the bluff is moderately strenuous, but the rest of the loop is easy. This description focuses on a miniloop from South Beach to North Beach that emphasizes the geologic features in the park, however, the entire loop is highly recommended. There is an excellent description of this trail in *Nature Walks in and Around Seattle* by Stephen Whitney.

Drive north on Elliott Avenue from downtown Seattle. Veer right as Elliott becomes 15th Avenue West; continue on 15th to the Dravus Street exit. Turn left (west) on Dravus. Continue to 20th Avenue/Gilman Avenue West and follow the Discovery Park signs to the entrance on West Government Way. Your first stop should be at the Environmental Education Center on the south end of the east parking lot (just inside the entrance to your left). At the education center, view the natural history displays, and on the weekends, if you don't have time to hike the whole loop trail, catch a shuttle bus that will drop you off at a parking lot near the Metro Treatment Plant. Parking at the Metro plant is restricted to those with special needs.

From the Metro Treatment Plant parking lot, hike southeast on the South Beach Trail along the base of the sea cliffs. At low tide you can walk out onto a broad wave-cut bench to view the distinctive layering in the cliffs above. The reddish and yellow brown sandy layers at the base are part of the stream-deposited Olympia non-glacial deposits. A little over 50 feet up the cliff the dark gray clay-rich Lawton Clay deposits begin. Fallen blocks of Lawton Clay can also be found at the base of the cliff.

At the 160-foot level there is a transition from the lake clays into the stream deposits of the Esperance Sand. In addition to the Ice Age climate change, the other story here is the instability of these slopes. Using old marine charts, it can be estimated that these bluffs are being cut back by shoreline erosion and landslides at a rate of as much as 80 feet per century. This could be much greater if the tide flats were not there as a buffer. Several currently active landslides can be seen along this section of the bluff. Recognize these by scarps (patches of bare ground at the top of the slide) and by "drunken forests" (trees that have been tilted in different directions by slide movement).

From the beach, head back toward the road until you intersect the South Bluff Trail, which ascends the bluff in a series of switchbacks through the forest. At the top, there is an overlook which faces directly down on the scarp of one of the active slides. On either side of the log barricade, look carefully for two brass medallions named "HARRY." These are National Geodetic Survey Horizontal Control marks that are used for a variety of studies ranging from slope stability to earthquake hazards.

At the junction with the main loop trail, head north, crossing some sand dunes that probably developed from outwash deposits formed when the Puget

Lobe retreated from the Seattle area between 14,000 and 15,000 years ago. After about 0.25 mile, the trail intersects the road where you can return to the Metro parking area or continue to wander among numerous trails within the park. Look over the extensive facilities of the Metro sewage treatment plant on your way back. When the site was excavated in 1990, geologic mapping revealed evidence that during the past few thousand years this place has been a tidal marsh, a beach, and a midden for Native people. It has also been buried by a debris flow and ripped by a tsunami wave generated by movement on the Seattle fault about 1000 years ago. Just think what could happen here in the future!

DOUBLE BLUFF

Hike 12

Stroll along the base of towering cliffs of sediment to observe the depositional products of the last Ice Age, processes of shoreline erosion, mass wasting in action, and evidence for a major active fault in the Puget Lowland.

DISTANCE ■ 1.5 miles

ELEVATION ■ Sea level

DIFFICULTY ■ Easy

TOPOGRAPHIC MAP ■ USGS Maxwelton

GEOLOGIC MAP ■ USGS 91-147 Seattle

KEY REFERENCES ■ Easterbrook (1994); Johnson and others (1996)

PRECAUTIONS ■ The shoreline is described under moderate to high tide conditions. At low tide the exposed area at the base of the cliff extends much further out to sea. At very high tides the path will be impassable. Check tide tables to avoid being stranded or forced to climb the cliffs.

About the Landscape: During the Pleistocene Ice Age which began about 2.4 million years ago, the Puget Lowland was repeatedly invaded by ice from British Columbia. Because the most recent advance was quite extensive, it obliterated most of the evidence of earlier glacial events. However, at this location three different tills can be seen, including the Vashon (about 15 thousand years old), the Possession (>80 thousand years old), and the Double Bluff (around 250,000 years old). Also seen are sediments of the Whidbey Formation, which were deposited during a warmer period between glaciations about 125,000 years ago. The Possession Drift at Double Bluff consists of glaciomarine drift, the debris dumped by tidewater glaciers during the waning stages of a glacial advance.

Along the shore of Useless Bay, the silt and sand layers of the Whidbey Formation are twisted into bizarre folds. This apparently marks the trace of the South Whidbey Island fault. Because such recent sediments have been contorted, the fault must be considered active and capable of generating dangerous earthquakes.

Unlike the accreting beaches of Dungeness Spit (Hike 4) and Westport (Hike 6), the shoreline of Puget Sound from Useless Bay to Double Bluff is rapidly eroding, probably at a rate of more than 100 feet per century. Thus, the landscape

Layers of sand in these cliffs have been twisted by movement along the South Whidbey Island fault zone.

is constantly changing and some of the features mentioned in this description may disappear with time.

Trail Guide: From Clinton on the southern end of Whidbey Island, take SR 525 to just before milepost 17. Turn south (left) on Double Bluff Road. Continue about 2 miles until the road makes a sharp left bend and turns into Shore Road. Instead of turning, go straight ahead into a parking lot behind a sign saying "Public Beach Access." This is a level walk along the shore of Useless Bay with a few short scrambles over landslide blocks and fallen trees.

The first 0.1 mile crosses a broad apron of sand at the base of the sea cliffs that serves as a buffer against erosion, as indicated by the vegetation covering the cliffs. Fingerlike sand spits and sandbars point south, indicating the sediment was transported from actively eroding areas ahead. You don't have to look far to find the source. As the beach abruptly narrows, bare cliffs rise more than 300 feet above the shoreline with only a few determined plants still clinging to the near-vertical slopes. The upper part of the cliffs consist of the Esperance Sand, which was deposited as outwash during the initial stages of the last glaciation. The lower two-thirds of the cliffs are composed of sand and silt layers that make up the Whidbey Formation. These sediments were deposited by streams about 125,000 years ago during a period between glaciations when the climate was actually a bit warmer than it is at the present. Most of the Whidbey sediments form neat horizontal layers, but about 0.15 mile northwest of the parking area, look about 50 to 70 feet up on the cliff face and you will see layers that are twisted like a pretzel. Some of the contortions could have been created by slumping shortly after deposition, but there are also places where sand has been injected into fractures, which is an indication of **liquefaction** along a fault zone. Scientists of the US Geological Survey now believe this area lies along the trace of a major zone of active fault movement, the South Whidbey Island fault. This structure apparently extends all the way across the Puget Lowland and into the Cascade foothills, and is probably capable of generating earthquakes of magnitude 6 or greater.

At about the half-mile mark, there are a series of landslides. One is much larger than the others (about 100 feet across) and is quite active. Small to very large blocks of silt and clay tumble almost continuously down the slope. This is not a good place to tarry!

At about 0.75 mile, two dark-brown to reddish beds of peat can be seen in the slope about 40 to 60 feet above; pieces can also be found along the beach. These are durable blocks, almost like thick chunks of leather because the organic peat has been compressed by the weight of the overlying sediments as well as by several thousand feet of ice during the episodes of glaciation. Further ahead, at about 1.25 miles, the clays underneath one of the peat layers are brick red and baked, due to fires that burned in the peat after it was deposited.

At the 1-mile mark, the high cliffs suddenly diminish to a low swale and there is a distinct change in the nature of the sediments. Instead of the layered look, the sediments now resemble concrete, except for the seashells found embedded here and there. This is a small section of Everson Glaciomarine Drift, deposited toward the end of the Fraser Glaciation about 13,000 years ago. At that time, tidewater glaciers were abundant and the Puget Sound probably looked a lot like the present day Glacier Bay National Park in southeast Alaska. The glaciomarine drift was deposited on the seafloor by the floating glacial ice, thus accounting for the presence of shells.

Just around the southern point of Double Bluff at about 1.1 miles, the sediments look almost the same, but are much older. This is the glaciomarine portion of the Double Bluff Drift. A technique called **thermoluminescence** indicates these sediments were deposited during an ice advance that occurred about 250,000 years ago.

Continue onward for a closer look at the peat-fire baked clay about 50 feet up in Double Bluff, or retrace your steps to the parking area.

Hike 13

ROSARIO BEACH

This shoreline reveals the twisted history of microplate accretion in the Pacific Northwest.

DISTANCE ■ 2 miles

ELEVATION ■ Sea level to 50 feet

DIFFICULTY ■ Easy

TOPOGRAPHIC MAP ■ USGS Deception Pass

GEOLOGIC MAP ■ USGS Misc. Inv. Map I-1198-G Port Townsend

KEY REFERENCES ■ Brown and others (1979); Gusey and Brown (1989)

About the Landscape: Although the San Juan Islands look vastly different than the North Cascades, the underlying geology is essentially the same. The bedrock of the San Juans and adjacent areas, like Lummi Island and Fidalgo Island, consists of several sheets of rock thrust faulted one on top of another to form a big stack of terranes. From Rosario Head to Lighthouse Point, you will walk along the boundary between the Lopez and the Decatur terranes. Because these terranes have been crunched together like a rush-hour auto accident on I-5, you would expect some damage, and this is readily apparent. Almost everywhere you go on this hike, the rocks have been twisted like taffy and sliced like salad vegetables in a food processor. In geologic terms, folds and faults are everywhere. You cannot walk more than 300 feet without finding evidence for faulting.

Trail Guide: The turnoff to Rosario Beach is at Pass Lake on SR 20, 9 miles north of Oak Harbor and 16 miles from I-5, Exit 230 in Burlington. Turn onto Rosario Road and head uphill for just over 1 mile to a left turn marked, "Rosario Beach." The trailhead is in the parking lot at the end of the road. This is an easy hike along beaches with short climbs over headlands.

A cliff composed of a dark green rock that was once basalt rises above the parking lot of the Rosario Beach unit of Deception Pass State Park. The cliff has been transformed by cooking in hot fluids under the seafloor to a rock type called spilite. If this rock was part of the seafloor, why is it now here on land?

Layers of chert and shale, deposited on an ancient sea floor, have been folded and uplifted by a collision between terranes.

Part of the answer can be seen in what looks like big cat scratches all over the cliff face, a feature geologists call slickensides or slickenlines. These are formed as blocks of rocks grind past each other along fault zones. Clearly, these rocks at Rosario Beach have been moved by faults here, there, and everywhere! Sliced and diced is a good description, and this is not surprising; you are standing along a terrane boundary where two great blocks of rocks, the Decatur terrane and the Lopez terrane, have smashed into each other.

From the parking lot, walk down through the blackberry bushes and a storm-tossed berm of logs to Rosario Beach. Note the discoid pebbles, also known as "skipping stones," that are here in abundance. These rocks are found along beaches where waves swash in and out, gradually flattening rounded stones in the process. Walking south along the beach toward Rosario Head, notice that the pebbles gradually diminish in size until only sand is found along the shore—an example of size sorting by longshore currents. The energy of breaking waves decreases as it moves along the shore toward Rosario Head, until there is only enough energy to move sand.

Along the beach, you have crossed the terrane boundary between the Decatur and Lopez terranes. At the far end of the beach, the first rocks of the Lopez terrane are **graywackes.** This rock type forms from the clay, silt, and sand that come from weathering of volcanic rocks. So, we have the wreckage of an ancient volcanic island that was spread out on the seafloor.

Taking the trail to the top of Rosario Head, the next rock type to appear is ribbon chert, a "graveyard rock" composed of microscopic silica crystals from the exoskeletons of a marine plankton called Radiolaria. When the silica hardens into solid rock it is called radiolarian chert. The ribbons formed as the plankton periodically bloomed and died, raining their skeletons down to the seafloor. Between bloomings, only clay settled out to form dark layers of shale alternating with the chert.

The top of Rosario Head is composed of pillow basalt that originated as blobs of lava extruded on an ancient seafloor. As you can see, all of these rocks have been twisted and broken by the force of the terrane collision. Rosario Head itself is a fold called an anticline that has warped the original flat lying graywacke, chert, and basalt into a giant arch.

Continue on the trail around Rosario Head and back to the cedar sculpture called the Maid of Deception Pass just above Rosario Beach. Beyond the dock and a small stone building, the trail heads east toward Bowman Bay. The rocks exposed are weakly metamorphosed **tuff,** lava, and volcanic sandstones of the Decatur terrane. Similar rocks can be seen more clearly in the roadcuts at the north end of the Deception Pass bridge.

If the tide is out, walk along the beachfront of Bowman Bay. Near the dock, in the intertidal zone, seeps of freshwater are draining the marshy area onshore. At higher tides, these are submarine springs. At the end of the bay, a sandy **tombolo** connects the mainland with the former island that includes Lighthouse Point. The cliffs at the south end of the tombolo are composed of a swirly mixture of light and dark plutonic rock called **plagiogranite.** Follow the trail inland, staying to the left at the junctions. Hidden in the woods is yet another terrane boundary, so by the time you reach Lighthouse Point you are back in the Lopez terrane. The steep, narrow channel cutting across Lighthouse Point is caused by a major fault that has chopped up the rocks and made them more susceptible to wave erosion. If you dare, climb the rickety aluminum ladder for a visit to the lighthouse, which is constructed on the same chert as Rosario Head. Then return via the same route or continue on the loop trail to see more of the same rocks plus a great view of Deception Pass bridge from sea level.

Hike

14

CATTLE POINT

A wave-eroded, wind-swept point reveals Pleistocene glacial grooves on rocks of ancient, exotic terranes.

DISTANCE ■ 1 to 6 mile loop

ELEVATION ■ Sea level to 77 or 170 feet

DIFFICULTY ■ Easy

TOPOGRAPHIC MAPS ■ USGS Richardson (short hike), False Bay (western part of long hike)

GEOLOGIC MAP ■ Brandon and others (1988)

KEY REFERENCES ■ Russell (1975)

PRECAUTIONS ■ Potential hazards include slippery rocks and logs, and logs thrown from big waves.

About the Landscape: San Juan Island is fascinating historically, botanically, zoologically, and geologically. The infamous "Pig War" was almost fought here at a time when both the United States and Canada claimed the San Juan Islands. From 1860 to 1872 the English forces were based at Garrison Bay on the west coast of San Juan Island; this coast is not unlike that of England except for San Juan's nearby forests. During the same period, the American Camp was on southeastern San Juan Island (near the hike); this grassy wind-swept site is like much of the western United States.

San Juan Island has a great variety of rocks because so many exotic terranes are stacked together. The southeastern end of San Juan Island witnessed glaciers, wind, and waves during the Quaternary period. Glaciers have

Lighthouse in dune field above Cattle Point

come and gone many times, eroding perhaps the most spectacular grooves in the Pacific Northwest. The wind has deposited sand on top of the glacial deposits. Waves have eroded the surficial deposits and the underlying bedrock, creating landforms from sea bluffs more than the 120 feet high to small tide pools.

There are seaweeds and many phyla of animals along this coast: bald eagles, harbor seals, and possibly orcas, and invertebrates on the rocks such as barnacles, snails, and limpets. There are anemones and chitons in the tide pools.
Trail Guide: From Friday Harbor, drive south across San Juan Island toward the American Camp of San Juan National Historical Park. Drive east all the way through the American Camp, and head downhill toward the lighthouse at Cattle Point. Note the topography near the lighthouse (you will not see this hummocky topography while hiking on the beach and rocks below the lighthouse). These hummocks are sand dunes that formed after this area was deglaciated about 13,000 years ago. The sand was blown from the southern beach by the prevailing southwesterly winds.

Where the road turns left (north) at the bottom of the hill, you can park and then walk on a trail to the lighthouse and to the dunes. An information sign includes an aerial photograph showing that the dune field was bare sand as recently as 1978. The area had been overgrazed by sheep and/or rabbits. In the middle of an exposure in the south side of a dune, just north of the lighthouse, is a dark layer, a type of **paleosol** (ancient soil) called a buried soil. Deposition of sand by the wind has alternated with soil formation. There was sand deposition, then a period of stability while the soil formed, then more eolian (by wind) deposition to bury the soil, and finally the formation of the thin modern soil. After visiting the lighthouse and dunes, return to your vehicle and drive a short way north to a parking lot.

From the parking lot, descend eastward to the beach where there are rock outcrops to the north and south. The rocks at the north end of the beach have layering that strikes to the northwest and dips about 45 degrees (down toward the northeast). They feel like sandpaper because they are sandstone, a sedimentary rock composed of sand-sized particles. The sediments that accumulated on the seafloor were compacted and cemented into rock as they were buried. This portion of seafloor moved eastward toward North America and was partially subducted beneath the continent. These sandstones are part of the Lopez terrane.

The southernmost rocks of this exposure are sheared because there was movement along a fault between these rocks and those at the south end of the beach. The fault is located beneath the beach, strikes toward the northwest, and dips down toward the northeast, parallel to the shearing and the bedding in the rocks. The fault is a terrane boundary, with the Lopez terrane at the north end of the beach, and the rocks of the San Juan terrane to the south. About 100 million years ago, the San Juan terrane was subducted toward the northeast under the Lopez terrane and North America.

As you walk south along the beach, notice some large boulders as well as the cobbles, pebbles, and sand. The sediment on this beach is derived from the glacial deposits (drift) in the bluff just to the west of the beach. (There are better exposures of glacial deposits right at Cattle Point and farther west.) At times of high tide and storm waves, the bluff of drift is eroded. Occasionally the bluff will be eroded enough to cause a landslide. The waves redistribute the landslide sediments, leaving sand and bigger particles on the beach, and moving finer silt and clay offshore.

There are many rocks on the beach that are not at all like the sandstones and the other rocks in outcrops north and south of the beach. These rocks are termed **erratics** (or glacial erratics); they were transported south from farther north in the San Juan Islands and from British Columbia. About 14,000 years ago there was a glacier here more than a mile thick. The glacier eroded rocks to the north and deposited them on southern San Juan Island. Most of the largest boulders are granitic (a term including relatively lightly colored, coarse-grained igneous rocks like granite, granodiorite, and diorite).

At the south end of the beach, and all the way around Cattle Point to the south and west, are rocks of the San Juan terrane. These rocks are of the Constitution Formation and are similar to those of Mount Constitution on Orcas Island (Hike 16). The Constitution Formation is about 150 million years old. The northernmost rocks are argillite, not quite sedimentary and not quite metamorphic rock. This argillite started as mud on the seafloor; it was buried and compacted to shale or mudstone (sedimentary rocks), and then underwent increases in pressure to become an argillite. Had the metamorphism been greater, due to higher temperature and/or pressure, the argillite would have become a metamorphic rock like a slate or phyllite. Note that the dark rock is smooth due to its fine-grained nature. Once again, the layering in the rock strikes northwest and dips down to the northeast at about 45 degrees.

Cattle Point is the southeast point of San Juan Island. Here you can still see the northwest trending layers of the Constitution Formation. However, at almost a right angle, note linear features striking northeast-southwest. These are glacier tracks (glacial grooves and striations) eroded by rocks embedded in the base of the glacier, perhaps 18,000 to 13,000 years ago. The large glacier that came from British Columbia was headed southwest toward the Olympic Peninsula. Ice is not hard enough to erode rocks, but the rocks at the bottom of the ice were grinding against the bedrock beneath.

The glacial erosion is on three scales. Fine-grained sediment at the base of the glacier polished the bedrock, making it very smooth. Sand and pebbles at the base of the glacier created striations, scratches parallel to ice flow. Larger rocks eroded grooves up to 3 feet wide and 3 feet deep. It seems as if rocks at the base of the glacier got in the groove, digging a channel ever deeper. In places, the sides of the grooves are overhanging and polished. Note that some of the grooves and striations are not perfectly parallel; this indicates minor changes in the direction of ice flow.

How could these glacial erosion features, particularly the striations, be preserved in the 13,000 years since the ice left? Why weren't they eradicated by wind, waves, and rain? They were preserved because until recently, geologically speaking, they were buried under drift. As the drift eroded, glacier tracks were exposed.

There are two types of sediment in the gray drift above the bedrock at Cattle Point. The lower unit is poorly sorted, containing everything from mud to cobbles. It does not have internal stratification (layering) suggesting deposition by meltwater, and it is too coarse to have been deposited by wind. This lower drift layer is called till. It was deposited right at the base of the ice, which compacted it.

The unit above the till is looser, has stratification, and is sorted, with some layers of mud, some of sand, and some of sandy gravel. This unit is recessional drift, or sediment deposited as the ice was retreating. The mud (fine-grained) may have been deposited in a pond (low energy). The sandy gravel was probably deposited by glacial meltwater, a more energetic environment.

From Cattle Point, continue walking west over the dark, layered, sandy and muddy rocks. Before the next small beach there are a few pods (about 3 feet across in size) of gray rock called limestone. They are somewhat anomalous, but are also found in volcanic rocks at Deadman Bay to the northwest (Hike 15). West of the limestone pods is a small gravelly beach, and another small point of bedrock. From the limestone pods it is possible to ascend the bluff where it's not particularly steep. It is a short walk north along the west part of the dunes and then along the road to the parking lot.

An alternative is to continue walking north beyond the small beach and the small rocky point to 2-mile long South Beach. The bluff to the north of the beach is a relatively thick and competent till, too steep to ascend. Walk west along the beach for about 2 miles. At about 500 yards before the rocks at the west end of the beach, walk north to Pickett's Lane, then walk or get a ride back to the parking lot north of the lighthouse.

However, there is another terrane boundary about 500 yards west of the south end of Pickett's Lane. The first rocks to the west are more sandstone and mudstone/argillite (with tuff and chert) of the Constitution Formation, striking northwest and dipping about 45 degrees down to the northeast. Further west, the small beach hides the Rosario Thrust, another terrane boundary which strikes northwest and dips down to the northeast. The Rosario Thrust strikes northwest here; overall it winds northward across San Juan, Shaw, and Orcas Islands.

To the west of the Rosario Thrust (and beneath it) is the Deadman Bay terrane. This terrane is composed of Orcas Chert and other rocks that have been subducted northeast along the Rosario Thrust. Each terrane we have seen arrived at the west edge of North America later, to be subducted: first the Lopez terrane, then the San Juan terrane, and then the Deadman Bay terrane. These three terranes are only a few of the numerous terranes extending from the North Cascades to the Olympic Peninsula. As each terrane was added to North America, the Pacific shore moved further west.

As one would expect from the name there is a lot of chert in the Orcas Chert. A fine-grained siliceous rock, chert is deposited as silica ooze on the seafloor. Also present in the Orcas Chert are dark mudstone and basalt flows, and some tuff and sandstone. In places the basalt flows have pillows, an indication that they were erupted underwater. Tuff is a rock resulting from the consolidation of volcanic ash. The basaltic flows and tuff are green because they have been metamorphosed (to a rock called greenstone).

In addition, here the Deadman Bay terrane contains slices of Garrison Schist because of the close proximity to the Rosario Thrust. This rock became a schist when it was subjected to high-pressure metamorphism before the terranes were accreted to North America. In this area the Garrison Schist is brecciated (broken), fine-grained, and green. The exposures of the Deadman Bay terrane stretch about 0.5 mile west from the Rosario Thrust.

You can return to your vehicle north of the lighthouse by walking east to South Beach, and then using Pickett's Lane and the road to Cattle Point, or retracing your route along the coast.

Hike 15 — LIME KILN POINT

This scenic coastline is most famous for whale watching, but pillow basalts and Permian fossils in limestone make the geology an equal attraction.

DISTANCE ■ 1 mile

ELEVATION ■ Sea level to 150 feet

DIFFICULTY ■ Easy

TOPOGRAPHIC MAP ■ USGS Roche Harbor

GEOLOGIC MAP ■ Brandon and others (1988)

KEY REFERENCES ■ Brandon and others (1988); Brandon and others (1994)

About the Landscape: The San Juan Islands consist of at least five separate terranes that have been stacked one on top of another by low-angle faults. The rocks at Lime Kiln Point are part of the Deadman Bay terrane, which consists of the Deadman Bay Volcanics and the Orcas Chert. This terrane, which extends northward to the Roche Harbor area, is sandwiched between the Rosario thrust fault that runs across the mountainside just below Mount Dallas and the Orcas thrust fault, which is located somewhere offshore to the west. Radiolaria and conodont fossils from the Orcas Chert range in age from Triassic to early Jurassic (about 250 to 180 million years ago). The Deadman Bay Volcanics contain a few small pods of limestone with Permian fusilinid and conodont fossils (286 to 248 million years ago). These fusilinid fossils are very significant because some of them are Tethyan, indicating they must have originated in warm equatorial areas in the Paleo-Pacific Ocean. The Deadman Bay terrane is exotic, then, and perhaps has been transported northward more than a thousand miles from its point of origin to its present location in the San Juan Islands. The volcanics of Deadman Bay are mainly pillow basalts that may have once been part of an oceanic island volcano chain like the present-day Hawaiian Islands.

The lighthouse at Lime Kiln Point is built on chert, marble, and lava of the Deadman Bay terrane.

Trail Guide: From the ferry terminal at Friday Harbor on San Juan Island, drive uphill onto San Juan Valley Road. At 1.7 miles, turn south on Douglas Road. Go another 1.4 miles west and turn onto Bailer Hill Road, which becomes the West Side Highway. Continue for 5.5 miles, just beyond the second switchback along the coast, to the entrance of Lime Kiln State Park. The trailhead is at the south end of the parking area. The trail from Deadman's Bay to the lime kiln is well maintained and nearly level with only a few short uphill segments. You can walk a 1-mile loop along the coastal cliffs, past the lighthouse to the ruins of the lime kilns, and back through an attractive forest of fir, cedar, and madrona.

From the trailhead near the outhouses, zigzag down to the shoreline on the north side of Deadman Bay. The rocks forming the shoreline cliffs on this side of the bay are pillow basalts of the Deadman Bay Volcanics; recognizable by the blob shape that looks something like a big stack of squashed meatballs. Across the bay on the south side, the blocky red and green outcrops are part of the Orcas Chert. These rocks also crop out along the West Side Road. The narrow canyon at the head of Deadman Bay marks the trace of a thrust fault that separates the Deadman Bay Volcanics from the Orcas Chert. If you hike up the hillside toward Mount Dallas, you'll cross the Rosario thrust fault zone, where you can see big blocks of Garrison Schist mixed into the chert, similar to the rocks of the Cattle Point area (Hike 14).

As the trail heads northward toward the Lime Kiln Lighthouse, notice several blocks of gray-colored rock embedded in the brownish green pillow basalts. These were originally masses of limestone, but now they have been metamorphosed to marble. For geologists, these rocks are of major interest because aragonite—a relatively rare mineral—is present in these marbles instead of common calcite, indicating these rocks were once buried at least 50,000 feet deep. The marbles also contain recognizable fusilinid and conodont fossils from the Permian and possibly the Triassic periods.

Look at the cliff just south of the lighthouse to see an especially good display of pillow structure in the basalts. Continuing northward beyond the lighthouse, the trail passes some slabs of marble. These stand out as ribs in the hillside because, in the relatively dry climate of the San Juan Islands, this rock type is more resistant to erosion than is basalt. The end of the trail overlooks a large limestone body that is the site of several lime kilns. From the 1860s to the 1950s, lime production was a major commercial enterprise in this area. The Roche Harbor Resort was home to one of the quarry owners. From here you can retrace your path back along the coast and do some whale watching or take a shortcut through the woods to the parking area.

Hike

16

MOUNT CONSTITUTION

Hike from the top to the bottom of a huge batch of sedimentary and volcanic rocks deposited along an ancient continental margin.

DISTANCE ■ 2.1 miles

ELEVATION ■ 2410 feet to 360 feet

DIFFICULTY ■ Easy (coming down)

TOPOGRAPHIC MAP ■ USGS Mount Constitution

GEOLOGIC MAP ■ Brandon and others (1988)

About the Landscape: Mount Constitution and the surrounding area are composed mainly of the Constitution Formation. This is a pile of sandstone, mudstone, chert, and a few **pillow lava** flows accumulated along the edge of a continental margin sometime during the late Jurassic or early Cretaceous time. The exact age of these rocks is uncertain, but they probably formed about 140 to 150 million years ago and are associated with the older rocks of the

The snow and ice covered peak of Mount Baker and a steep fault on the west side of Lummi Island are seen in the view across 150 million year old sedimentary rocks near the summit of Mount Constitution.

Garrison terrane (Hike 14). During the Fraser Glaciation (18,000 to 13,000 years ago) the San Juan Islands were covered by thousands of feet of ice. Most of the bedrock exposures, therefore, show evidence of glacial erosion, and large parts of Orcas Island consist of debris deposited by the ice sheet.

Trail Guide: From the ferry landing on Orcas Island take the Orcas-Olga Road 13 miles past Eastsound to the entrance of Moran State Park. Then follow the Mount Constitution Road to a parking area at the summit. The trailhead is at the south end of the parking lot. This is one of those rare hikes that is all downhill from the summit of Mount Constitution to Cascade Lake. If you can't arrange a shuttle and have to hike back up, you can take the West Boundary Trail to the summit for a change in scenery.

Before you begin this hike spend some time enjoying the spectatcular views from the top of Mount Constitution. To the northwest you have the horseshoe-shaped outcrops of Sucia Island formed by a geologic structure called a plunging syncline. Also, still looking to the northwest, you can see the Canadian Gulf Islands and Vancouver Island. To the north and east are the peaks of the Canadian Coast Range and the sand spit of Sandy Point. To the east Mount Baker and the Twin Sisters rise above the Nooksack and Skagit River deltas, with the steep east slope of Lummi Island in the foreground (this is probably a major fault).

The trail down starts just behind the TV towers. About 0.5 mile down there is an excellent view over Cascade Lake which features an island within an island. Summit Lake, just off the trail at about 1 mile, is a glacially eroded depression that looks like a **tarn,** except it was carved by the Cordilleran Ice Sheet rather than a small alpine glacier.

At 1.5 miles the trail crosses the road to the summit and 0.1 mile further is a cold spring that formed where fractures in the bedrock allow ground water to flow out at the surface. A cistern contains the spring water flow. Continuing along the trail, several small lakes and wetlands demonstrate that the water table is at or near the surface.

About 0.4 mile from the road, turn left at a junction and descend steeply downslope to Cascade Lake through scattered outcrops of metamorphosed volcanic and plutonic rocks of the Turtleback Formation, probably the oldest rocks on the San Juan Islands at about 400 million years.

Chapter 3
NORTH CASCADES

Black Peak in the North Cascades

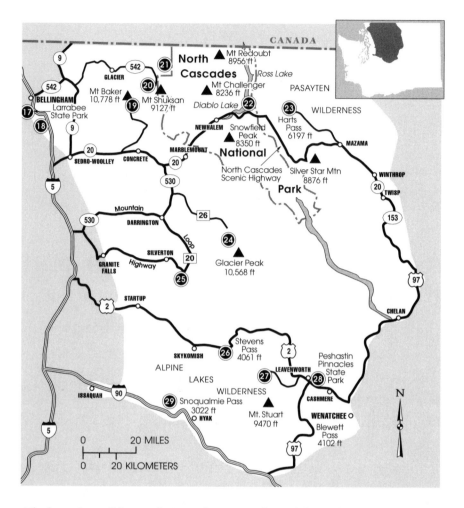

The boundary of the North Cascades is complicated, but to keep things simple, the limits can be roughly defined as I-5 to the west, I-90 to the south, US 97 to the east, and the Canadian border to the north.

The North Cascades were assembled by plate tectonic processes into a collage of several blocks of rock bounded by faults that developed in different places at different times. Most of the range consists of immigrant rock masses that arrived successively from their origins south and west. Some geologists think that the points of origin were the southeast Pacific and Central America. The blocks are known as terranes; packages of terranes that traveled together are called domains. Geologists have used many different names for these domains and terranes in the North Cascades. To provide some consistency, we will use the terminology of Roland Tabor and Ralph Haugerud in *Mountain Mosaic,* a splendid book on the geology of the North Cascades.

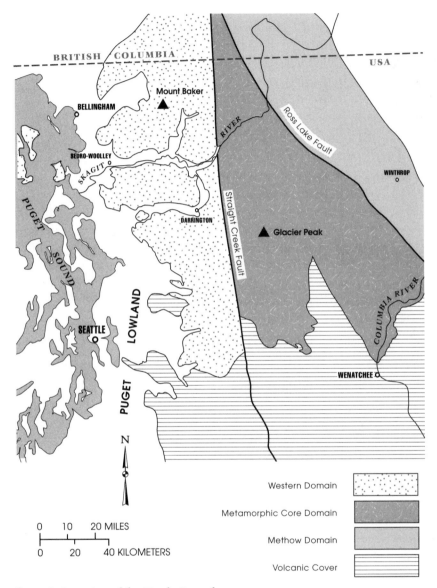

figure 6. Domains of the North Cascades

The three domains of the North Cascades are the Western, the Metamorphic Core, and the Methow (see figure 6). The Metamorphic Core domain is separated from the Methow by the Ross Lake fault and from the Western by the Straight Creek fault.

The Western domain includes four terranes (see figure 7). The Chilliwack River terrane probably originated as part of an island arc (like present-day

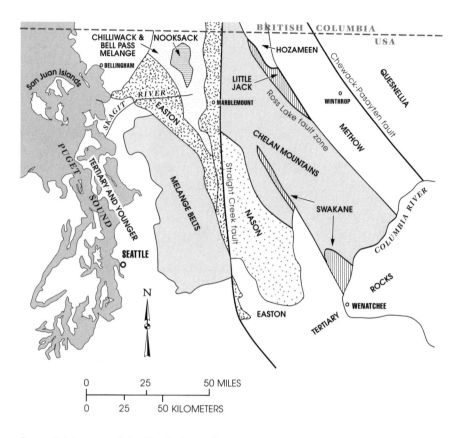

figure 7. Terranes of the North Cascades

Indonesia) between 375 and 170 million years ago. The rocks have been slightly metamorphosed, transforming the volcanics to greenstones and the sediments to phyllites which make up many of the exposures on the Chain of Lakes Trail (Hike 20).

The Nooksack terrane of lava flows and sedimentary rocks was most likely deposited along the continental margin of the ancient supercontinent of Gondwana 170 to 120 million years ago. These can be seen east of the town of Glacier along SR 542 on the way to Hikes 20 and 21.

The Easton terrane, originally seafloor basalts and marine clays, ranges in age from 160 to 105 million years. Today, the rocks are mainly schists and phyllites after having been pushed down a subduction zone and squeezed back out. They are well displayed along the trail to Bat Caves (Hike 18). A distinctive kind of metamorphosed basalt, called blueschist, occurs in many places within the Easton terrane, especially around the summit pyramid of Mount Shuksan.

The last block of the Western domain is not really a terrane, but rather a hodgepodge of chopped up rocks called the Bell Pass melange—the French word for mixture. Bits and pieces of sandstone, shale, chert, basalt, gneiss, and ultramafic rock are chaotically churned together, probably in a setting similar to the Cascadia subduction zone off the Washington coast today (Hike 1).

The Metamorphic Core domain also consists of four terranes. The rocks in this domain are mainly schists, gneiss, and granitic plutons or dikes that formed deep within the earth and were uplifted by tectonic forces to form the crest of the range.

The Nason terrane contains high-grade schists and gneisses, but these metasediments and metavolcanics originated along an ancient continental margin 210 to 190 million years ago. View the Chiwaukum Schist, a distinctive unit in the Nason terrane, on the Icicle River Canyon hike (Hike 27). Almost identical schists have been found in the Harrison Lake area of British Columbia along the Straight Creek fault, indicating that they have been moved as much as 90 miles northward from their original location near Leavenworth. Rocks of the Swakane and Little Jack terranes are not seen in *Hiking Washington's Geology*. For the curious, however, monotonous biotite-gneisses of the Swakane are exposed on SR 97 near Rocky Reach Dam. Schist and amphibolite of the Little Jack terrane can be seen along SR 20, about 2 miles east of the turnoff to the Ross Lake trail (Hike 22).

The Methow domain includes only two terranes: the Hozameen and the Methow, although some geologists believe that the Little Jack terrane and the northern part of the Chelan Mountains terrane are simply the metamorphosed equivalent of the Methow. The Hozameen terrane consists of the remnants of a seafloor formed between 350 and 220 million years ago. These are now schists, amphibolites, and metacherts that crop out east of Ross Lake from Jack Mountain to Hozameen Peak.

The Methow terrane consists mostly of marine sedimentary rocks deposited between 135 and 90 million years ago in an ocean floored by Hozameen rocks. In the vicinity of Harts Pass (Hike 23) are thousands of feet of these sandstones, shales, and conglomerates bent up so the layers are almost vertical. Eventually, the Methow ocean filled with marine sediments, succeeded by stream deposits that formed great deltas and floodplains along the Cretaceous margin of North America.

About 90 to 100 million years ago the microcontinent of Wrangellia was involved in a collision with North America near where the North Cascades are located today. The geologic debate is this: was it a head-on or a sideswiping collision? Whatever the scenario, it wreaked havoc, with most of the existing rocks in the Cascades suffering at least some degree of metamorphism, while huge batches of melt formed in the lower crust and pushed upward to form plutons throughout the Metamorphic Core domain. Minimum damage was done in the Methow terrane, where the rocks were only twisted into folds and broken into faults (Hike 23). The Chelan Mountains terrane suffered the maximum effect with sedimentary and volcanic rocks buried to depths of as much as 90,000 feet resulting in complete recrystallization and even partial melting (Hike 22).

After the Wrangellian crunch, the tectonic opposite occurred 55 to 45 million years ago as parts of the North Cascades were stretched by the so-called "Eocene extensional event." As the Cascades were pulled apart, great slabs of the crust sank, creating rift basins that filled with sand, gravel, and clay from large rivers flowing from mountains to the east. Around Chuckanut Mountain (Hike 17), almost 20,000 feet of sandstone, shale, and conglomerate were deposited along with thick coal layers. Rocks of similar origin also form Peshastin Pinnacles (Hike 28).

The Cascadia subduction zone has produced abundant volcanic and plutonic rocks for the past 43 million years. However, beginning 15 to 10 million years ago, uplift and erosion in the North Cascades have been so great that nearly all of the older volcanics have been stripped away, revealing numerous granitic plutons that crystallized 3 to 10 miles below the surface, such as those seen at Denny Creek (Hike 29) and Deception Falls (Hike 26). Volcanism continues at the present time in the North Cascades because subduction is still an ongoing process off the Washington coast.

Within the past 3 million years, two calderas, each comparable to Crater Lake in Oregon, have produced immense ash eruptions that devastated the landscape of northwestern Washington. The remnants of one caldera can be found near Hannegan Pass (Hike 21), and another below Kulshan Ridge (Hike 20). Recent explosive eruptions have also deposited thick pyroclastic flows in the White Chuck River valley (Hike 24). The most obvious results of subduction however, are the two huge volcanic cones of Mount Baker (Hikes 19 and 20) and Glacier Peak (Hike 24) that have formed mainly within the past 700 thousand years.

If glaciation, streamflow, and gravity didn't exist, the North Cascades would be at least 100,000 feet high. The present shape of the range is a balance between construction by volcanism and tectonics, and destruction by erosion and mass movement downslope. Glacial erosion abounds on the Chain of Lakes Trail (Hike 20). The deposits of huge landslides and mudflows from Mount Baker are seen on the Schreibers Meadow trail (Hike 19), and landforms due to stream erosion dominate along the Icicle River canyon (Hike 27) and Deception Falls (Hike 26).

Geophysical evidence indicates the uplift of the Cascade Range continues. Our magnificent mountains will not be reduced to mere hills anytime during the next few million years.

TEDDY BEAR COVE

This hike begins in an abandoned gravel pit displaying sediments from the last glaciation, continues along an old rail bed with spectatular exposures of an Eocene sandstone, and ends up along a picturesque shoreline.

DISTANCE ▪ 1 mile

ELEVATION ▪ 200 feet (at highest point) to sea level

DIFFICULTY ▪ Moderate

TOPOGRAPHIC MAP ▪ USGS Bellingham South

GEOLOGIC MAP ▪ USGS Misc. Inv. Map I-854-B

KEY REFERENCES ▪ Johnson (1991); Mustoe and Gannaway (1997)

PRECAUTIONS ▪ In rainy weather, clays on the trail heading down to the shoreline can be slippery in places.

About the Landscape: There are three major geologic themes on this trail: The first is the Chuckanut Sandstone deposited during the Eocene between 52 and 46 million years ago. At that time, Washington was much warmer and flatter than it is today. The Cascades did not exist, so large river systems meandered across the state much like the Mississippi as it flows to the Gulf Coast. Sand and gravel deposited in stream channels were eventually buried as much as 20,000 feet deep where they hardened into sandstone and conglomerate; clays and remains of abundant vegetation on the floodplain became shale and coal deposits. Fossils found in the Chuckanut indicate that the climate of northwestern Washington was about the same as San Diego today, probably a consequence of worldwide global warming caused by carbon dioxide emissions from extensive volcanism.

The second theme also relates to climate, the climate of the last glaciation, during which the Cordilleran Ice Sheet more than 5700 feet thick covered Bellingham. The signature of Fraser Glaciation is thick outwash of sand and gravel deposited as the glacier advanced and retreated. Sandwiched between these outwash deposits is glacial till that looks something like concrete, consisting of pebbles and cobbles randomly embedded in sand and mud.

The third and last geologic theme relates to the relentless attack of the sea on the shore. At Teddy Bear Cove, both the effects of erosion and the products of deposition by wave action can be clearly seen.

The bizarre outcrops at Teddy Bear Cove are formed from Chuckanut Formation conglomerates that were deposited about 50 million years ago.

Trail Guide: The trailhead is in a parking lot at the junction of Chuckanut Drive (SR 11) and California Street about 1 mile south of Bellingham. The hike is partly along the Interurban Trail that leads from Bellingham to Larabee State Park.

Sand and gravel extracted from the pit at the trailhead were deposited by great floods of meltwater that washed over a barren landscape as part of the Cordilleran Ice Sheet invaded the Puget Lowland about 20 thousand years ago. As you zigzag upslope, the sandy outwash layers are overlain by a pebbly till that represents the rock material deposited underneath the ice sheet. If you need proof of the glacial origin of this till, check out the sandstone boulder exposed where the trail joins the Interurban Trail and crosses California Avenue. The faceted face of the boulder is marked by grooves and scratches formed as it was dragged along the bedrock by the glacier moving south.

Unlike many stream canyons, the canyon on the left as you continue along the Interurban Trail has a flat bottom instead of a V shape. In 1993 the canyon was filled in by a debris flow that originated from a development upslope on Chuckanut Mountain. Fortunately, little damage was done by this event, but it is a clear message that we need to be careful when clearing land and building on steep slopes.

Further along, the Interurban Trail becomes a narrow slot between bedrock walls of the Chuckanut Formation. These are sandstones and shales with crossbedding and fossils such as palms that indicate deposition in a delta environment with a much warmer climate than we currently experience in the Pacific Northwest. Notice also that these layers of rock have been bent upward to an angle of about 70 degrees—one side of a giant arch called an anticline that forms Chuckanut Mountain. One geologic interpretation of the arch is that originally horizontal layers of the Chuckanut were bent out of shape as the Olympics were shoved into the edge of the continent to become part of Washington about 40 million years ago.

At about 0.5 mile from the trailhead, follow the sign and take a right off the Interurban Trail, cross Chuckanut Drive, and head down a steep slope of glacial till toward Teddy Bear Cove. Just before reaching the railroad track, look to the right to observe an excellent example of a layered soil profile consisting of loose topsoil, a compacted hardpan, and weathered sandstone underneath.

The destination of this hike, Teddy Bear Cove, is formed by a big knob of rock consisting of sandstone and conglomerate that are resistant to erosion and thus tend to form ribs and ridges across the landscape. Standing atop the south end of this headland provides an excellent opportunity to view the effects of longshore drift. Along this shoreline, sediments are being moved from the north toward the south as demonstrated by the fact that sand has built up behind a line of boulders extending out from the shore just south of the headland.

The rocks at Teddy Bear Cove have been carved into spectacular shapes by a combination of weathering and wave erosion. The conglomerates have the consistency of blocks of concrete, forming slabs and towers that punctuate the shoreline; in contrast, the sandstone has been worn away into recesses.

Geologists are particularly interested in the pebbles and cobbles found in the conglomerate as a possible means to identify where the headwaters of the rivers might have been before flowing into the Chuckanut Basin. It appears the Chuckanut sediments were derived from local sources such as the San Juan Islands, the Cascades, and the Canadian Coast Range. So, unlike other rocks in western Washington, the Chuckanut sediments must have been deposited where they presently exist rather than moving in on a microplate from somewhere to the south.

Hike 18 — BAT CAVES

This hike is definitely aerobic exercise, but the view from the top and the unique geology will be well worth the climb.

DISTANCE ■ 2.5 miles

ELEVATION ■ 305 feet to 2085 feet (Oyster Dome)

DIFFICULTY ■ Strenuous

TOPOGRAPHIC MAPS ■ USGS Bow and Bellingham South

GEOLOGIC MAP ■ DGER 98-5 Bow and Alger

KEY REFERENCES ■ Gallagher, and others (1988)

PRECAUTIONS ■ The rocks of the Bat Caves talus field are precipitous and very slippery when wet. Also, the Townsend's big-eared bats that inhabit the caves are a protected species and should not be disturbed from fall through spring.

About the Landscape: One hundred sixty million years ago, the rocks along the trail to the Bat Caves were volcanic islands on an ancient seafloor. Sometime between 160 and 120 million years ago these rocks were metamorphosed. On this hike you will see three different rock types that are part of the Easton terrane (also known as the Shuksan Metamorphic Suite). These rock types include marine clay and silt that has been transformed to phyllite, semi-schist derived from volcanic sand, and meta-igneous rocks formed by metamorphism of basalt lava flows, volcanic ash, gabbro, and diorite. The Easton is one of several exotic terranes that have come from far away to form the western part of the United States and Canada.

The Bat Caves were formed by huge blocks of meta-igneous rock that most likely fell from the cliffs above during one or more of the great earthquakes (magnitude 8 or greater) that shook the Pacific Northwest in prehistoric time.

Trail Guide: The trailhead is at mile 10.1 on SR 11 (Chuckanut Drive). Look for the sign that says "Pacific Northwest Trail" on the east side of the road. The hike involves a climb of about 2000 vertical feet with most of the vertical in the first miles and in the last 0.5 mile. The trail is excellent and well maintained.

This route begins on the Pacific Northwest Trail, which ascends Blanchard Mountain through a Douglas fir and western hemlock forest. There is not much bedrock to be seen initially, but about 0.2 mile past the first switchback is a small outcrop of phyllite. A well-defined metamorphic foliation gives this rock a thinly sheeted appearance; notice that the foliation is almost horizontal. The next outcrop along the trail, about 0.2 mile to the north, has a near vertical foliation indicating there are some large-scale folds not apparent in the separate outcrops. Geologists can sometimes figure out the overall structure of the rock by taking measurements at many of these small outcrops.

After a steep ascent of about 1000 feet, there is currently a clearcut with a spectacular view over Samish Bay. The flatlands here are part of the delta of the Samish River, but clearly, the present day stream is too small to have deposited all of this sediment. One possible sediment source is the Skagit River, which now lies to the south, but might have flowed into Samish or Padilla Bays

The imposing cliffs that rise above the Bat Caves on Chuckanut Mountain are composed of metamorphosed lava flows that were part of a small ocean basin 160 million years ago.

in the recent past. Another possible sediment source is one or more giant mudflows from Mount Baker or Glacier Peak. Additionally, at the end of the Fraser Glaciation, meltwater would have made the Samish River at least as voluminous as the Skagit. There is some evidence that as recently as 10,500 years ago, glaciers from Mount Baker suddenly advanced all the way down the Skagit and Nooksack River valleys to the lowlands, so that much of the material in the deltas may be of glacial and volcanic origin.

At 1.8 miles there is a junction where you leave the Pacific Northwest Trail and head northward on the Oyster Dome Trail. In about 0.1 mile, the trail crosses a small section of bedrock that doesn't look like much, but is definitely worth a pause. On closer examination, you can see a stretched pebble conglomerate that formed deep within the earth where it was so hot and the pressure so high that the pebbles of the original conglomerate were squeezed out, with the result that they are long and thin instead of rounded.

Continue another 0.4 mile to the junction with the old Bat Caves Trail, then start upward past several large outcrops on the Oyster Dome Trail. Stop at the first outcrop in order to see two very different rocks that are both part of the meta-igneous unit. One variety is metamorphosed lava called greenstone; it is so hard that even if you hammer on it you'll be lucky to break off a small piece. The other rock type is a talc schist, which is one of the softest geologic materials—so soft you can scratch it with your fingernail.

At the next large outcrop, about 0.1 mile up the trail, someone has provided an interpretive sign proving the old adage you should not believe everything that you read. This sign, entitled "Ice Age," says, "Grooved striations atop this particular matrix of Chuckanut Sandstone were made by regolith slowly rumbling along about 8000 years ago under the pressure of glacier one mile high." It's hard to tell what to focus on, the geologic or grammatical errors! Let's just deal with the geologic problems. First, the bedrock here is not Chuckanut sandstone; it is a much older metamorphic rock. Second, all of the glacial ice in the Puget Lowland had melted away by 8000 years ago. However, at the glacial maximum about 15,000 years ago, there was more than a mile of glacial ice covering this locality on Chuckanut Mountain, but the whole idea of "regolith rumbling" is inaccurate. What was happening beneath the glacier was a slurry of shattered rock being moved like sandpaper along the bedrock underneath the glacier. This produced the grooves, scratches, and channels in the bedrock. You can see these marks for yourself if you take a short scramble up onto the rock cliffs to the west of the trail. You'll also be rewarded by an excellent view out over the San Juan Islands.

From here, keep going onward and upward for another 0.1 mile until you reach another sign saying "Talus Trail," the route to the Bat Caves, which are about 0.15 mile from the junction. The caves are actually spaces between huge blocks of metamorphic greenstone. These rocks fell from the cliffs that rise vertically 300 feet above this immense pile of talus. Born as a basalt on the seafloor, they were stuffed down a subduction zone to a depth of 50,000 feet or more, creating heat, pressure, and incredible stress, conditions the original minerals in the basalt couldn't tolerate, so they broke down and formed new metamorphic minerals that could coexist with these conditions. Thus, a greenstone is formed from a basalt by metamorphism, like butterflies from larvae.

Many hikers turn back here, but if you want the ultimate scenic reward, keep hiking up Oyster Dome by heading back to the main trail and then continuing ever upward another 0.25 mile to a junction. Take a left at the junction, and follow the trail along a ridge to the top of Oyster Dome, which is a glacially scoured outcrop of greenstone. You are now at the crest of the Chuckanut Range, where there are splendid views over the San Juan Islands and directly down the vertical cliff to the Bat Caves talus below.

Hike 19 SCHREIBERS MEADOW

A hike to view the products of volcanic eruptions, alpine glaciations, and catastrophic mass wasting events in fields of fire and ice.

DISTANCE ■ 1 to 4 miles

ELEVATION ■ 3200 feet to 5450 feet (Park Butte)

DIFFICULTY ■ Moderate to strenuous

TOPOGRAPHIC MAP ■ USGS Baker Pass

GEOLOGIC MAP ■ USGS Mount Baker 30' x 60' quadrangle

KEY REFERENCES ■ Gardner and others (1995)

PRECAUTIONS ■ This is one of the most popular areas in the North Cascades; be prepared for company during July and August. If done on snowshoes or cross-country skis during winter months, carefully assess avalanche hazards if you go on steep terrain.

About the Landscape: Within the past 10,000 years, Schreibers Meadow was first covered with glacial ice, then a flank eruption produced a cinder cone, extensive ash deposits, and lava followed by an immense debris flow, which devastated the area. Since then, life in these meadows has been kept interesting by at least one major cycle of advance and retreat by the Easton Glacier, ash eruptions, plus great mudflows from Mount Baker.

If you continue on to Park Butte, you will encounter the Yellow Aster Complex, the oldest rocks in the North Cascades. From Morovitz Meadow to Park

The jumble of rocks found in the valley of Rocky Creek were probably deposited by a flood of meltwater from the Easton Glacier.

Butte, the rocks are at least 400 million years old, and elsewhere, Yellow Aster rocks may be more than a billion years in age.

On the Scott Paul Trail you will observe the most recent geologic events in and around Mount Baker. The bedrock is composed of lava flows as young as 11,000 years. After that, fire and ice alternated on the flanks of the mountain. The ridges and valleys on the upper part of the Scott Paul Trail are a series of glacial valleys and lateral moraines formed within the past 10,000 years. Banks along all of the trails in the area display conspicuous layers of ash erupted from several volcanoes, including Mount Baker, Glacier Peak, and the cinder cone in Schreibers Meadow. The coarse red cinders from this eruption are especially prominent along the Scott Paul Trail.

Trail Guide: From Sedro-Woolley, drive 14.5 miles east on SR 20 and turn left onto the Grandy Lake road (also signed for Baker Lake). Proceed another 12.5

miles to FR 12 and turn left again. In 3.5 miles, turn right onto FR 13 at the Mount Baker National Recreation Area sign. Follow this road 4 miles to a parking area at the end. The trailhead is near the restroom. The Schreibers Meadow Trail meanders a little over 1 mile through forests and meadows to the recently deglaciated valley of the Easton Glacier. For extensions to the hike you can continue another 2.5 miles and 2000 vertical feet to the Park Butte lookout, or you can hike the 8-mile loop of the Scott Paul Trail (with another 2500 feet of elevation gain). Snow persists here through late June (late July at Park Butte and the Scott Paul Trail), and the insects are voracious in July.

Begin your hike at the trailhead by scrambling down into the bed of Sulphur Creek to get a close-up view of an andesite lava flow that originates in Schreibers Meadow and continues at least 9 miles downslope into the Baker River valley. This is the youngest known flow from the Mount Baker eruptive center. Continue up the trail observing the many small ponds (mosquito hatcheries) dotting the lumpy landscape of the meadows. On a clear day, your northern horizon will be the imposing hulk of Mount Baker. If the relative humidity is right, steam plumes can be seen rising from Sherman Crater just below the summit. You'll smell the sulfurous odor from the crater if the wind is from the north, and you may begin to wonder if this is a safe place to hike. A valid question, because all those lakes and lumps in the meadows are formed on the rubble of a gigantic avalanche (debris flow) that occurred about 6800 years ago when a large sector of the rim of Sherman Crater collapsed (Hike 35, the Hummocks hike at Mount St. Helens, is a modern comparison). Some of the avalanche debris rumbled over this site and on down the Sulphur Creek valley; the rest of it surged along the Middle Fork of the Nooksack and probably continued out into Bellingham Bay. This deposit, consisting of angular blocks of lava embedded in clay and ash, is seen in drainage ditches along the trail.

About 0.5 mile from the trailhead, look to the south at the tree-covered hills rising about 300 feet above the meadows. These two overlapping cinder cones are the source of the Sulphur Creek flow. Each cinder cone has a small crater lake at the summit that reportedly contains fish! This Mount Baker flank eruption happened about 8500 years ago. In addition to lava, the Schreibers Meadow cinder cone also produced thick deposits of scoria, which covered slopes to the east, forming the bright red roadcuts seen for a mile or two approaching the trailhead parking area.

Beyond the meadows is a short stretch through the forest where streambeds expose a volcanic mudflow deposit that overlies the older avalanche material. Emerging from the trees at about 1.2 miles, the great gash of the Easton Glacier valley gives testimony to the incredible erosive ability of flowing ice, and the rapidity with which glaciers in the Cascades have retreated during the past century. The terminus of the glacier is now about 1 mile upslope from where the trail crosses the valley—only 100 years ago the terminus was about 0.25 downstream. Now the valley is occupied by a meltwater stream rushing amongst the jumble of characteristic glacial moraine and volcanic debris flow deposits: rock, sand, and mud. Further up the valley, the trough deepens and is flanked by a spectacular pair of ridges—the lateral moraines that constitute Railroad Grade.

This hike is just the beginning of some of the most remarkable scenery on earth. If you have the time and energy, explore! Continue up to Park Butte or Railroad Grade, hike a loop on the Scott Paul Trail, or just scramble up the Easton Glacier valley.

Hike 20 CHAIN OF LAKES

A high traverse through a volcanic landscape that is being transformed by the forces of glacial erosion, gravity, and the simple processes of freezing and thawing.

DISTANCE ■ 6 mile loop

ELEVATION ■ 4250 feet (Bagley Lake) to 5740 feet (Table Mountain)

DIFFICULTY ■ Moderate to strenuous

TOPOGRAPHIC MAPS ■ USGS Shuksan Arm; Green Trails No. 14 Mount Shuksan

GEOLOGIC MAP ■ USGS 94-403 Mount Baker

KEY REFERENCES ■ Hildreth (1996)

PRECAUTIONS ■ Depending on snow conditions it may be necessary to complete this route in reverse during any months other than July through October.

INFORMATION ■ The hike is entirely at subalpine elevations of 4000 feet to more than 1 mile high. If you can arrange a car shuttle from the visitor center to Artists Point you will save 1000 feet and more than 1 mile at the end of the hike. A trail park pass is required and can be obtained at the Heather Meadows Visitor Center.

About the Landscape: Interesting geology starts at the trailhead and never quits on this hike. Standing in the parking lot at Artists Point, you can see as much geology in a 360-degree sweep as in almost any other locality in the world. Start with Mount Baker, a dormant volcano that will erupt again, rising nearly 11,000 feet, and filling the southwest skyline. The cone you see has been constructed within the past 700,000 years, and the construction process is not finished. Beneath these recent lavas are flows of the Chilliwack Volcanics that originated as part of an ancient island arc hundreds of millions of years ago. Mount Shuksan, rising more than 9000 feet to the west, is part of a much younger seafloor, only a little over 100 million years old.

All these volcanic rocks of different ages and origins found in the same place indicates the complex geology of the Cascade Range. Immense faults have moved these rocks at least hundreds and perhaps thousands of miles from their birthplace to be assembled into the gigantic collage that constitutes the older part of the Cascade Range. Mount Baker is a geologic infant by comparison, but this volcano has packed a lot of action into its brief history. You can picture that action like this: think about huge lava flows churning down river valleys burying everything; cataclysmic explosions of red hot ash totally incinerating everything in their path clear to the Puget Lowland; the Cordilleran Ice Sheet and alpine glaciers grinding great valleys into the volcanic landscape; and last but not least, think of gravity, which brings gigantic pieces of this landscape crashing downwards, devastating the valleys and lowlands below.

Trail Guide: Take SR 542 from I-5 in Bellingham to the Heather Meadows Recreation Area (55 miles). The trailhead is at Artists Point at the end of the road.

The hike begins at Artists Point with a spectacular side trip to the summit of Table Mountain, rising 500 feet above the parking lot. The Table Mountain Trail begins in a rubble of andesite shattered into fragments by ice in cracks that pervade the mountain's cliffs. In the jumble of rocks along the trail you can also find blocks of a blue green rock containing angular chunks of brown or gray lava. This is a volcanic breccia of the Chilliwack Group, a faulted slab of metamorphosed volcanic and sedimentary rocks that formed the landscape upon which the Mount Baker volcanics were extruded. Along the steeply winding trail are spectacular examples of platy jointing, thin sheets of fractured andesite that probably formed when lava was extruded on or adjacent to snow and ice.

On the flat top of Table Mountain there are numerous boulders of Chilliwack Group rocks—an enigma because the closest outcrop of Chilliwack is at least a couple hundred feet downslope. How could these rocks have defied gravity and moved to the top of the mountain? The answer is the Cordilleran Ice Sheet that pushed down into the Puget Lowland from Canada and was so thick about 15,000 years ago that it pushed its way up the Nooksack Valley and over the 5700-foot top of Table Mountain. The Chilliwack Group rocks on top were most likely ripped off the top of Bagley Peak, carried south, and left behind as the ice melted. The scoured, striated surface on top of Table Mountain also demonstrates that glacial erosion has been a major force in creating this landscape as do the rest of the jagged peaks, U-shaped valleys, and tarns apparent in the spectacular view from the summit.

Returning to Artists Point, head out onto the Chain of Lakes loop. For the first mile, the trail runs almost horizontally along the base of the lava cliffs of Table Mountain. To your left, the deep valley of Swift Creek carves into the highly erodible ash deposits that fill the Kulshan Caldera. This caldera collapse feature, similar to Mount Mazama (Crater Lake), resulted from a catastrophic explosion that sent huge clouds of incandescent ash rolling out into the Puget Lowland a little over a million years ago, long before the current cone of Mount Baker was constructed. The only remnant left from this event, besides the caldera deposit here, is about a foot of ash near Lake Tapps, east of Tacoma. All the rest was swept away by Ice Age glaciers.

After walking 1.2 miles from the Artists Point parking lot, you will come to a junction. To the left is a trail out to the knobby spire of Coleman Pinnacle, the remnant of a lava flow extruded within the Kulshan Caldera about 300,000 years ago. It is about the same age as the Table Mountain flow, but it must be from a different eruption because these lavas contain the mineral hornblende, in contrast to the flows of Table Mountain that contain pyroxene.

Turn right to continue the Chain of Lakes loop. About 0.25 mile from the junction, look southwest toward Lasiocarpa Ridge which is capped by pyroxene andesite flows. The conspicuous tan to pink dacites beneath are also part of the ash that filled the caldera.

About 0.5 mile from the junction a unique cliff of Table Mountain andesite deserves your attention. The uniqueness of this outcrop, the horizontal rather than vertical columns, indicates the flow must have originally come down a valley. Subsequent glacial erosion has removed the valley walls, leaving Table Mountain as a high plateau, what geologists call topographic inversion. The andesite consists of white chunks of feldspar embedded in a glassy black matrix, indicating the lava cooled quite rapidly, probably flowing out onto snow or ice.

Mazama Lake is another 0.25 mile. This is a tarn that occupies a depression scooped out by a Little Ice Age glacier between 1300 and 1900. The most obvious feature of Mazama Lake is a pile of rubble dividing the lake into two segments; perhaps a recessional moraine from the same Little Ice Age glacier that created the depression the lake occupies. Alternatively, the lake basin may have been formed by an earlier, more extensive glaciation, which, if true, means the rubble is the terminal moraine of a Little Ice Age glacier.

Iceberg Lake, named for big blocks of ice from the cliffs above that float on the lake conspicuously in midsummer, is another 0.25 mile along the trail. Looking across the lake from the trail, you'll clearly see the contact between the Table Mountain lava and the U-shaped glacial valley it flowed down. This

The cliffs above Iceberg Lake are composed of andesite lava that flowed down a valley from Mount Baker more than 300,000 years ago. Now the erosion-resistant andesite forms the high plateau of Table Mountain.

is one of the most spectacular exposures of an intracanyon lava flow found anywhere in the world. Iceberg Lake was probably scooped out by glacial erosion about 8000 to 9000 years ago, judging from the age of cirque moraines in the upper part of Swift Creek. Hayes Lake is separated from Iceberg Lake by a knob of bedrock mantled with glacial till.

To take a sidetrip to Hayes and Arbuthnot Lakes, head north on the Galena Camps Trail. At the north end of Hayes Lake there is an unusual black sand beach consisting mainly of glassy andesite and feldspar grains. The source of this sediment is obviously a lava flow, but since none of the nearby flows are glassy like this sand, the flow that provided the sediment has most likely been eroded away.

At the end of Hayes Lake, outcrops of altered Chilliwack Group rock contain large amounts of potentially valuable minerals like chalcopyrite (a copper ore) and galena (a lead ore). In fact, some early miners were so excited about the prospect of finding ore in this area they drove a tunnel through the bedrock hoping to drain Hayes Lake into Arbuthnot Lake with the expectation of more ore below the waterline. There was no such luck, and the dreams of mining glory have long since faded.

Returning to the main trail, head eastward and steeply upward to Hermann Saddle, a glacial col (or low pass) separating two cirques. If you can tear your eyes away from the glorious view of Mount Baker soaring skyward on one side and Mount Shuksan on the other, check out the bedrock at the saddle, a volcanic breccia that is part of the Chilliwack Group—the same rock type as the erratics atop Table Mountain. The distinctive blue green color of the fine-grained lava matrix indicates that the rare metamorphic mineral pumpellyite is present.

From the saddle, the trail heads down a cirque headwall toward Bagley Lake. About halfway there, the trail twists its way through the jumbled boulders of a large rock avalanche that must have occurred in prehistoric time judging from the size of some of the lichen colonies growing on these rocks. Most of the avalanche blocks are Chilliwack greenstone and breccia, but a few samples of an unusual hornblende andesite can also be found. If you look uphill toward the obvious scar at the source of the avalanche, you can see a few scraps of columnar andesite clinging to the nearly vertical cliffs. This is the last remnant of lava that flowed down a canyon from Coleman Pinnacle about 300,000 years ago. Obviously the landscape has been rearranged in a big way since that time, mostly due to the erosive effects of alpine glaciers still working in this cirque during the Little Ice Age, only a few hundred years ago.

A bridge through another accumulation of big angular boulders of Chilliwack at the east end of the scooped out tarn of Bagley Lake could be the remains of a moraine that dammed the lake, but a quick glance upward reveals another landslide scar on the mountainside. Clearly these steep slopes are not resisting gravity very well.

From the bridge, hike about 0.25 mile up past a tarn, and across a spectacular glacially eroded surface where you can clearly see the pentagonal to hexagonal pattern of the top of a columnar andesite flow. As you continue on to the US Forest Service Visitor Center, you'll see that some of the columns have been used as steps.

From the visitor center, you can take the Wild Goose Trail back to the parking lot at Artists Point, or you can hike the Fire and Ice Loop, a barrier-free hike of about 0.7 mile starting and ending at the visitor center. In fact, if you don't have time to complete the Chain of Lakes Trail, you can see most of the main geologic features of the Chain of Lakes Trail: columnar andesite flows, tarn lakes, an overlook of the Bagley Lake cirque, and the talus slopes of Table Mountain, on this short hike. Interpretative signs along the trail provide information on the geology and ecology.

Hike 21 COPPER RIDGE

Journey through glacial landforms into the heart of the North Cascades for a spectacular view of the volcanic and plutonic rocks produced by the Cascadia subduction zone.

DISTANCE ■ 10 miles

ELEVATION ■ 4400 feet to 6840 feet (Copper Ridge)

DIFFICULTY ■ Strenuous

TOPOGRAPHIC MAPS ■ USGS Mount Shuksan and Copper Mountain; Green Trails No. 14 Mount Shuksan and No. 15 Mount Challenger

GEOLOGIC MAP ■ USGS Mount Baker 30' x 60' quadrangle

KEY REFERENCES ■ Tepper (1996)

About the Landscape: For more than 40 million years, the Juan de Fuca Plate has plunged under the west coast of Washington to form what is now called the Cascadia Subduction Zone. At a depth of about 50 to 60 miles, the plate begins to dehydrate and partially melt releasing fluids that rise into the mantle and lower crust, causing even more melting. The result is like a big factory that continuously produces great batches of molten rock and then ships them upward into the basement of the Cascade Range directly above the melt zone. Some of the melt makes it all of the way to the surface and builds great volcanic peaks like Mount Rainier, Mount St. Helens, and Mount Baker. However, much of it runs out of energy deep underground and solidifies to form masses of granitic rock called plutons.

On this hike, you will see both the volcanic and plutonic products of subduction. The plutonic rocks form the high ridges of Goat Mountain, Mount Sefrit, Nooksack Ridge, Ruth Mountain, and the whole landscape from Egg Lake north to the Canadian border. The volcanic scenario is centered in the vicinity of Hannegan Pass where about 3.5 million years ago a huge mass of molten rock rose to within a mile or two of the surface. After a series of eruptions vented the molten rock to the surface, there was a major collapse into the vacated space. The result was catastrophic. Huge explosions of glowing ash, interspersed with lava flows, devastated everything within tens of miles of the eruption and undoubtedly made life difficult hundreds of miles away (see also Hike 20). The evidence for this event is a huge pile of light-colored ash hundreds to thousands of feet thick found around Hannegan Pass.

Trail Guide: Turn left onto FR 32 from SR 542 about 13 miles east of Glacier. Drive 6.5 miles to the trailhead at the end of this dirt road. This hike involves more than 4000 feet of elevation gain over two passes. Add another 1000 feet of climbing and 2.4 miles if you plan to continue on to Copper Lake. Boundary camp at 5 miles from the trailhead is the best place to stay if you have planned an overnight trip because it is on the other side of Hannegan Pass just before you start up again toward Copper Ridge. Permits to stay at all campsites must be obtained at the Glacier Ranger Station.

The first mile or so is a gentle rise through the alders and willows that have sprouted on the floodplain of Ruth Creek. The size of this vegetation is an indication of how long ago the last flood occurred. To the south, across a U-shaped glacial valley, Nooksack Ridge rises 4000 feet, almost vertically, and is capped by the glacial horn of 7191-foot Mount Sefrit.

Scattered outcrops along the trail reveal several different plutonic rock types of the Chilliwack **batholith.** The first is a granodiorite, looking like salt and pepper with shiny black specks of biotite embedded in light-colored quartz and feldspar. Further up the trail, you'll encounter coarser grained tonalite and diorite that both contain small black prisms of the mineral hornblende. The main difference between them is that tonalite contains lots of gray-colored crystals of quartz, and the diorite has none.

At about 4 miles out, the trail begins to switchback steeply up toward Hannegan Pass. Here the first outcrops of the Hannegan volcanics can be seen where a series of springs emerge from ash deposits oxidized to form red and orange iron minerals. These are the last scraps of a thick sheet of ash that once filled the whole Ruth Creek valley. By the time you get to the turnoff to Hannegan Camp, the underlying granodiorite is again exposed.

At Hannegan Pass (5100 feet), the trail branches three ways. The left-hand trail goes to Hannegan Peak (6186 feet) through a stack of ash flows from the Hannegan caldera. To the right, a climbers' scramble trail traverses through ash flow deposits onto the granitic rocks of Ruth Peak. These are both great choices for a day trip.

If you plan a longer hike with overnights, proceed straight ahead for the descent to Boundary Camp. On the way down, you will have one of the world's best views of the interior architecture of a caldera complex. Thanks to the extensive glacial erosion of the high Cascades, you can clearly see the immense pile of white to pink ash deposits cut by dikes and sills of andesite. The rim of cliffs that surround Boundary Camp is very close to the edge of the caldera, so you can get an idea of its dimensions.

The trail from Boundary Camp to Egg Lake ascends through the caldera deposits, which can be examined in detail where the trail crosses Hells Gorge.

Just before the trail crosses the stream, layers of a quartz-rich dacite tuff are cut diagonally by a basalt dike. The round white crystals in the basalt are amygdules that consist of calcite and zeolite that filled vesicles (gas bubble cavities).

Continue onward and upward for another 0.3 mile where the trail finally flattens out (temporarily) and traverse along the top of a huge north-facing cirque headwall that plunges down into the headwaters of Silesia Creek. Just over the edge, about 20 feet below the trail, a unique glassy rock similar to obsidian crops out in a band about 3 feet thick. This is a vitrophyre that formed when the base of one of the ash flows was heated beyond the melting point and then rapidly cooled. Small shards of rock scattered around the outcrop indicate that Native Americans may have used this site as a source for tools and projectile points.

Between 8 and 9 miles out, two unusual varieties of plutonic rock can be found. Near Silesia Creek are pink megacrysts of potassium feldspar, some more than an inch across, embedded in a granodiorite. The origin of these huge crystals is still a topic of debate among geologists. Near the turnoff to Egg Lake Camp, appropriately, are dark diorite egg-shaped inclusions in the light-colored granodiorite; probably these bits of rock broke off as the pluton pushed its way upward through the crust of the earth.

At about 9 miles the trail begins to climb steeply toward the Copper Ridge

Uplift of the Cascades during the past 15 million years has revealed the once deeply buried mass of granodiorite exposed in these cliffs above the Hannegan Pass trail.

lookout at 6260 feet. About halfway up, a very steep and narrow gorge on the right side of the trail probably represents a fault zone with shattered rocks that have been more easily eroded than the surrounding rock. There are also a few outcrops of conglomerate that seem totally out of place in the midst of all of these plutonic rocks. Careful examination will show that the conglomerate has been baked, presumably by the heat of the surrounding pluton, therefore, this rock must be part of a roof pendant, a small remnant of the country rock that was intruded. The rest of the country rock has been eroded away to reveal the plutonic rocks below.

The lookout is built on a 34-million-year-old diorite and gabbro pluton that extends from here to Copper Lake, about 1 mile away. Note that layers of almost pure black hornblende prisms can be found in both the diorite and the gabbro. The rock which forms Mount Sefrit, seen at the beginning of the hike, is very similar, but much younger at 23 million years.

The view from the lookout is certainly one of the best in the North Cascades. The jagged summits of the Pickett Range and Mount Challenger to the southeast, Mount Redoubt rising nearly 9000 feet to cap the northeast skyline, and Slesse Peak just across the Canadian border to the northeast are composed mainly of the Skagit Gneiss Complex and plutonic rocks of the Chilliwack batholith.

From Copper Ridge you can return by the same route, or if you have an extra day, continue northward to the Chilliwack Valley and complete an 8.5-mile loop back to Boundary Camp. This will provide a lot more scenery, but the geology remains essentially the same.

ROSS LAKE

Hike

Descend into the Skagit River Gorge to view high-grade metamorphic and igneous rocks that were 80,000 feet below the surface of the earth before the uplift of the present-day Cascades. This rock serves as the buttress for Ross Dam, so there are also some interesting aspects of geological engineering.

DISTANCE ■ 1 to 7 miles

ELEVATION ■ 2100 feet to 1600 feet (Ross Dam)

TOPOGRAPHIC MAPS ■ USGS Ross Dam and Pumpkin Mountain

GEOLOGIC MAP ■ DGER GM-23 Marblemount

KEY REFERENCES ■ Babcock and Misch (1989)

About the Landscape: One of the most extensive geologic units in the North Cascades is the Skagit Gneiss Complex. The last word of the name tells the story; these are not simple rocks. Their history began about 220 million years ago in an ancient sea where erupting volcanoes were building volcanic islands, much like the present day Aleutians or Indonesia. The seafloor deposits consisted mainly of sediments eroded from the volcanic islands and lava flows of andesite or basalt. About 90 million years ago, the crustal block containing these volcanic and sedimentary rocks was plunged to great depths within the earth—80,000 to 100,000 feet deep in some places.

What caused this tectonic burial event is an ongoing geologic controversy. One hypothesis is that there was a head-on collision between a tectonic plate called Wrangellia and the North American Plate. As Wrangellia pushed inland, the western edge of North America was forced downward. The result was metamorphism with sediments converted to schists and volcanics to amphibolites. The alternative view is that Wrangellia never crashed over the top of North America. Instead, the collision was more of a sideswipe, causing metamorphism when huge amounts of molten rock were generated and buoyantly rose toward the surface. The magma-loading, or sideswipe, hypothesis is that the weight of all this molten material pushed the surrounding rocks down to levels deep enough that they were metamorphosed.

The second part of the story in the Skagit Gneiss Complex also involves melting. Between 90 and 45 million years ago, the deepest rocks got so hot they began to melt, but not completely. The light-colored quartz and feldspar melted and formed a kind of rock slush with dark unmelted crystals of hornblende and biotite. As the slush was squeezed to and fro, a complicated mixture called a **migmatite** was formed. Where melting was more extensive, huge pools of molten rocks (magma) formed and began to rise upward through the migmatites. These were also squeezed by tectonic forces as they crystallized, forming a rock with aligned crystals called an **orthogneiss.**

Marble is a rare rock type in the Skagit Complex. These small bodies of rock may be the metamorphosed fossil remnant of calcareous algae mats that were deposited here and there amidst the sediments of the ancient Skagit sea.

Trail Guide: Drive on SR 20 to milepost 134 about 14 miles east of the town of Newhalem. The trailhead is at a large parking area on the west side of the road. This is a good early-season hike that is generally snow free by mid-May. The trail is very well maintained and serves as an access route for day hikers who want a close-up look at the imposing concrete structure of Ross Dam or who are heading for Ross Lake Resort. The trail continues to Big Beaver Creek, which is the habitat for gigantic trees that comprise one of the last stands of old growth western red cedar in the Pacific Northwest. It is also a perfect habitat for inumerable mosquitoes that discourage sightseeing. The main disadvantage of this hike is that it is all downhill at the beginning, and thus, all uphill at the end. Ross Dam is more than 500 feet below the trailhead, and the powerhouse is another 500 feet below that.

The rock buttresses that anchor the ends of Ross Dam are composed of Skagit gneiss.

The trail begins on the right side of the parking area and heads downward through a scrubby forest of Douglas fir, pine, and hemlock. All along the trail are well-weathered outcrops of orthogneiss containing aligned crystals of biotite, quartz, and feldspar. About 0.25 mile from the trailhead is a glacially polished outcrop crossing the trail, clearly showing the trend of the foliation in a northwest direction. Just a bit further on, the trail crosses Happy Creek, which lives up to its name, tumbling exuberantly downslope. Just out of sight, however, the whole stream runs into a tunnel that diverts the flow into Ross Lake. Continuing along the trail, the rock outcrops become more prominent, forming low cliffs of banded gneiss and biotite schist cut by pods and veins of quartz-feldspar **pegmatite.** Just below the cliffs, huge blocks of gneiss scattered on the slope look like some kind of rockfall, but considering the topography, they are probably glacial erratics.

Where the trail intersects with a service road, turn right for a brief side-excursion. Continue past more cliffs of schist, gneiss, and migmatite. Cross a bridge above the Happy Creek diversion tunnel and go to the boat landing at the end of the road. Just up the lake are some gray marble outcrops exposed when the level of Ross Lake is low during the summer. In addition to the gray to white calcite, some very unusual minerals can be found including phlogopite, spinel, humite, tremolite, diopside, and scapolite.

Retrace your steps to the junction of the Happy Creek Trail. Continue on until this road intersects with another that leads to Ross Dam. Head downhill to the dam through a huge roadcut in orthogneiss. This orthogneiss is variably foliated and is immediately recognizable because it is much more uniform in composition than the schist and gneiss outcrops. Notice all of the fractures in the rock and the dark, streaky fault surfaces called slickensides. Because this rock forms the buttresses of Ross Dam, it was important for geological engineers to recognize this weakness in the rock and grout the rock together with concrete to provide increased stability.

Walking out on the dam notice the waffle iron pattern of the front face, which rises 540 feet above the river bottom. This was the mold for an intended addition of another 120 feet to the dam by increasing the height and thickness. Also view the panorama of surrounding peaks: Sourdough Mountain to the west; Colonial, Snowfield, and Pyramid Peaks to the south (from left to right); Ruby Mountain to the west; and Jack Mountain to the north. All are composed of Skagit Gneiss except Jack Mountain, which consists mainly of metachert and amphibolite.

From here the trail continues northward along the west bank of Ross Lake with numerous outcrops of orthogneiss. About 0.5 mile from the dam, a very different rock type, a mica-schist formed by the metamorphism of sediment deposited on an ancient seafloor, is exposed in the bed of a small creek. This schist contains both biotite and muscovite mica along with quartz and feldspar and is so well foliated that it forms sheets like pages in a book.

At 0.7 mile from the dam, a spur trail leads down to the Ross Lake Resort. Here the outcrops are orthogneiss, although there are abundant fragments of schist in the rubble along the shoreline. The West Bank Trail continues northward through alternating outcrops of schist, banded gneiss, and orthogneiss. There is an especially good outcrop of orthogneiss near the mouth of Pierce Creek. At 5.2 miles the trail reaches the Big Beaver Valley, which in its lower part consists of a series of marshes formed when big rock slides and debris flows from the steep glacially sculpted walls blocked the drainage. From here, return to the trailhead, or if you are equipped for several days of hiking go up the Big Beaver Trail to Little Beaver Valley and some of the most spectacular glacial scenery in the world.

HARTS PASS

Explore the depths of the Methow Graben from a subalpine zone perspective.

DISTANCE ■ 2 to 6 miles

DIFFICULTY ■ Moderate

ELEVATION ■ 6260 feet (Windy Pass) to 6840 feet (Grasshopper Pass)

TOPOGRAPHIC MAPS ■ USGS Washington Pass and Pasayten Peak; Green Trails No. 50 Washington Pass and No. 18 Pasayten Peak

GEOLOGIC MAP ■ DGER 90-5 Robinson Mountain

KEY REFERENCES ■ Barksdale (1975); McGroder and others (1990)

PRECAUTIONS ■ Generally, the Harts Pass Road is snowbound until at least early August.

About the Landscape: The Methow region has been called the Rosetta stone of Cascades geology because it consists mainly of sedimentary and volcanic rocks that preserve a story of the conditions of the earth in the Pacific Northwest at the time they were deposited. The rocks tell a story of land areas adjacent to the Methow moving up and down like pistons in an engine; first the land to the east rose, then the land to the west rose, and then the east again. The oldest of these rocks, the Twisp Formation, represents submarine landslides along the continental margin prior to 170 million years ago.

Sometime between 155 and 135 million years ago the volcanic and sedimentary rocks of the Newby Group were deposited. These form the basement upon which the Harts Pass rocks were deposited. The Goat Creek, Panther Creek, and Harts Pass Formations consist of sandstones, shales, and conglomerates mainly derived from granitic mountains to the east 125 to 105 million years ago. About 105 million years ago, there was a sudden change as the Virginian Ridge Formation was deposited. The source of sediments switched to the west as terranes like the Hozameen arrived and smashed into the western margin of North America. Gray and black pieces of chert from these western terranes were carried into the Methow Basin and can be found as a distinct component of the sandstones and conglomerates in the Virginian Ridge Formation.

After the western terranes became part of North America, they were stitched together by plutons and dikes of the Black Peak batholith indicating that the Methow and Crystalline Core terranes had merged by 90 to 88 million years ago. The combined terranes had arrived at their present latitude in Washington by 48 million years ago when the Golden Horn batholith was intruded. The dikes seen on both legs of the hike resemble Golden Horn intrusives, although their exact ages have yet to be determined.

Trail Guide: This hike is on two trails in the vicinity of Harts Pass. One is the Windy Pass Trail heading north from the road to Slate Peak. The other is the Grasshopper Pass Trail that heads in a southerly direction from Harts Pass Road. Both trails are part of the Pacific Crest Trail. Both hikes could be accomplished in a long day, but it would be far better to spend the night at the glorious Meadows Campground and enjoy one hike a day at a more leisurely pace. Note that trailers are not allowed on the road to the Meadows Campground.

From Mazama drive 9 miles on FR 1163 to the junction with the Harts Pass Road (FR 5400). Turn right and continue about 11 miles to Harts Pass. For the

The high alpine meadows in the vicinity of Harts Pass are underlain by glacially eroded sandstones of the Harts Pass Formation.

Grasshopper Pass trailhead, turn left and proceed 2 miles south on the Meadows Campground Road. For the Windy Pass trailhead, continue upwards toward Slate Peak for 1.5 miles to the trailhead, which is at the first switchback above Harts Pass.

Both trails start well above 6000 feet in the subalpine zone and climb gently only a few hundred feet on well-maintained paths. Late August and early September are prime times for wildflowers in these expansive meadows.

From the Windy Pass trailhead, the trail ascends gently through an alpine meadow with groves of larch. The first outcrops, about 50 yards from the trailhead, are sandstones of the Harts Pass Formation composed mainly of quartz and feldspar eroded from granitic highlands to the east. In about 0.5 mile, the trail reaches a crest and begins a long descent. At about 1 mile the trail crosses a series of springs. Notice how different the vegetation is in these wetland areas (for example, monkeyflowers are found almost exclusively in these damp spots).

At about 1.5 miles, just beyond a talus slope below the Slate Peak lookout, a well defined rhyolite or dacite dike runs parallel to the trail for about 25 yards, before cutting uphill through dark shales of the Virginian Ridge Formation. The dike rock is pink with gray phenocrysts of quartz and white phenocrysts of feldspar. On surfaces of the lava there are convolute patterns of reddish brown stripes on a brownish background due to chemical weathering that concentrated iron oxides in bands called leisegang. Continuing along the trail, you can see scattered outcrops of Virginian Ridge shale, sandstone, and the notorious chert-pebble conglomerate. Most of these rocks are black because they contain lots of graphite formed by the decomposition of organic material. You can actually write with pieces of Virginian Ridge shale.

If you are planning to complete both trails in one day, Buffalo Pass, at 2 miles, is a good turn-around point with a glorious view down the U-shaped glacial valley of the Pasayten River. If you have plenty of time, continue on to Windy Pass and more fabulous views of the Pasayten Wilderness and some not-so-pretty vistas of some of the mineral development work that is still being done in this area.

The Grasshopper Pass trail starts at the end of a road that continues south from the Meadows Campground. Join the Pacific Crest Trail from a short spur that leaves the north end of the parking area near a bulletin board. You can take a short side trip up the road to the abandoned Brown Bear Mine. If you spend a lot of time chipping away at the white quartz veins in the more extensive upper workings, you will probably find at least a fleck or two of gold. This can be distinguished from the more common pyrite (fool's gold) by the fact that you can smear the gold out on the rock with the tip of a knife.

The main trail below passes through a pair of cirques filled with talus from the outcrops above. These are frost-shattered blocks of the Harts Pass Formation. Some of these display classic sedimentary structures, like cross-bedding, graded bedding, and scoured channels. The sandstones have been tilted to a nearly vertical inclination. Looking east, across the valley of Rattlesnake Creek, you can see that almost horizontal beds of Virginian Ridge Formation have been deposited across the truncated tops of the Harts Pass Formation. This angular **unconformity** probably formed as some chert-rich terrane to the west smashed into the Methow.

The trail continues a moderate uphill climb to a hairpin bend at about 1 mile, where it begins a long westward descent toward Tatie Peak. Great ribs of Harts Pass sandstone, which are more resistant to erosion than the layers of shale in between them, run down the slopes. The view from here is spectacular: to the southwest, the granitic spires of the Golden Horn batholith including Silver Star Mountain, the Needles, Tower Mountain, and the Golden Horn itself. Further north is the serrated skyline of Ragged Ridge in the Black Peak batholith, and closer up, the looming presence of Azurite Peak, composed of Harts Pass sandstone.

As the trail begins to climb again, a swarm of igneous dikes can be seen. These are composed of rhyolite or dacite with abundant phenocrysts of gray quartz and white feldspar. Further up the trail, some of the dikes contain rapakivi feldspars, a very unusual texture—something like rabbit eyes staring out from the rock with a pink feldspar surrounded by a white rim. Similar rocks are found in the Golden Horn batholith to the west, so these dikes may have been injected from the same batch of magma. If so, they are about 50 million years old.

Continuing uphill beneath Tatie Peak, there is a sudden change from light sandstone to black shales. This is the contact between the Harts Pass Formation and the older Panther Creek Formation. When you reach this point, walk back about 10 yards to see a textbook example of one of the rhyolite dikes. Most of the dike contains abundant white phenocrysts of feldspar, but along the contact with the black shale, there is a 0.5-inch wide band of very fine-grained rock. This is a chilled margin, where the molten rock of the dike has cooled so rapidly that only tiny crystals were able to grow. Notice that the shale along the contact has been baked by the heat of the dike into a hard splintery contact metamorphic rock called hornfels. Similar pieces of baked shale can be found as inclusions in the dike.

The black Panther Creek shales crop out for only about 50 yards along the trail. They abruptly end with the recurrence of more sandstone beds, but unlike the Harts Pass Formation these sandstone beds contain numerous flecks of black chert and abundant layers of black shale. The Goat Creek Formation crops out from here to Tatie Pass where the trail flattens at a saddle on the southwest ridge of Tatie Peak. From a geologic viewpoint, this is a good place to turn around; from here on, a series of faults repeats the rocks already seen. If you continue, the trail stays high, with wide and handsome views until Grasshopper Pass, which is about 5 miles from the trailhead.

KENNEDY HOT SPRINGS

Although the springs are now only lukewarm, there is abundant evidence of hot times in the White Chuck Valley.

DISTANCE ■ 5 miles

ELEVATION ■ 3300 feet to 4300 feet (hot springs)

DIFFICULTY ■ Moderate

TOPOGRAPHIC MAPS ■ USGS Sloan Peak and Glacier Peak; Geographic Glacier Peak Wilderness; Green Trails Nos. 111, 112

GEOLOGIC MAP ■ USGS 88-692 Sauk River

KEY REFERENCES ■ Beget (1992); Mastin and Waitt (1995)

About the Landscape: Like Mount Baker to the north, Glacier Peak is a stratovolcano that has recently been extruded on top of older rocks of the Cascade Range. The older rocks exposed are schists and gneisses of the Nason terrane. As shown on the terrane map (figure 7) this block of igneous and metamorphic rocks extends all the way from central Washington to the North Cascades. Two very different rock types can be seen along the trail: the first is a gneiss with distinct black and white layers, the other is the Chiwaukum Schist, which also can be seen in the Icicle River Canyon (Hike 27). Both are probably of Cretaceous age.

Glacier Peak can only be seen in a couple of peek-a-boo views, but the deposits from this volcano at one time filled the White Chuck Valley to the brim. Between 12,500 and 13,000 years ago there were nine ash eruptions, the largest of which blew out three times more ash than the 1980 eruption of Mount St. Helens. This huge eruption covered the entire landscape around the volcano, but most of it blew to the east on the prevailing winds. During this same eruptive period, possibly hundreds of lahars roared down river valleys on the west side and out into the Puget Lowland. Less numerous, but equally devastating, were pyroclastic flows of pumice and ash that filled the valley hundreds of feet deep—flows mainly due to collapse of lava domes at the summit of the peak. Most consisted of loose pyroclastic material, but some of the flows were hot enough to fuse into light-colored layers of **welded tuff,** a process that takes a temperature of 1500 to 2000 degrees Fahrenheit. Another batch of lahars reached as far as the Skagit Valley between 6300 and 5900 years ago. A more recent mudflow extended as far as the confluence of the White Chuck and Sauk Rivers.

The remnants of lahar and pyroclastic flow deposits now form terraces on either side of the White Chuck River and are collectively known as the White Chuck fill. The trail travels through these terraces and provides a good opportunity to contemplate the hazards of living in this valley.

Trail Guide: Drive 9.5 miles south of Darrington on the Mountain Loop Highway and turn left (east) onto the White Chuck River Road (FR 23). Continue 10.5 miles to the trailhead at a large parking area on the right. This hike is on a well-maintained trail with a few rocky spots and a couple of narrow log bridges to negotiate. You have to climb over 1000 feet on the way in and another few hundred feet coming back out, but there are enough switchbacks to keep the climbing intensity moderate. The elevation is fairly low, so the trail should generally be accessible by late May or early June. Try this as a cross-country ski trip in midwinter, but be cautious of avalanches.

The journey to Kennedy Hot Springs begins on a high terrace remnant of the volcanic debris that once filled the valley of the White Chuck River. The zone of devastation is now masked by a forest of Douglas fir, cedar, and hemlock, but here and there along the trail the evidence of a past disaster can still be found. The first indication is a bank full of volcanic boulders exposed just beyond the Glacier Peak Wilderness Area sign. The andesite, dacite, and pumice fragments found here could only have originated on the flanks of Glacier Peak, more than 6 miles to the east.

Farther along the trail, metamorphic schists and gneisses of the Nason terrane are as much as 160 million years old. If you are hiking in the sunshine look carefully at the dirt along the trail. It glitters with tiny flakes of mica eroded from the metamorphic rocks.

At about 1.2 miles, the trail crosses a bridge over Fire Creek. The boulders in the streambed are a mixture of Glacier Peak volcanics and Nason terrane metamorphics. The most distinctive is a large boulder of quartz-feldspar pegmatite along the bank just upstream from the bridge.

Beyond the turnoff to the Meadow Mountain Trail at 1.3 miles, there is a short ascent and then a descent toward the White Chuck Valley. Just beyond the crest is an excellent exposure of one of the lahars that fills this valley with cobbles and boulders of lava (andesite and dacite) embedded in sand-sized volcanic ash. About 50 yards beyond the log bridge over Pumice Creek (at about 1.5 miles), the trail flattens out on a terrace alongside the White Chuck River and is obstructed by a series of big rocks that have fallen from the cliffs above. These are the same volcanic boulders that were seen in the lahar exposure, but here the deposit forms cliffs a hundred or more feet high. This is only a small remnant of the volcanic debris that once filled this valley.

After crossing through several small lahar terraces just above river level the trail switchbacks up and around a landslide. Just beyond the last switchback

Geologist Sue DeBari soaks in the murky water of Kennedy Hot Springs.

are gray rocks of a welded tuff from a pyroclastic flow so hot when it came down the valley that it incinerated everything in its path, then welded itself together as it settled out. These rocks are best examined in fresh exposures where the trail begins to descend. Looking carefully, you can see shiny black prisms of pyroxene or hornblende, and nearly clear crystals of quartz surrounded by gray ash. Fragments of pumice are also part of the mix. These tend to weather out into cavities, giving the tuff a pockmarked appearance.

The trail again descends to near river level and continues almost level for about 0.5 mile along terraces before it begins to ascend again. Just as the trail rises, a light-colored ash makes up the banks along the side of the trail. Unlike the pyroclastic flows from hot ash avalanches down the side of the volcano, this deposit is from the slow but steady settling of particles from ash clouds produced by an eruption.

At about 3.5 miles, after switchbacking up to another crest along the trail, a deep canyon cuts into the sidewall of the main valley. At the very top is a section of light-colored airfall ash underlain by a thick section of volcanic ash embedded with numerous dark fragments of lava. This pyroclastic flow unit forms a flat-topped terrace that caps the valley fill. Radiocarbon dates from charcoal in the ash indicate this was generated as an immense cloud of ash that rushed down the White Chuck Valley during a major eruption of Glacier Peak between 12,500 and 13,000 years ago.

After descending again, the trail goes along the White Chuck River flood-plain. About 0.6 mile beyond the Glacier Creek crossing there is a ghost forest of snags formed from trees buried by a very recent debris flow that apparently came from Glacier Peak down Kennedy Creek and into the White Chuck Valley. At 5.1 miles is the junction with the Kennedy Ridge Trail, and in another 0.2 mile a log bridge crossing Kennedy Creek. Just beyond the crossing is a guard station with a spring in the hillside to the east. To reach the hot springs, cross the bridge over the White Chuck River, turn left and follow the trail upstream about 100 yards.

If you are expecting the hot springs to be hot, they are not. Small, lukewarm (85 degrees Fahrenheit), and murky is an accurate description. But some very interesting deposits of bright orange carbonate form little terraces on the boulders as the springs drain toward the river. The color may be in part from the iron-rich bacteria that thrive in the tepid water.

The campground is an ideal base for further exploration of the Glacier Peak area. The steep 2-mile hike to Lake Byrne provides some excellent exposures of Nason terrane schists and gneisses. The Kennedy Ridge Trail also has impressive outcrops of contorted metamorphic rocks and some conspicuous rockslides.

Hike

25

BIG FOUR ICE CAVES

Caves cut in ice formed at the base of a huge snow avalanche deposit.

DISTANCE ■ 1 mile

ELEVATION ■ 1900 feet to 2100 feet

DIFFICULTY ■ Easy

TOPOGRAPHIC MAP ■ USGS Silverton

GEOLOGIC MAP ■ USGS 88-692 Sauk River

PRECAUTIONS ■ Although it is tempting on a hot day, DO NOT ENTER the ice caves. They are subject to collapse without warning; unwary hikers have been fatally injured.

About the Landscape: During the winter months, huge snow avalanches roar down a nearly vertical 4000-foot rock wall of Big Four Mountain to accumulate on a plateau at the base of the slope. Much more snow builds up during the winter than melts in the summer, so the deposits at the base are under constant pressure from the weight of the snow above causing metamorphic recrystallization from snow to ice. This is similar to the process forming glacial ice, except that the Big Four ice does not flow downslope. Instead, during the late summer months, most of the overlying snow disappears and meltwater streams cut pathways through the base of the ice. These tunnels are enlarged by warm air flowing through; at the end of the summer they are tens of feet high and wide.

Trail Guide: From Everett, take US 2 east to SR 9. Drive north and turn off on SR 92, going 8 miles to Granite Falls. From Granite Falls, drive east about 25 miles on the Mountain Loop Highway to the Big Four picnic area on the south side of the road. A trail park pass is required. This and information about the area can be obtained at the US Forest Service Visitor Center in Verlot. The well-maintained trail, which is especially suitable for families, meanders through a forest and up a hill before emerging onto an open plateau at the base of Big Four Mountain. The ice caves generally emerge in late July and are at their best in August.

For the first 0.5 mile, trail 723 is a walk through a western hemlock, Pacific silver fir, and western red cedar forest with boardwalks over a montane wetland. At about 0.4 mile, cross the Stillaguamish River on a suspension bridge. If the water is low, note the bedload of boulders, which are moved downstream during high water and flood conditions. Just a bit further, a second bridge crosses over a tributary stream where the bedload boulders are bigger yet, even though the stream is much smaller. Streams flowing down steeper slopes have higher velocities, and thus more energy to move larger-size sediments.

As the trail starts to rise from the river valley, clays can be found that must be lake deposits with their fine layering and lack of the pebbles and boulders of till deposits. Presumably, the lake formed due to a landslide downstream, or due to the Puget Lobe of the Cordilleran Ice Sheet pushing up the Stillaguamish Valley from the Puget Lowland.

At about 1 mile, the trail reaches a short open plateau at the base of the nearly vertical north face of Big Four Mountain. The rock debris covering the trail has fallen from the cliffs above. Looking at sandstone blocks the size of a small cabin, you get the impression that this would not be the place to build your dream home. In fact, if you are here early in the summer, keep back a safe distance to avoid avalanches. The ice caves emerge from under their snowslide cover about the end of July or the beginning of August. Generally there are two or three caves providing a natural air conditioning system as meltwater and equally chilly air flow through them. The cool downdrafts minimize vegetation on the rocky plateau and allow subalpine wildflowers to grow at an unusually low altitude. The ice walls show a characteristic blue color caused by the fact that ice molecules absorb all of the frequencies of sunlight

Meltwater has cut these caves into a mass of ice formed from snow avalanche deposits that accumulate during the winter at the base of Big Four Mountain.

except the highly energetic blue band, which escapes to reach your eyes. Large blocks of ice around the entrances give testimony to the unstable nature of the caves as the ceilings periodically collapse.

Hike 26

DECEPTION FALLS

An intriguing streamside walk through an old-growth forest with interesting rocks and puzzling landforms.

DISTANCE ▪ About 0.7 mile

ELEVATION ▪ 1800 feet to 1720 feet (lowest point on loop)

DIFFICULTY ▪ Easy

TOPOGRAPHIC MAP ▪ USGS Scenic Quadrangle

GEOLOGIC MAP ▪ USGS I-1963 Skykomish River

KEY REFERENCES ▪ Erikson (1977); Macloughlin (1994)

About the Landscape: There are two interrelated geologic stories displayed on this short hike. The first is about intrusion of the Mount Stuart batholith and the other is about how Deception Creek and the Tye River flow through the rock of the batholith.

The Mount Stuart batholith is a huge mass of plutonic rock that consists of two major phases: an eastern pluton that was intruded about 93 million years ago and a western pluton at about 85 million years. Both are composed mainly of granodiorite and tonalite. The Mount Stuart batholith is geologically controversial because it has been magnetized in a way that suggests it

125

may have been intruded as much as 1500 miles to the south of here, in Baja California, then transported northward by plate tectonic processes. An alternative interpretation is that the entire batholith has been tilted along faults so that the magnetic inclinations observed give a false impression. Another controversy is the origin of the batholith. It could be the result of heat and pressure generated by terranes smashing together, but maybe it is the product of the same kind of subduction process along a continental margin that has produced the more recent granitic rocks of the Cascade Range.

The other geologic activity here is watching the rivers flow. Deception Creek crashes down over a series of waterfalls to its junction with the Tye River. The blocks of rock over which both of these streams flow are formed by joints. Remember that these plutonic rocks originally crystallized several miles deep within the earth. Now at the surface, a lot of pressure has been removed, resulting in expansion of the rock; and as it expands it cracks into big blocks forming a pathway for the rivers. Fault lines of shattered rock can also provide pathways for streamflow, but are much less common than joints.

Trail Guide: The trailhead is at a rest area near mile 57 on US 2, about 8 miles east of Skykomish. This loop trail is partly barrier free. Most of the walk is through an old-growth forest, but there are splendid vistas out over rushing waters of the Tye River and Deception Creek.

The hike begins just to the right of the restrooms in the parking lot. The first part descends through western hemlock, Douglas fir, and western red cedar to a streambed that serves as an overflow channel for Deception Creek when it is at flood stage. On the right side of the far end of the bridge over the creek, is a large outcrop of biotite-hornblende granodiorite with numerous dark gabbro xenoliths and a cross-cutting andesite dike. Also notice the potholes that have been ground into the granodiorite in the stream bed.

At the first overlook of the Tye River, observe the size of the boulders in the channel. During flood stage these boulders are easily carried as bedload by the force of the flowing stream. The relatively straight channel of the Tye River here probably follows joints providing a path of least resistance.

At the second overlook, the river suddenly makes a sharp bend into a narrow cleft that runs in a perfectly straight line 100 feet or more. The interpretive sign suggests three possibilities for this very unusual feature: (1) diversion of the stream by a log jam; (2) erosion of a soft layer of rock; and (3) a fault. The first suggestion makes no sense at all. How could a log jam of wood force a stream to cut a vertical slot into solid bedrock? To do so the log jam would have to persist without rotting away for maybe a million years or so. Number two is plausible. The slot is about the same width as dikes seen upstream in Deception Creek, but there the dikes seem to be just as resistant to erosion as the granodiorite. The best possibility is a fault or series of closely spaced joints that would break the granodiorite into easily erodible chunks. At least two generations of dikes that have not been eroded into slots can be seen in the stream bed: an older generation of dark andesite or basalt dikes is clearly cut by younger light-colored granitic dikes.

At the third turnout (second platform) notice that the river valley is U-shaped with a narrow V-shaped channel cut into the bottom. The interpretive sign "From Peaks to Puget Sound" claims that the U shape is due to glaciers that melted away 14,000 years ago. This refers to the Puget Lobe of the Cordilleran Ice Sheet. That ice, however, did not make it this far up into the Cascades; in fact, there is a huge terminal moraine from this ice sheet a few miles east of Skykomish. Instead, this glacial valley was probably formed by an alpine glacier that flowed down from the crest of the Cascades about 20,000 years ago and melted away due to a locally warming climate by the time the ice sheet occupied the Lowland.

Before returning to the parking lot, cross the bridge and pass under US 2 to a viewpoint that looks up Deception Creek. Here again, you can see the older dark dikes and younger light dikes cutting through the granodiorite. At the overlook, the sign says that the Mount Stuart batholith crystallized 85 million years ago, but there is evidence that the granodiorite here is 93 million years old.

ICICLE GORGE

Hike 27

Take a long walk to observe the products of erosion and deposition by a typical mountain stream, including a gorge composed of some of the most spectacular metamorphic rocks found anywhere in Washington.

DISTANCE ■ 4 mile loop

ELEVATION ■ 2700 feet to 2900 feet (high point on loop)

DIFFICULTY ■ Easy

TOPOGRAPHIC MAPS ■ USGS Chiwaukum Mountains; Green Trails No. 177 Chiwaukum Mountains

GEOLOGIC MAP ■ USGS I-1661 Chelan

KEY REFERENCES ■ Macloughlin (1994)

PRECAUTIONS ■ If you go off-trail to examine schists in the Gorge, be careful of slippery rocks.

About the Landscape: There are two separate stories to be told on this hike. The first is about the Nason terrane, composed of the Chiwaukum schist bedrock exposed in the inner gorge and surrounding cliffs. This rock started out as sediments on a Cretaceous seafloor that were first regionally metamorphosed to schist about 220 million years ago and then contact metamorphosed by intrusion of the Mount Stuart batholith about 90 million years ago. This dual metamorphism is unusual; but it can also be found in almost identical schists located to the north across the border near Harrison Lake, British Columbia. Geologists believe that the Harrison Lake schists were once part of the Chiwaukum unit but were moved about 120 miles northward along the Straight Creek fault. This is one of the few places where good geologic evidence of northward terrane movement can be found.

The other feature to observe along Icicle Creek is mountain stream mechanics. Unlike their rather staid lowland counterparts, mountain channels show great variations in form and flow. They are also quite prone to sudden changes that might result from something as subtle as a tree falling from the forested banks.

Trail Guide: From US 2 at the west end of Leavenworth, turn onto the Icicle Creek Road and drive 16.5 miles to a parking area on the left. This is the trailhead for the River Trail, 0.1 mile west of the Chatter Creek Guard Station. This is an easy loop trail that meanders in and out of the forest in Icicle Gorge with only a couple hundred feet of up and down climbing. The trail can also be accessed from Chatter Creek and Rock Island Campgrounds for shorter out-and-back trips.

The hike begins in a parking lot that is so large it seems more suitable for a suburban mall than a trailhead. But such is the popularity of areas accessing the Alpine Lakes Wilderness. The parking area is strewn with glacial erratics, mainly Mount Stuart granodiorite. These boulders have flat surfaces (called facets) that were ground into the rock when they were dragged down the Icicle Gorge valley by the same glacier that produced the broad U shape which can be seen from the perspective of the adjacent ridges.

Taking the loop counterclockwise, follow the trail, which wanders through the woods for about 0.25 mile before ascending a bedrock knob composed of mica-schist. At the top of the knob, a near-vertical cliff overlooks the confluence of Jack and Icicle Creeks where a huge fan of boulders and cobbles has forced the Icicle to flow across the valley and up against the base of the cliff. Because the size of sediment transported by streams depends mainly on a steep streambed rather than volume, it is typical for steep tributary streams in canyons to dump a load that cannot be moved by the main stream—which has a more gentle gradient. If you are a rafter, get ready for action where the steep tributary streams occur because these are the conditions that create rapids.

Beyond the knob, the trail descends to river level. As you hike westward toward Rock Island Campground you can observe the various modus operandi

Abundant garnets can be found in outcrops of the Chiwaukum schist that make up the walls of Icicle Gorge near Chatter Creek Campground.

of the Icicle. Most of this section of the stream has a pool-riffle pattern. This pattern generally indicates the stream is getting more of a load than it has energy to haul, so a bunch of the sediment is periodically dumped in the channel. It is apparent that many of the boulders are too big to be moved by ordinary flow conditions. Some of these are residual boulders, immovable objects left behind as the stream has cut down into glacial deposits on the valley floor; others can actually be rolled and skipped along during flood conditions. Be sure to notice that here and there pools are formed by large logs that have fallen from the banks into the streambed or as the result of flooding. This large woody debris can be a vital part of the habitat for fish and other creatures living in or near the water. In mountain streams, the kind of woody debris present can be a powerful influence on the nature of stream flow.

As the trail approaches the Rock Island Campground a different stream pattern appears: the slope is steeper and thus the power to erode is greater. Instead of a rocky bank, the Icicle is cutting directly into the Chiwaukum Schist bedrock and rapids abound. This is called a cascade channel. Rock Island itself is a block of bedrock around which the Icicle has split into two channels, probably following faults or joints that form zones of weakness in the rock.

Finding the continuation of the loop trail through the campground is a bit tricky. Go across the bridge just beyond campsite number 22 where the trail goes into the woods on your left. This part of the loop is mainly through the forest on a flat terrace, which flanks the present stream. The presence of the terrace indicates that sometime, not so long ago, the Icicle must have been a much larger river that every now and then flooded, moving a whole lot more sediment than it does in present conditions. This was probably during the Little Ice Age from 1300 to 1900 when glaciation was much more extensive in this area than it is now. With the addition of large quantities of meltwater, the Icicle was probably capable of scouring out a large part of the valley during extreme conditions.

The highlight of this hike is at the eastern end of the loop where the trail comes back across Icicle Gorge near Chatter Creek Campground. If you don't have time for the whole hike, at least be sure to see this cascade section of the river. The bedrock exposed here is absolutely spectacular, but be careful of the slippery banks if you go down for a closer look. The river-polished schist in the gorge presents an almost agonized display of metamorphic foliation, twisted and folded by at least two major episodes of mountain-building activity. After that, the metamorphosed rocks were cracked deep within the earth by great earthquakes, then molten rock filled the fractures to crystallize out as granite dikes. The schist contains quartz, mica, fibrolite (a form of sillimanite), feldspar, and garnets galore. Another uncommon mineral found here is cordierite. It occurs as bluish gray chunks that formed when the Chiwaukum schist was baked by the heat of the nearby Mount Stuart batholith.

If you want to collect garnets or cordierite, a safe place to prospect is in the bed of Chatter Creek, about 0.25 mile up the Gorge Trail from the bridge. Some of the dikes also contain garnet of igneous origin—a fairly rare occurrence.

Other unusual rocks can be seen in a short side trip from the Icicle Creek bridge. Go up the access trail to the Icicle Creek Road and walk east to some outcrops on a knoll to the north of the road just beyond the Chatter Creek Guard Station to see sheets and pods of metaperidotite. Rockhounds will love the minerals to be found here, including olivine, tremolite, talc, and anthophyllite. Complete the loop by walking another 0.5 mile up the Gorge Trail or along the Icicle Creek Road.

PESHASTIN PINNACLES

Hike a short steep ascent through a climber's mecca to view layers of sedimentary rock that filled a giant rift in central Washington.

DISTANCE ■ Up to 1 mile

ELEVATION ■ 1040 feet to 1480 feet (high point on loop)

DIFFICULTY ■ Moderate

TOPOGRAPHIC MAP ■ USGS Peshastin

GEOLOGIC MAP ■ USGS I-1661 Chelan

KEY REFERENCES ■ Gresens and others (1981); Evans (1994)

About the Landscape: Between 55 and 37 million years ago, the central part of Washington began to tear apart in a manner similar to the present-day rift valleys of East Africa. During this time, a big block extending from Leavenworth on the west to Wenatchee on the east and at least to Lake Chelan on the north, sunk more than 30,000 feet. As the block dropped, sediments from the surrounding hills of granite were transported by streams to accumulate layer by layer in the Chiwaukum Graben, the geological name for this structure. Between 37 and 34 million years ago, the **graben** was squeezed together as the western side moved northward relative to the eastern side. Geologists call this **dextral transpression**. But whatever you call it, the result was that the initially flat layers of sedimentary rock were folded so that they now point skyward, forming the pinnacles.

Trail Guide: On US 2 about 2 miles west of Cashmere, turn off on North Dryden Road. Follow the signs about 1 mile to Peshastin Pinnacles State Park. This hike can be as easy or as tough as you want to make it. You can reach an outcrop that tells most of the story in a short stroll, or if you are capable, rope up and do some rock climbing to get intimately familiar with the texture and structure of these rocks. Even if you are here for a casual stroll on the trail to view the geology, you will probably see some serious rock climbers in action.

The trail upward to the Pinnacles begins at a gate on the northern end of a grassy picnic area. The first big mass of rock on your right is Orchard Rock consisting of coarse sandstone alternating with a pebbly conglomerate. The sandstone is mostly quartz and feldspar grains that are hard to identify without magnification. The pebbles in the conglomerate are easy to recognize, mostly chert, sandstone, and granite. Notice the excellent example of cross-bedding in the north wall indicating these rocks were originally part of a sand bar or delta.

From Orchard Rock, take the switchback up toward Martian Slab, through

The dramatic rock slabs of the Peshastin Pinnacles are composed of well-cemented sandstone that is more resistant to erosion than the surrounding rocks.

slopes of shale and fine sandstone that are less resistant to erosion than the big slabs of sandstone that are a climber's delight. Martian Slab is a thick layer of sandstone rising skyward at an angle of about 60 degrees. Notice the perpendicular fractures that cut the slab into blocks. These joints occur whenever rocks that were once deep within the earth expand as erosion removes the crushing weight of thousands of feet of overlying material.

Dinosaur Tower is a spectacular projection of rock at the top of the ridge. The odd knoblike shapes on the skyline are the result of **differential weathering**, which is probably related to differences in the cementation of the sandstone. Where the calcite is abundant, the sand grains are solidly glued and resistant to erosion. These form the knobs that may or may not look like dinosaurs to you.

The story of differential weathering is the same for Sunset Slab and Austrian Slab, between which you will travel on your way back down to the picnic area. As you head down the slope, be sure to notice the broad flat areas that have been exploited for orchards in the Wenatchee River valley. The sediments in these terraces are outwash from local alpine glaciers, and/or deposits associated with huge floods up the Wenatchee River from the east. (See Columbia Basin chapter.)

Hike
29

DENNY CREEK

Have fun at the famous Sliding Rocks in Denny Creek and, if you are adventurous, scramble up into Mineral Gulch where spectacular skarn can be found.

DISTANCE ■ 1 to 1.5 miles

ELEVATION ■ 2750 feet to 3500 feet (Mineral Gulch)

DIFFICULTY ■ Moderate to difficult

TOPOGRAPHIC MAPS ■ USGS Snoqualmie Pass; Green Trails 207 Snoqualmie Pass

GEOLOGIC MAP ■ USGS 84-693 Snoqualmie Pass

KEY REFERENCES ■ Erikson (1969)

PRECAUTIONS ■ There is danger from rockfall and very rough terrain in Mineral Gulch, so use good judgement. This hike is best done from late July through November. It may be inaccessible or dangerous other times of the year due to snow and high meltwater flows.

About the Landscape: The Snoqualmie batholith is a huge mass of granodiorite formed by several batches of molten rock that rose from the Cascadia subduction zone between 19 and 25 million years ago. One of these big blobs of magma pushed up into the earth about 20 million years ago beneath what is now Snoqualmie Pass. It never made it to the surface, but instead crystallized about 3 to 5 miles deep into a granodiorite. The sedimentary rocks, shale and limestone, along the margin of this mass were baked by the heat of the intrusion and penetrated by hot fluids. This created a rock type called skarn that is one of the wonders of the mineral world. The skarns on Denny Mountain contain lots of really spectacular minerals that are prized by rockhounds. **Trail Guide:** Turn off I-90 at Exit 47, just west of Snoqualmie Pass. Drive east 2.5 miles on Denny Creek Road (FR 58). Take the first left beyond the entrance to Denny Creek Campground and drive about 0.5 mile to a large parking lot at the trailhead. The trail to Sliding Rocks is a moderate uphill grade. This part is ideal for families with children. The hike is short, not too strenuous, and there is the reward of sheer fun in the chutes and pools at the end.

It is a different story if you continue on to Mineral Gulch. This is a rock-hopping, cliff-climbing scramble up the bed of Denny Creek, including the ascent of several waterfalls. There is an alternative trail up the west side of Denny Creek, but it can be just as treacherous.

Fill out your trail permit for the Alpine Lakes Wilderness then walk about 0.25 mile through an old-growth forest before beginning a moderate ascent along the west side of Denny Creek. In 0.5 mile, cross a bridge and notice the large boulders that have been tumbled down the streambed by great floods of the past. Just above the bridge, the trail passes beneath the giant stilts on which I-90 has been elevated. Hiking under an interstate highway in a primitive forest is a totally unique sensation!

As the trail returns to parallel the east side of Denny Creek, look across the valley to see an excellent example of exfoliation, great slabs of granite peeling off the glaciated rock walls like layers of an onion. A few hundred feet up the trail, cross into the Alpine Lakes Wilderness area and in another 0.25 mile you will arrive at Sliding Rocks, an expanse of stream-polished granodiorite exposed in the valley of Denny Creek. On a hot summer day, kids (and adults) can have great fun slipping down the stream channel over the smooth rocks from pool to pool for several hundred feet.

For rockhounds or any curious hikers, there is some great geology to be seen. In the middle of the main part of the polished rock exposure is a unique feature, a synplutonic dike. First an injection of molten basalt into a fracture split a cooling crystal mush of granodiorite. The basalt crystallized out immediately to form a solid dike, but the granodiorite mush was still moving about, so it broke the dike into several separate pieces, and in turn, injected some molten rock into the fractures. The broken, injected dike ends up looking like the snake in the famous "Don't Tread On Me" flag.

Look in the pool at the top of the Sliding Rocks exposure for a well-developed **intrusive breccia** that formed when blocks of the solid surrounding rock were ripped off the walls of the granodiorite pluton as it ascended through the earth. Other bits and pieces of ripped-off rock called xenoliths can be seen scattered throughout the granodiorite. Last but not least, look at the predominant granodiorite. Up close you can see gray crystals of quartz, white crystals of plagioclase feldspar, pink crystals of potassium feldspar, and black shiny flakes of biotite mica.

To get to Mineral Gulch from here, look carefully for a trail that goes up through the forest on the west side of Denny Creek or take a little rock climbing

A dark, synplutonic dike cuts through granodiorite in bedrock exposures polished by the flow of Denny Creek at Sliding Rocks.

expedition up the bed of the stream over three waterfalls. At the top of the third waterfall, or the end of the side trail, is a major canyon that heads up to the northeast. This is Mineral Gulch. You don't need to go very far to find fabulous crystals in skarn rock including clear calcite rhombs, blades of yellow-green epidote, small prisms of dark green diopside, flakes of silvery specular hematite, and brown crystals of grossularite garnet. The further you go, the steeper the climb, and the greater the danger of getting bashed by falling rock. Keep this in mind and good luck on your rock hunt.

Chapter 4
SOUTH CASCADES

Crater of Mount St. Helens, with Mount Adams in the background

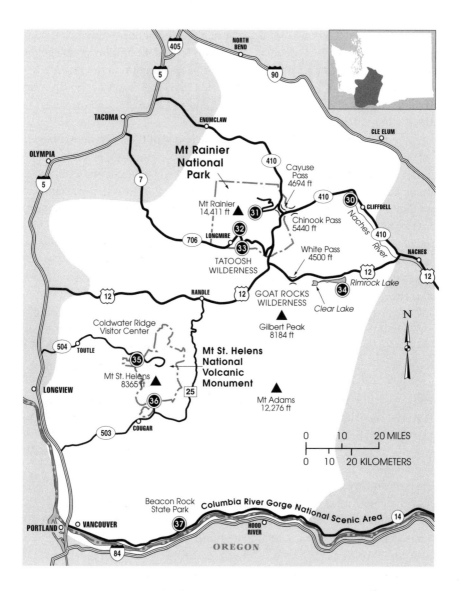

There is no distinct boundary between the North and South Cascades, but it is convenient to divide them along I-90 in the vicinity of Snoqualmie Pass. North of this boundary, more extensive uplift and erosion reveals large patches of Mesozoic and Paleozoic igneous and metamorphic rocks. To the south, these patches are almost completely covered or intruded by Eocene and younger rocks. An exception is the vicinity of Rimlock Lake (Hike 34) where scattered bits of metamorphic schist and amphibolite are the last remnants of a Jurassic seafloor.

The rest of the South Cascades' story begins with sandstones, shales, conglomerates, and coal beds deposited between 55 and 42 million years ago on a vast coastal plain that extended from central Washington to the Puget Lowland. Rocks of this age have different names in different places: on the east side of the range they are the Naches Formation (Hike 30), and on the west side, the Puget Group (Hike 10).

Beginning about 42 million years ago, volcanoes of the Cascade Arc began to erupt due to subduction of the seafloor off the Washington coast. In the South Cascades, the volcanics were mainly basalts of the Northcraft and Goble Formations. Between 37 and 27 million years ago, much of western Washington was flooded by a vast inland sea. Here and there, volcanic islands emerged, erupting lava flows and pyroclastics of basalt, andesite, and rhyolite. Sediments eroded from these volcanoes were deposited on the relatively shallow seafloor. These rocks occur throughout the South Cascades and are generally known as the Ohanapecosh Formation, named for outcrops near the campground in Mount Rainier National Park with the same name.

Another surge of volcanism occurred between 27 and 20 million years ago, mostly basalt to andesite flows and pyroclastics called the Fifes Peak Formation in the vicinity of Mount Rainier, and the Skamania volcanics around Mount St. Helens and the Columbia Gorge. One of several immense blasts of ash that thundered across the landscape, the Stevens Ridge Formation, forms outcrops as much as 3000 feet thick along the Stevens Canyon Highway in Mount Rainier National Park. At the same time volcanoes were growing, they were shedding huge mudflows. Near the Columbia River Gorge, the mudflows were so extensive they formed a separate geologic unit called the Eagle Creek Formation that can be seen on the trail to Hamilton Mountain (Hike 37).

As volcanoes were erupting on the surface, vast plutons of granitic rock crystallized underground. Much of the basement rock upon which Mount Rainier is built consists of granodiorite of the Tatoosh pluton, with ages ranging from 26 to 14 million years. The Spirit Lake pluton, with an age of about 21 million years, was intruded at about the same time as abundant volcanic rocks of Oligocene and Miocene age in the vicinity of Mount St. Helens.

An outpouring of flood basalts began in the Columbia Basin about 16 million years ago. More than twenty of these flows came down the ancestral Columbia River and several lapped up onto the South Cascades, which had just begun to rise. Altogether, more than 2000 feet of basalt flows accumulated in the Columbia River Gorge area. These can be seen around Hamilton Mountain (Hike 37) and Boulder Cave (Hike 30).

Volcanic activity was scattered throughout other parts of the South Cascades from 14 million years ago to the present. The big finale was the construction of the major volcanic cones of Mount Rainier, Mount Adams, and Mount St.

Helens, plus the Indian Heaven, Simcoe Mountains, and Goat Rocks (Hike 34) volcanic fields. The latter two have been inactive for hundreds of thousands of years, but the rest have erupted within the past few thousand years.

The oldest major volcano appears to be Mount Rainier, where there is evidence of activity as much as 3 million years ago, even though most of the cone construction is younger than about 500,000 years. Lavas that now form ridges radiating from the lower slopes of the mountain erupted mostly between 130,000 and 90,000 years ago. These lavas moved down valleys or parallel to glaciers during the early stages of cone building. The flows that formed the upper part of Mount Rainier began erupting 40,000 years ago (Hike 32).

About 5600 years ago, a major collapse removed a large part of the summit and created the Osceola mudflow that covered a large part of the Puget Lowland in the Seattle-Tacoma area (Hike 31). In the past 10,000 years, more than sixty lahars of varying sizes have originated from Mount Rainier, along with at least eleven substantial ash eruptions.

The onset of major eruptions at Mount Adams began with a basaltic shield volcano about 940,000 years ago. Around 520,000 years ago the main stratovolcano began building on top of the shield. From 450,000 to 100,000 years ago, persistent activity, with a surge from 120,000 to 100,000 years ago, formed an apron of volcanics extending more than 9 miles from the present summit, making Mount Adams the second largest volcano in the Cascade Range. Eruptions constructed the present summit cone from 40,000 to 10,000 years ago. The last small lava flow originated on the flanks of the volcano more than 3500 years ago, however, there have been many lahars and small ash eruptions since then. The adjacent Indian Heaven volcanic field has approximately sixty volcanic centers that were active as recently as about 8000 years ago.

Mount St. Helens is by far the youngest and most active of the Cascade volcanoes. The oldest known deposits associated with the present cone are 40- to 50-million-year-old dacites found in Ape Canyon. The volcanic history of Mount St. Helens has been divided into a series of eruptive stages and periods. The Spirit Lake Stage has been ongoing for 4000 years with seven eruptive periods, including 1980 to the present. The four most recent eruptive periods have all involved pyroclastic blasts and dome building similar to the present-day activity. The lava flows, pyroclastics, debris avalanches, and lahars of Mount St. Helens are among the best studied volcanic rocks in the world (Hikes 35 and 36).

Glaciation is the last part of the South Cascades' story. There were two extensive periods of glaciation late in the Pleistocene Ice Age: the Hayden Creek Glaciation, around 250,000 to 150,000 years ago, and the Evans Creek Glaciation from 25,000 to 15,000 years ago. During these intervals, the alpine glaciers on Mount Rainier extended as much as 40 miles down their valleys.

Due to global warming 8000 to 4000 years before the present, the glaciers melted away to minimal size, only to advance again during Little Ice Age beginning about 3500 years ago. One hundred years ago the Nisqually Glacier (Hike 32) was more than 1 mile further down its valley, near where the highway bridge presently crosses the river.

The future of the South Cascades is easy to predict. Subduction of the Juan de Fuca Plate continues off the Washington coast, so there will inevitably be new volcanic activity. For the short term, most of the glaciers will continue to retreat, but eventually another change in climate will bring them back down their valleys. And, since the laws of gravity have not been repealed, gigantic mudflows and avalanches will devastate the landscape around the big volcanoes, including populated areas of the Puget Lowland. Buyers beware!

Hike 30

BOULDER CAVE

Not an ordinary cavern: walk through a cave formed by stream erosion.

DISTANCE ■ 0.75 mile

ELEVATION ■ Start, 2460 feet; high point, 2600 feet

DIFFICULTY ■ Easy

TOPOGRAPHIC MAP ■ USGS Cliffdell

GEOLOGIC MAP ■ DGER 87-16 Mount Rainier

KEY REFERENCES ■ Campbell (1975)

PRECAUTIONS ■ Boulder Cave is closed to all visitors from November 1 through April 1 to protect Townsend's big-eared bats.

About the Landscape: There are many types of caves and caverns. Some, like limestone caverns (Hike 53) and lava tubes (Hike 36), may be quite long while others, like sea caves and meander caves, are generally quite short (often wider than they are long). Boulder Cave (also called Boulder Creek Cave) is unusually long (about 400 feet) for a cave produced by mass wasting and a stream. According to the trail guide, "Caves are unusual in the Northwest, and Boulder Cave is the largest, most extensive cave of its kind." It is a good idea to borrow one of these guides and to bring a flashlight or lantern along.

Trail Guide: Cliffdell is a community about halfway between Chinook Pass and Naches on SR 410 (Chinook Pass is closed in the winter). Southeast of Cliffdell are the Tertiary Fifes Peak and Stevens Ridge Formations, composed of volcanic and volcaniclastic rocks. Edgar Rock, a cliff on the southwest side of the Naches River 1 mile southeast of Cliffdell, is part of a large Miocene volcano. Northwest of Cliffdell is the Miocene Grande Ronde Basalt.

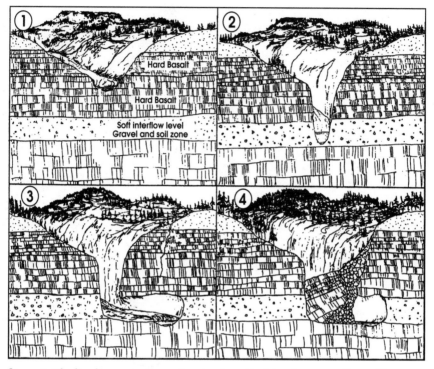

figure 8. Idealized cross-sections showing how Boulder Cave was formed by undercutting of resistant basalt.

One quarter mile northwest of Cliffdell, leave SR 410 and cross the bridge over the Naches River. Drive 1.25 miles up the southwest side of the river to a parking lot and campground. There is a $5.00 fee per vehicle.

From the parking lot, take the Boulder Cave Trail southwest along the northeast side of Devil Creek. The bedrock here is Grande Ronde Basalt (about 16 million years old), part of the extensive Columbia River basalts. Here the Grande Ronde lava flows are, in places, separated by interflow sediments.

Devils Creek began to cut through the lava flows (see upper left portion of figure 8). The fact that the canyon cut by Devils Creek is much deeper than it is wide attests to the resistant nature of the lava flows (see upper right portion of figure 8). Once the creek encounters an interbed of erodible sediments, it is relatively easy for it to cut laterally and a meander cave may develop on the outside of a bend in the creek (see lower left portion of figure 8). Look down from the canyon rim to see small meander caves.

If the meander cave gets too big, its roof may collapse (see lower right portion of figure 8). According to the trail guide, this series of events led to the formation of Boulder Cave about 25,000 years ago. Perhaps the roof col-

Colonnade of Columbia River basalt flow at lower cave entrance

lapse occurred during an earthquake; however it happened, the collapse did not completely dam Devils Creek, so the creek eroded the loose material under the big block of basalt thereby enlarging the cave.

Continue upcanyon (straight ahead) at the junction after the trail starts to descend from the canyon rim. At the canyon bottom the trail doubles back to the left and into the cave. Here and at the lower cave entrance is a basal colonnade, the lower portion of a lava flow with large polygonal columns (the upper part with smaller less regular columns is called an **entablature**). Look up at the cave roof to see the polygonal columns end on. The white coating on the rocks is a mixture of calcite and silica deposited by groundwater that seeps through the rocks above and evaporates in the cave. At the lower entrance, the trail turns sharply left and ascends to the canyon rim.

143

Hike 31

EMMONS GLACIER

The largest chunk of ice in the lower forty-eight states was buried by a rock avalanche from Little Tahoma Peak.

DISTANCE ▪ 2 miles

ELEVATION ▪ 4300 feet to 5000 feet

DIFFICULTY ▪ Strenuous

TOPOGRAPHIC MAP ▪ USGS Sunrise

GEOLOGIC MAPS ▪ USGS Misc. Inv. Map I-836; USGS Bulletin 1288; USGS Professional Paper 444

KEY REFERENCES ▪ Crandell (1969, 1973, 1983); Crandell and Fahnestock (1965); Fiske and others (1963)

PRECAUTIONS ▪ Mount Rainier makes its own weather; take rain gear and warm clothes in addition to the Ten Essentials. Do not get too close to the Emmons Glacier (danger of rockfall) or the White River (fast and cold). Do not attempt to climb onto the Emmons Glacier unless you are an experienced ice climber with ice axe, rope, helmet, and other safety equipment. And don't let the 2-mile distance fool you; allow all day for this hike.

About the Landscape: Mount Rainier has half of all the ice in the lower forty-eight states. The Emmons Glacier, the largest glacier south of Alaska and Canada, starts at over 14,000 feet on the northeast part of Mount Rainier's summit, and in a little over 4 miles descends to about 5000 feet in the White River valley. The Emmons Glacier has carved cliffs in Steamboat Prow and Mount Ruth on the northwest, and Disappointment Cleaver and Little Tahoma Peak on the southeast; these are the steep sides of a glacial trough. About 5600 years ago, one of the largest mudflows on earth occurred here: the Osceola mudflow originated high on Mount Rainier and rushed down the White River valley to the Puget Lowland.

In December 1963 rockfalls from Little Tahoma Peak formed avalanches which buried the lower Emmons Glacier and the adjacent White River valley. On the north side of the snout of the Emmons Glacier, and for about a mile downvalley, are moraines built in the last 500 years. At the base of the glacier terminus (blue ice partly covered with rock debris) is a tunnel from which the White River pours. The White River starts with a bang, not a whimper, and is a textbook example of a braided stream on an outwash plain.

Trail Guide: The White River entrance to Mount Rainier National Park is off SR 410, 3 miles north of Cayuse Pass (closed in winter) and 38 miles southeast of Enumclaw. From SR 410 drive 5 miles up the south side of the White

River valley (a glacial trough with a braided meltwater stream). The bedrock along this route is Miocene granite (actually granodiorite and quartz monzonite) of the Tatoosh pluton. The surficial deposits include drift, mudflow deposits, and alluvium.

Much of the road is on sediments of the Osceola mudflow. Two of the best exposures of this mudflow deposit are in roadcuts at the White River Ranger Station and in streamcuts by Inter Fork along the Glacier Basin Trail. The Osceola mudflow was one of the largest lahars (volcanic mudflows) known on earth. Its sediments include boulders as much as 15 feet in diameter. The presence of a remnant of the Osceola mudflow on Steamboat Prow (9702 feet) indicates that it originated higher on Mount Rainier, probably from collapse of summit rocks which were likely weak from hydrothermal alteration.

Explosions may have been responsible for landslides; the mixing of clay-rich material with melting ice could have generated the enormous lahar about 5600 years ago. That lahar temporarily filled White River valley to more than 500 feet deep before it rushed 70 miles to the Puget Lowland. Many towns including Enumclaw, Buckley, Sumner, and Auburn are along the route of the Osceola mudflow. Should a similar event reoccur, about one hundred thousand people are at risk.

Cross the bridge over the White River and turn left (west), driving one mile to White River Campground, which includes a ranger station, a picnic ground, and parking for hikers. The Glacier Basin Trail begins at the west end of the White River Campground. Before entering the forest, take a look around you. You're on the floor of a glacial trough, carved when glaciers in general, and the Emmons Glacier in particular, were much more extensive. The floor of the glacial trough is covered with alluvium and mudflow deposits.

The lower half of both sides of the glacial trough is Miocene granite of the Tatoosh pluton, which invaded the rocks of the ancestral Cascades. These old rocks include the Eocene Ohanapecosh Formation and the Oligocene to Miocene Stevens Ridge Formation, both comprising Goat Island Mountain (7288 feet) to the south. Yakima Park to the north is capped by Pleistocene andesite from Mount Rainier and by Evans Creek Drift.

The first part of the trail is on Holocene alluvium and mudflow deposits that lie between Inter Fork (south) and the granitic side (north) of the glacial trough, then you'll encounter the outermost moraines of the Garda Drift. South of Inter Fork the moraines were built just before 1749, 1850, and 1902 (we know this based on counting tree rings).

About 1 mile west of White River Campground a fork in the trail (elevation 4760 feet) gives you three choices; time permitting, all three are recommended. One choice would be to continue west on the Glacier Basin Trail to see excellent exposures of Osceola mudflow sediments on the south bank of

Inter Fork. In some places the creek has cut through the yellowish mudflow deposit and down into underlying gray Evans Creek till.

FIGURE 9

Stratigraphy of the Emmons Glacier Area

CENOZOIC	Quaternary	Holocene	Rock avalanche deposits from Little Tahoma Peak (1963)
			Garda Drift (about 2000 years ago to present)
			Interbedded mudflow deposits and alluvium
			Osceola Mudflow deposits (about 5600 years old)
		Pleistocene	Evans Creek Drift (about 20,000 years old)
			Andesites of Mount Rainier volcano (chiefly lava flows)
	Tertiary	Miocene	Tatoosh pluton: granodiorite and quartz monzonite
		Oligocene(?)	Stevens Ridge Formation: mostly rhyodacitic ash flows
		Eocene	Ohanapecosh Formation: volcanic breccia, sandstone, and siltstone

Another choice is to cross Inter Fork here and follow the trail westward about 1 mile along the top of the moraine complex to get a spectacular view (weather permitting) from the moraine crest. From closest to farthest, note the steep south side of the moraine, the hummocky topography at its base, the White River, the Emmons Glacier, and Little Tahoma Peak (11,138 feet). The south side of the moraine is so steep because it was supported by the Emmons Glacier until only about a century ago. The hummocky topography is a result of three factors: first, glacial deposits are irregular in thickness; second, stagnant ice in the drift is melting, leading to collapse; and third, the rock avalanche deposits from Little Tahoma Peak are irregular in thickness.

The White River is born of meltwater from the Emmons Glacier and carries a load of outwash. The 1963 rockfalls from Little Tahoma Peak produced most of the debris on the Emmons Glacier. Note that the volcanic strata in the north cliff of Little Tahoma Peak dip to the east, indicating a source from higher to the west, perhaps a taller Mount Rainier.

Little Tahoma Peak, Gibraltar Rock, Steamboat Prow, and other bedrock high on Mount Rainier are andesite flows and breccia that erupted before the present glaciers dissected the volcano. The ridge to the southwest end (elevation about 5400 feet) of the moraine trail has Miocene granite intruded into Eocene Ohanapecosh Formation at the base, and Mount Rainier andesite at the top. Evans Creek Drift is found up to an elevation of about 6400 feet, indicating that the former ice cover was much thicker.

The third choice is to cross Inter Fork, leave the trail, and carefully work your way about 1 mile southwest toward the snout of the Emmons Glacier and the source of the White River. Note the route you take so that you can easily return to the Glacier Basin Trail.

It has already been stated that much of this area is underlain by stagnant ice. Depressions resulting from the melting of blocks of stagnant ice are called **kettles** (or kettle lakes if there is water in the bottom). Collapse has exposed buried stagnant ice in the sides of some kettles, a sight you're unlikely to see anywhere else closer than Alaska. The rock debris, including giant boulders, is mostly Garda Drift at first, and then mostly rock avalanche deposits. The rockfalls from Little Tahoma Peak occurred in December 1963; the debris totaled about 14 million cubic yards. The rockfalls and resulting avalanches dropped more than 6000 feet as they traveled from Little Tahoma Peak to more than 1 mile beyond the snout of the Emmons Glacier. One rock left on the Emmons Glacier was about 160 feet long and 60 feet high. The trees are so small because the vegetation here had to get a new start after the 1963 rock avalanches.

The lower part of Goat Island Mountain just southeast of the snout of the Emmons Glacier is the Eocene Ohanapecosh Formation. Notice how a former thicker and longer Emmons Glacier steepened the side of the glacial trough. You may be able to see a **trimline** on this slope: this former ice position slopes

Kettle lake in stagnant ice beneath drift and the 1963 rock avalanche deposit

gently to the northeast, and has older more abundant vegetation above; below this trimline the vegetation is younger because the ice covered the slope to this height only two or three centuries ago.

Angle toward the White River where the discharge varies considerably because of annual and daily changes in the rate the glacier melts. If the river is low, you can see terraces, channels, and bars indicating that it is sometimes higher. Notice how well the river sorts the debris provided by the glacier: the outwash is dominantly sand, pebbles, and cobbles because most of the boulders are left behind and most of the silt and clay stay in suspension and are carried to the Puget Lowland. Grinding at the base of the glacier produced the fine-grained sediment, called rock flour, that gives the White River its name.

The climax of this hike is the toe of the Emmons Glacier. Remember not to climb on the ice or get close enough to be hit by material falling, sliding, or flowing from the snout. Particularly if it is a warm day, you are likely to observe mass wasting on the steep ice front. The White River is loud (and cold) where it issues from the tunnel at the base of the ice. You can see rocks beneath, within, and on the glacier. The foliation (banding) in the glacier is produced as the ice flows; the foliation shows because there are alternating bands of coarse-grained and fine-grained ice, and/or different concentrations of air bubbles.

If you can safely obtain a piece of glacier ice here or at one of the kettles, look at it closely. You can probably detect large intergrown ice crystals; imagine the tiny snowflakes that fell near the top of Mount Rainier and were slowly transformed into glacier ice.

PARADISE

Hike 32

The name does not exaggerate! This is a route through an incomparable alpine meadow and along the great abyss of the Nisqually Glacier with incredible views of Mount Rainier rocks and glacial landforms.

DISTANCE ■ About 0.7 to 4 miles

ELEVATION ■ 5400 feet to 6900 feet (Panorama Point)

DIFFICULTY ■ Moderate to strenuous

TOPOGRAPHIC MAPS ■ USGS Mount Rainier West and Mount Rainier East

GEOLOGIC MAPS ■ USGS Map I-432; DGER 87-16 Mount Rainier quadrangle

KEY REFERENCES ■ Crandell (1983); Decker and Decker (1996); Driedger (1986); Fiske and others (1963); Lescinsky and Sisson (1998); Pringle and others (1994); Sisson (1995)

About the Landscape: A map of Paradise area trails can be obtained from the Jackson Visitor Center information desk.

The andesite lava flows and pyroclastics that make up the bulk of Mount Rainier are gradually being ground into cirques and valleys by the majestic flow of glacial ice.

The focus of this hike is the construction versus the destruction of Mount Rainier. This is the story of all of the Cascade stratovolcanoes. Volcanism builds the cone—and a combination of glaciation, stream erosion, and gravity tear it down. The dominant force varies as time goes by. For the past few thousand years, volcanic activity at Mount Rainier has been minimal, only a few ash and steam vent eruptions plus a small scale extrusion of lava at the summit about 2000 years ago. So the destructive forces, especially gravity, have prevailed.

The impact of glaciation depends upon the current climate conditions. The Nisqually Glacier is a classic case in point. During the peak of alpine glaciation in the Cascades (called the Evans Creek Stade), ice extended all the way to the outskirts of the town of Ashford. By the late 1850s it had retreated more than 25 miles, but still extended to the point where the SR 706 bridge crosses the river on the way up to Paradise. From the late 1800s to 1945, more than a mile of the Nisqually Glacier melted away. Following this major retreat, the terminus of the glacier has behaved like a yo-yo. It advanced in the 1950s and retreated in the 1960s and early 70s. In the late 70s and early 80s it advanced again. Since then the terminus has been fairly stationary. The glacier has proven itself to be an indicator of short-term climate that might be quite valuable to scientists studying global climatic changes.

From the Paradise trails you get an awesome view of the stratified volcanics of Mount Rainier. These are especially well displayed at a prominent ridge on the skyline just to the left of the summit. Also look carefully at the steep cliff that rises above the terminus of the Nisqually Glacier. Both of these exposures show that Mount Rainier is composed of layers of ash and pumice (10 percent) alternating with lava flows (90 percent). This means that most of the recent mountain building eruptions were relatively quiet extrusions (lava) sometimes punctuated by explosive outbursts (ash).

The construction of the Mount Rainier volcano apparently began about 500,000 years ago. Within the past 100,000 years the main cone was built and great lava flows came down glacial valleys. These flows now form ridges that radiate like spokes from the summit (e.g. Rampart Ridge and Mazama Ridge).

Another part of the Mount Rainier story is gravity. Periodically parts of the mountain collapse and rush downslope to become volcanic debris flows called lahars. One of the biggest was the Paradise lahar about 6000 years ago. It covered the meadows of Paradise with debris from the summit and then rumbled on down the Nisqually River valley all the way to the Tacoma area, where it built great delta deposits that extended the shoreline many miles out into the Puget Sound. Remnants of this great lahar can be found hundreds of feet above the floor of the Nisqually Valley, indicating the immense thickness of the flow. The scary thing is that geologic history could repeat itself, but now many people live in the path of this future catastrophe.

Trail Guide: Drive SR 706 to the Paradise Visitor Center of Mount Rainier National Park. Head directly west from the visitor center to the stairs at the west end of the parking area. Go up the stairs and follow the signs to the Nisqually Vista Trail.

Be aware that this hike starts at an elevation more than a mile high, so if you have just driven up here from sea level, you may have to work to catch your breath coming back uphill. If you are in the mood for aerobics, you can extend this hike several miles and a few thousand vertical feet by taking the various loop trails available. The snow sometimes lingers well into August on the high trails, so be prepared for slippery conditions. But don't worry, there are barricades to keep you from falling into the deep abyss of the Nisqually glacial trough. If you can hike this trail in August, you will have the additional reward of remarkably beautiful subalpine flower fields.

About 0.1 mile from the beginning of the trail, check out a large ice-transported boulder of andesite that stands prominently on the right side of the trail and contains a huge round gas bubble hole that formed in the molten lava. This is called a vesicle and its size is exceptional—perhaps a block of ice was mixed into the flow and flashed to steam. At the beginning of the loop trail there is a fabulous view out toward the summit and the layers of lava and ash that make up the mountain. You can also see a cirque in the making at the top of the Nisqually Glacier. Walking further down the trail notice the boulders with flat surfaces (facets) ground onto the rock as they were dragged downvalley by a glacier. There are also thin layers of ash in the banks of a creek where it crosses the trail at the lower end of the meadow.

After a short walk through a subalpine forest of mountain hemlock and subalpine fir you reach the first overlook of the great valley carved by the Nisqually Glacier. Looking down from here, with even better views from the second and third viewpoints, you can see the brown, rock-covered face of the present terminus of the glacier, which has retreated more than a mile from its position during the late 1800s. Much of the lower part of the glacier is covered by rock debris that represents landslides off the cliffs above the valley. To get an idea of how much larger the glacier was during its heyday, look at the trimline defined by bare ground above the present-day surface of the ice. Clearly, the glacier we see now is only a small remnant of its most recent maximum stand. In fact, during the glacial maximum, the Nisqually Glacier filled this valley clear to the visitor center.

If you have the time and energy, a worthwhile extension is to complete the loop and then head uphill on the Dead Horse Creek Trail. As you emerge from the trees into the upper meadows, look up toward Gibraltar Rock on the right skyline below the summit. This is a stack of andesite lava flows truncated on its upper end. If you mentally project the uppermost flow toward the summit, you can see that Mount Rainier must have once been at least a thousand feet higher than it is now. The missing part collapsed about 5600 years ago to form the immense Osceola and Paradise lahars. Just before the junction with the Moraine Trail there are some big blocks of highly oxidized reddish andesite embedded in sandy ash that might have once been part of the summit area.

Turning off on the Moraine Trail, you climb gently to the crest of a moraine deposited during the maximum stand of the Nisqually Glacier during the Evans Creek Stade about 22,000 years ago. Look down at the remnant ice below and picture the glacier filling the valley to the level where you are now standing. The trail descends to the crest of another moraine that was deposited during the neoglacial maximum in the 1870s. This is still well above the existing level of the glacier, so you get a clue of the current climatic trend in the Cascade Range.

Hike 33

PLUMMER PEAK

Climb through a col to a horn for a magnificent view of Mount Rainier.

DISTANCE ▪ 1.5 miles

ELEVATION ▪ 4867 feet to 6370 feet

DIFFICULTY ▪ Moderate

TOPOGRAPHIC MAP ▪ USGS Mount Rainier East

GEOLOGIC MAP ▪ USGS Professional Paper 444

KEY REFERENCES ▪ Crandell (1969, 1983); Crandell (1973); Fiske and others(1963)

About the Landscape: The Tatoosh Range experienced intense alpine glaciation, and, weather permitting, offers a spectacular panorama of the entire south half of Mount Rainier, the highest volcano in the United States. The last eruption of Mount Rainier was a small one in 1882, but because Mount Rainier contains half (this is not a misprint) of the ice in the conterminous United States, even a moderate eruption could cause a disaster in populated western Washington. Indeed, a lahar can reach the southeastern Puget Lowland without a significant eruption. For example, about 600 years ago the Electron mudflow originated on the west flank of Mount Rainier and raced 35 miles down the Puyallup River to Orting where its deposit is 16 feet thick.

Plummer Peak is in the Tatoosh Range on the south flank of Mount Rainier. There are three kinds of rock in this area. The oldest are Tertiary volcanic and volcaniclastic rocks associated with the ancestral Cascades. Of these rocks, the unit present at the top of Plummer Peak and nearby summits is the mid-Tertiary Stevens Ridge Formation, dominated by ash flows. Next came the late Tertiary intrusions of granitic rocks (mainly granodiorite and quartz monzonite). The main intrusive body is the Tatoosh pluton which is about 26 to 14 million years old.

The youngest rocks are Mount Rainier andesites, most of which are from the Quaternary period, and most of these are intracanyon lava flows. When lava is erupted, it fills the valleys before it can cover an entire landscape. These thick valley fills of lava are particularly resistant when the landscape is lowered by erosion and may become ridge formers as the nearby less resistant rocks are eroded. This is an example of topographic inversion: a place that had been a valley becomes a ridge.

Repeated glaciation took place in the Quaternary. The Tatoosh Range has small but textbook examples of horns, cols, cirques, and tarns, with giant glacial troughs to the south. It is interesting to look at the radiating valley glaciers and cleavers on Mount Rainier, and imagine the scene 20,000 years ago with ice nearly to the top of Plummer Peak. Or imagine watching a future eruption of Mount Rainier from Plummer Peak; even though lava flows, ash flows, and lahars surround you, you're probably safe from all but a little ash fall.

Trail Guide: The trailhead is on the south side of the parking area for Reflection Lakes, in south-central Mount Rainier National Park. There are two ways to reach Reflection Lakes. One is from the west, using SR 706 to the Nisqually entrance of the park. Drive eastward along the Nisqually River (through Longmire) and bypass Paradise; Reflection Lakes are about 1.5 miles from the Paradise junction. The other route to Reflection Lakes is via SR 123 and the Stevens Canyon entrance (about 1.5 miles north of Ohanapecosh). Drive westward about 17.5 miles from the Stevens Canyon entrance; you will drive up Stevens Canyon itself before reaching the Reflection Lakes parking lot.

The trail south from the Reflection Lakes parking area leads across granites of the Tatoosh pluton upward toward the older rhyodcitic ash flows of the Stevens Ridge Formation. (If you want to see younger Mount Rainier andesites, try the trails just north of Reflection Lakes; the lakes lie exactly at the base of the volcano.) The basins of Reflection Lakes were excavated by Quaternary glaciers. The rocks beneath the basins are more erodible than those beneath the surrounding terrain, more erodible because they are a weaker lithology or because they have more fractures.

The vegetation along this trail is varied and beautiful. The forest trees include subalpine fir, mountain hemlock, and Alaska yellow cedar. In summer there is a great profusion of wildflowers. As you get higher, the trees get sparser

Plummer Peak is a horn carved from Tertiary igneous rocks; Mount St. Helens is on horizon.

153

and smaller, and rocks and alpine meadows dominate. Look and listen for marmots and pikas.

Note the banded appearance of the soil in the shallow cuts along the trail. The lighter layers are ashes from post-glacial eruptions of Cascade volcanoes: Mount Rainier, Mount St. Helens, and Oregon's ancient Mount Mazama (the Crater Lake ash is about 7000 years old). The darker layers are buried soils, organic rich just like the modern forest soil. The surficial materials record about 10,000 years of alternating ash fall and soil formation.

At about 5200 feet elevation is a big rock outcrop of granodiorite of the Tatoosh pluton. Notice the visible crystals of quartz and feldspar, coarse-grained because the magma cooled slowly within the earth's crust.

Near timberline the trail has switchbacks and there is lots of talus. The taluses have both coarse-grained (plutonic granodiorite) and fine-grained (volcanic) clasts, so the contact between the two rock types must be above in the cliffs of Pinnacle Peak.

The maintained trail ends at the col of Pinnacle Pass, just under 6000 feet elevation. The view from here is spectacular on a clear day. From southeast to south are the volcanoes Goat Rocks (Hike 34), Mount Adams, and Mount Hood, the highest peak in Oregon.

Observe the rocks and glaciers of Mount Rainier. On the east, Gibraltar Rock and the horn of Little Tahoma Peak are east-dipping volcanics. On the west skyline are west-dipping volcanics. If you project the volcanics on both sides upward, you might suspect that Mount Rainier once had eruptions from a summit higher than present. That old summit became rotten due to hydrothermal activity.

About 5600 years ago, perhaps at the same time as one or more eruptions, Mount Rainier was decapitated. From the summit a lahar swept south through Paradise and down the Nisqually River. At about the same time, one of the world's largest lahars, the Osceola mudflow, rushed down the northeast side of Mount Rainier and followed the White River valley to beyond Auburn!

The eastern part of Mount Rainier's summit plateau is two overlapping cinder cones built during eruptions a little more than 2000 years ago. The crater of the younger eastern cinder cone is full of snow except where hot vapors have melted tunnels.

If you look carefully just below and beside the termini of most of the glaciers on Mount Rainier, you can see moraines, ridges of till deposited at the margins of the glaciers when they were more extensive. From Pinnacle Pass, the moraines on the west side of the snout of Nisqually Glacier (Hike 32) are prominent (the Nisqually Glacier is the one closest to Pinnacle Pass; it descends from the summit to just northwest of Paradise). These moraines were built in the last 1000 years, many of them in the mid-1800s. In general, the glaciers are retreating because melting and evaporation exceed snowfall.

There are four peaks near Pinnacle Pass. One is Pinnacle Peak to the northeast, not recommended unless you are an experienced free climber and/or have rope and hardware. Pinnacle Peak is a horn, steep on all three sides and with plenty of "portable handholds" (loose rock). The same is true for The Castle, a horn just east of Pinnacle Peak. The third is Denman Peak, just west of Pinnacle Pass; Denman Peak is ascended by traversing the north slope of Plummer Peak, dropping to the saddle, and scrambling up the south ridge.

We recommend Plummer Peak, climbed so often that there is an unofficial trail from Pinnacle Pass. Go southwest to the base of Plummer Peak, and traverse west half way across its north slope to a pool of water. Often there is a spectacular reflection of Mount Rainier in this pool. Nearby is a pile of rocks with small black tourmaline crystals and an orange-brown coating of limonite. The iron-rich tourmaline, a silicate mineral, is weathering to limonite, a hydrous iron oxide.

The pool and tourmaline-rich rocks are near the top of the Tatoosh pluton. Turn south and follow the crude trail to the top of Plummer Peak; snowfields last late into summer on this north-facing slope. The summits of the four peaks are Tertiary rhyodacitic ash flows of the Stevens Ridge Formation; the rock is gray and fine-grained.

From the summit of Plummer Peak, on a clear day, you can see Mount St. Helens to the southwest. To the south-southeast is the giant glacial trough of Butter Creek. To the west is Cliff Lake, a tarn in the cirque surrounded by Lane, Denman, and Plummer Peaks. Pinnacle Pass to the northeast is a col. And, oh, what a view of Mount Rainier!

Hike 34

BEAR CREEK MOUNTAIN

Goat Rocks: Washington's sixth volcano, an old volcano much dissected by alpine glaciers.

DISTANCE ■ **3.5 miles**

ELEVATION ■ **6020 feet to 7337 feet**

DIFFICULTY ■ **Moderate**

TOPOGRAPHIC MAP ■ **USGS Pinegrass Ridge**

GEOLOGIC MAP ■ **DGER 87-16 Mount Rainier**

KEY REFERENCES ■ **Campbell (1975)**

About the Landscape: On this hike you will see the effect of the 1980 eruption of Mount St. Helens, Washington's fifth volcano, on Washington's sixth volcano, Goat Rocks. Most Washingtonians are familiar with our other four volcanoes: Mounts Rainier and Baker, which have had small historic eruptions, and Mount Adams and Glacier Peak, which have erupted often in the last 15,000 years.

Goat Rocks is a deeply eroded volcano active from the Miocene until the Pleistocene. Streams, landslides, and Quaternary glaciers dissected this volcano, exposing its roots, and the older rocks below it. Small glaciers remain on the highest peaks of the Goat Rocks volcano.

Trail Guide: The Goat Rocks Wilderness of the Wenatchee National Forest lies on the crest of the Cascades south of US 12. About 9 miles east of White Pass and just west of Rimrock Lake at the intersection of US 12 and Tieton Road is a sign to Clear Lake. Set your trip odometer at 0.0 at this sign. Go south and then counterclockwise around Clear Lake.

In the vicinity of Clear Lake are some of the oldest rocks in southwestern Washington. These Mesozoic rocks are likely part of an exotic terrane accreted to North America about 100 million years ago. These old rocks, mostly marine sediments and volcanics (metamorphosed in places), are the foundation upon which the Goat Rocks volcano was built. You will see roadcuts of these Mesozoic rocks for the first 8 miles south of US 12.

At mile 3.3 turn left and cross the North Fork of the Tieton River, and at mile 7 turn right on FR 1204. As you ascend the hill you will cross an unconformity, or break in the geologic record. At mile 7.9 you pass the highest roadcut of the Mesozoic exotic terrane with sandstones and mudstones deposited as turbidites on the seafloor. Turbidites are layers of sediment that become finer grained toward the top because the turbidity currents that deposited them slowed down.

At mile 8.3 is an exposure of Pleistocene andesite from the Goat Rocks volcano. This lava flow, about 1 million years old, has platy structure, or subhorizontal tabular sheets formed during cooling and contraction. The contact between the Mesozoic turbidites and the Pleistocene lava is not visible, but this unconformity represents about 100 million years of missing rock record.

From here to the trailhead the road is on top of the andesite flow and glacial deposits. Here and there is a roadcut in andesite, but mostly you see till and boulders left by late Pleistocene ice. There are many side roads; stay on FR 1204 until mile 14.6, where you turn right (uphill) on an unmarked dirt road. At mile 17.0 you'll reach the end of the road, the trailhead, and a register for the wilderness area. A trail park pass is required.

Just south of the parking area at the end of the road is Section Three Pond, which is worth walking around. On the floor of the very shallow pond are mud volcanoes. Gases bubble up through the mud to form the tiny volcanoes; the gases may be from decaying organic matter beneath the mud. How did this

Behind Section Three Pond is the andesite flow capping Pinegrass Ridge.

pond form? Possibilities include irregular deposition during glaciation, or hummocky topography associated with later landslides. Look for tadpoles and/ or frogs in the pond.

Travel southwest on the east side of Pinegrass Ridge, resistant andesite from the Goat Rocks volcano which stretches north from Bear Creek Mountain. To the west and east of Pinegrass Ridge, and 3000 feet lower, are the glacial valleys of the North and South Forks of the Tieton River. You'll hike through alpine meadows, prolific with wildflowers in the summer, and forests of fir, hemlock, cedar, pine, and spruce.

From the pond look west to a ridge with large columns of andesite about a million years old; the columnar joints formed as the lava flow cooled and contracted. The trail is just west of the pond, and soon enters the Goat Rocks Wilderness. The light-colored sandy ash from the 1980 eruption of Mount St. Helens is quite obvious.

Along most of the route, the trail crosses small bowls which have steep slopes to the west, and are open to the east. These bowls, typically with less vegetation than surrounding areas, and which may have springs on their floors, are small landslide scars. The weathered pyroclastics beneath the resistant andesite are weak and susceptible to mass wasting and erosion.

In about 1 mile, a trail (not marked) leads west over the ridge and down to the North Fork of the Tieton River. Beyond here, between the trail and the ridge crest is a talus of rocks that have fallen from the rocky ridge and piled up against it.

In another mile or so there are small colorful outcrops along the trail, particularly at creek crossings, of volcanic strata dipping beneath, and therefore older than, the andesite flow on the ridge. These are due to Miocene and Pliocene explosive eruptions and represent volcanic clouds rolling along the ground (pyroclastic flows) and rising high in the atmosphere to rain ash from the sky (pyroclastic falls).

After crossing the headwaters of Bear Creek there is a marked trail junction. One trail descends east to Conrad Meadows along the South Fork of the Tieton River. If you can arrange to have a vehicle at Conrad Meadows, this is an alternative route for the ascent or descent of Bear Creek Mountain. From this junction proceed steeply up (southwest) toward the summit. The trail ascends through a cirque, a hollow-shaped amphitheater carved by a small cirque glacier, that holds snowfields late in the season. The prevailing winds from the southwest blow lots of snow onto the northeast sides of mountains; snowmelt is reduced in this shady location.

In addition to the outcrops of andesitic bedrock, there are many loose blocks of andesite along the trail. Note the gray color of the very fine-grained matrix speckled with abundant large crystals (phenocrysts) of white plagioclase feldspar and spare crystals of black iron-rich minerals (mainly pyroxene).

In places beside the trail there is a deeply eroded older trail. In the sides of this little gully you can see alternating light and dark layers of ashes and soils representing ashfalls from Cascade volcanoes to the south and west and soils forming between eruptions. The most prominent ash layer is orange; it is from the collapse of Mount Mazama that formed Crater Lake about 7000 years ago. The ashes and soils here are all younger than deglaciation, perhaps 10,000 years ago. At the top is the 1980 ash from Mount St. Helens.

As you climb to the top of the cirque headwall, note the huge columns of the andesite flow. Also, look down to see the hummocky ridges of loose rocks on the floor of the cirque; these ridges are moraines deposited at the lower edge of the small glacier that occupied the cirque. From the top of the cirque headwall it's a short clockwise loop up to the summit, with the view getting more spectacular every minute. The trees near the summit are stunted from wind and cold.

To the south is Mount Adams, 12,276 feet high, and to the northwest is Mount Rainier, at 14,411 feet, the highest peak in the Cascade Range; both stratovolcanoes are obviously covered with glaciers. To the east are the Yakima folds (Hike 41) of the Columbia Basin. To the southwest is the heart of the deeply dissected Goat Rocks volcano, where eruptions occurred from the Miocene to the Pleistocene. Careful inspection (binoculars help) reveals thick lava flows, thin layers of pyroclastics, and vertical dikes where magma was rising toward the surface. Because the Goat Rocks volcano is resistant to erosion, this is the highest part of the South Cascades (with the exceptions of Mount Rainier, Mount Adams, and Mount St. Helens). And it is the most rugged! Glacial features abound.

The nearest peak is Devils Horn, steepened on all sides by glaciers, like the Matterhorn of the European Alps. On the northwest flank of Devils Horn is Devils Washbasin, a tarn or cirque lake. Devils Washbasin drains north into the deep glacial trough along the North Fork of the Tieton River.

Further to the southwest is the long ridge of Goat Rocks, an arête, sharpened by glaciers on both sides. To the west is the largest ice mass, the McCall Glacier beneath Old Snow Mountain and Ives Peak. To the southwest is Gilbert Peak, at 8184 feet the highest remnant of the Goat Rocks volcano. On its north and east flanks are the Conrad and Meade (cirque) Glaciers. Gilbert and Ives Peaks are horns.

If you're lucky, it's a clear and windless day, and this view is too magnificent to leave. When you do depart, descend northeasterly through the cirque, turn north at the trail junction, and return to Section Three Pond.

Hike 35

HUMMOCKS TRAIL

Meander through the Devastated Zone from the 1980 eruption of Mount St. Helens and contemplate the power of the earth to destroy and recreate.

DISTANCE ■ 2.3 mile loop

ELEVATION ■ 2400 feet to 2250 feet (Toutle River)

TOPOGRAPHIC MAPS ■ USGS Elk Rock US Forest Service Mount St. Helens National Volcanic Monument

GEOLOGIC MAP ■ DGER 87-4 Mount St. Helens

KEY REFERENCES ■ Decker and Decker (1993); Doukas (1990); Phillips (1987); Pringle (1993); Wolfe and Pierson (1995).

About the Landscape: The topography and varicolored rocks are reminiscent of the Painted Desert of Arizona, but the origin is very different. The May 18, 1980, eruption of Mount St. Helens began when a bulge on the north side of the mountain collapsed in a series of three huge landslide blocks. As the blocks disintegrated they produced debris avalanches. One roared downward through Spirit Lake and sloshed up and over Johnson Ridge into the Coldwater Creek drainage. Another churned down the North Fork of the Toutle River at speeds greater than 60 miles per hour. The avalanches were followed by an immense blast of gas and ash that rose nearly 12 miles into the stratosphere.

Another part of the blast formed a pyroclastic density current that thundered laterally across the landscape at more than 650 miles per hour. Lahars, generated when ash mixed with melted ice and snow, rolled down the South Fork of the Toutle River and the Muddy River. The biggest lahar was created from water squeezed out of the North Fork debris avalanche where it came to a halt in the Hummocks Trail area. This mass of mud and debris surged down the Toutle River ripping up everything in its path, including homes and bridges. It eventually reached the Columbia River where it disrupted shipping traffic for months. The hummocks are gigantic pieces of the former cone of Mount St. Helens that settled out of the debris avalanche when it slowed down due to a constriction in the Toutle River valley. For a current summary of recent activity at Mount St. Helens, visit the Cascade Volcano Observatory website at *vulcan.wr.usgs.gov/Volcanoes/MSH/.*

Trail Guide: From Exit 49 off I-5, drive east on SR 504 about 39 miles past the Coldwater Ridge Visitor Center to the turnoff for the Johnson Ridge Observatory. The parking lot and trailhead are on the right about 2 miles from the turnoff.

Taking the loop counterclockwise, the trail begins with a short traverse through mounds of many colors ranging in height from a few feet up to 80

A gigantic debris avalanche filled the Toutle River valley with these huge blocks of volcanic rock from the May 18, 1980, eruption of Mount St. Helens.

feet. The different colors come from different parts of Mount St. Helens mixed together (and sometimes smeared out) by the debris avalanche. Soft pink and tan rocks are dacite from lava domes that formed during the Pine Creek Eruptive Period 2900 to 2500 years ago. Most of these rocks are quite crumbly because they have altered by reaction with hot gas and water that circulates through the interior of the volcano. More durable blocks of dark to light gray dacite originated as lava flows during the Castle Creek (1800 to 1600 years ago) and the Goat Rocks periods (1800 to 1857). There are also black basalts of the Castle Creek Period and reddish brown andesites of the Kalama Period (1480 to 1770).

At about 0.25 mile, the trail winds down into a badlands topography of low rounded hills composed mostly of altered volcanics mantled by gray ash from the recent eruptive period that began in 1980. Drainage networks have not yet been established in the hummocks, so there are numerous ponds and just a few flowing streams. Vegetation, however, is rapidly recovering in these wetland areas with thickets of willow and cattails providing an ideal habitat for the numerous small frogs that lurk along the trail in crevices of crumbly volcanics.

At a little over 1 mile, the trail descends through a recently cut ravine to the present course of the Toutle River, which is rapidly cutting down through the erodible debris. The terraces along the river were formed by stream erosion combined with deposition of post-1980 lahars. Walking along the upper terrace, note the bright orange iron-rich bacteria that appear to be thriving in small seeps. After the 1980 eruption, bacteria, including *Legionella pneumophila*

(Legionnaire's Disease), were among the first life forms to return to the Devastated Zone. This area is part of a research site for the Pacific Northwest Forest and Range Experiment Station, so be sure to leave both rocks and vegetation undisturbed.

On the plateau above the river you can see several small, circular ponds, probably kettles, formed by the melting of blocks of ice carried along by the avalanche. A few bread-crust bombs are scattered across the surface. This area is too far away from the crater for the bombs to have been hurled here, so they must have fallen on top of the avalanche when it was close to the vent and then been rafted along to their present location.

To complete the loop, turn left at the junction with the Boundary Trail and hike another 0.5 mile along the ridge above several more ponds. This is a good place to view the trimline on the surrounding ridges created by the lateral blast. Virtually all of the vegetation was destroyed for a distance of up to 12 miles from the crater.

Hike 36 · APE CAVE

Explore a wonderland of lava tubes, lava casts, and an intracanyon lava flow formed by the Ape Cave basalt about 1900 years ago.

DISTANCE ■ 1 mile

ELEVATION ■ 2400 to 2800 feet for all segments

DIFFICULTY ■ Easy to moderate (except for those with acrophobia or claustrophobia)

TOPOGRAPHIC MAPS ■ USGS Mount St. Helens, Mount Mitchell, and Smith Creek Butte quadrangles

GEOLOGIC MAP ■ DGER 87-4 Mount St. Helens North

KEY REFERENCES ■ Decker and Decker (1993); Halliday and Larson (1983); Phillips (1987a); Pringle (1993)

PRECAUTIONS ■ Come prepared for rough ground with temperatures between 50 and 60 degrees Fahrenheit even in midsummer. Bring a lantern; an ordinary flashlight is not adequate. For hiking the Upper Cave you will want a headlamp. Three different light sources are recommended for each party.

About the Landscape: The volcanic activity that built Mount St. Helens can be grouped into four major eruptive stages. The initial eruptions that extended from 50,000 to 36,000 years ago are called the Ape Canyon Stage. The Cougar Stage (20,000 to 18,000 years ago) produced numerous lahars, pyroclastic flows, and dacite ash layers. The volcano was dormant until 13,000 years ago when the Swift Creek Stage began and extended to 10,000 years ago. This produced large volumes of ashfall and pyroclastic flow material.

After another long period of dormancy, the Spirit Lake Stage began around 1900 years before the present, and has been going on ever since. This stage includes seven episodes of major volcanic activity, called eruptive periods, including Smith Creek (3900 to 3300 years ago); Pine Creek (2900 to 2500 years ago); Castle Creek (2200 to 1600 years ago); Sugar Bowl (age uncertain); Kalama (1480 to late 1700); Goat Rocks (1800 to 1857); and the Modern Period (beginning in 1980). For more information, visit the USGS Mount St. Helens website at *vulcan.wr.usgs.gov/Volcanoes/MSH/*.

Trail Guide: From the town of Cougar take Highway 503/FR 90 about 7 miles north. Turn left onto FR 83 and drive west 1.6 miles to the Ape Cave parking lot.

The Ape Cave hike takes place in an underground lava tube with an accessible length of 12,810 feet. There are two possible starting points depending upon time available and tolerance for the underground experience. Those who want to complete the full length of the hike can take a surface trail approximately 1.5 miles through the forest to the upper entrance. However, the upper part of the cave is a very rough scramble over lots of fallen rock, so most hikers will want to take the main entrance, roughly in the center of the tube. This entrance is a steel staircase through a ceiling collapse structure (called a skylight) only a short walk from the visitor center. From here you can see most of the highlights of the lava tube by walking either up or down the tube.

Immediately after descending underground through the main entrance, some of the unique features of Ape Cave can be seen. First, there is an upper and a lower level, which in places forms an hourglass shape probably representing erosion by the underground lava as it cut deeper into its own solidified floor. Along the walls, a number of ledges remain from a succession of lava streams flowing through the tunnel, each leaving its own "bathtub ring" or high-water (lava) mark. The floor of the cave near the entrance is covered with what looks like sand, but is a coarse ash, which poured in through skylights during the Kalama eruptive period about 450 years ago.

Continuing downslope about 100 meters from the stairs into the lower part of the tube, notice the rubble of rock on the right hand side of the cave and the reddish ash exposed. This is a blowout structure probably caused by a steam explosion from the damp walls of the valley down which the Ape Cave lava flowed.

163

As you walk along, shine your light upward. In many places there are lava icicles hanging from the ceiling that were formed as superheated gases remelted the roof of the lava tube. About 0.3 mile from the main entrance, the passageway narrows and a distinct echo effect can be heard. A few hundred feet further is the meatball, a feature unique to Ape Cave. This rounded piece of lava was broken off the wall and rafted along the surface of a flow; as the flow level dropped, the meatball got jammed in a narrow part of the cave and is now stuck there, hanging above the floor.

In another 0.25 mile, the cave looks almost like a subway with railroad tracks. These "tracks" (lava levees) were formed as a bathtub ring by the last major flow coming down the tube. Then the floor was covered with Kalama ash, but the tracks were exposed when the ash was eroded, probably due to heavy rainfall and/or snowmelt that seeped through from the surface. Near the lower end, about 4000 feet from the entrance, the tube divides into upper and lower passageways separated by a thin lava floor/ceiling. Be careful if you ascend into the upper tube; the floor has collapsed in places making travel dangerous. The lower cave gradually narrows down to a crawl space blocked by sand.

Exploration of the upper cave is more adventurous because it involves a bit of climbing and scrambling over rubble and possibly wading. To begin, take a hard left at the bottom of the stairs going down into the lower cave just below the main entrance. This leads up into the "great room" of the upper cave. Check out the floor on the way up—it looks like ripples on a beach. This is the top surface of a lava flow type called by its Hawaiian name, *pahoehoe*. *Pahoehoe* flows quite easily, but as it cools it tends to pile up on itself, forming a characteristic pattern of ripples and ropes. Along the walls are wide lava ledges, whimsically called "Sasquatch feeding troughs." In the middle of the great room, fallen from the ceiling, are some large blocks of rock glazed with a thin film of volcanic glass that formed when the ceiling partially melted due to the rising heat of a lava flow moving through the tube. Notice the splash marks in the floor around blocks that fell from the ceiling into the lava stream.

To continue, scramble over a rubble heap at the upper end of the room into a passageway marked by groundwater seeps that have left colorful deposits of iron oxides on the walls. In about 0.5 mile is a sweeping bend in the cave with the distinct figure-eight cross-section. Just up from this passage there are numerous slump and peel structures that formed when multiple flows coated the tube walls with lava, and then the outer wall broke away to reveal the inner surface. Some of these look almost like a rind partially peeled off an orange. At the upper end of this section is a bright red wall of ash where the entire tube has either been broken or blasted away from the valley wall.

Just beyond is perhaps the most spectacular feature in the cave: a 10-foot high lava fall that developed when a flow collected in a pond behind an

The Muddy River has cut a spectacular gorge into the Ape Cave basalt at Lava Canyon.

obstruction in the tube. The only way to go on is to climb up the face of the falls; this is where a head lamp will come in handy, since the climb is a bit tricky while carrying a lantern. Above the falls the cave narrows to only a few feet in width, and in the summertime a cool breeze of up to 7 miles per hour can be felt. In the middle of the passageway is a big lump of dark lava known as the lava tongue, the front of a flow that made it only this far down the tube. A small lake covers the floor a short distance further, at least during the spring and early summer. You can get around the water by tiptoeing along the ledge or just splash on through if you don't mind getting your feet wet. In another 100 yards the upper lava falls is better described as a lava cascade because the drop is only a few feet.

Approaching the upper end of the cave, light begins to filter in from above. This is not the entrance, but rather a "skylight" that apparently developed during the active flow period because there is no rubble indicating a post-volcanic collapse. Do not try to climb out here. The stairs for the upper entrance are about 800 feet further through a narrow, multicolored, multitextured passage. Before exiting, continue on to a large room that is the upper end of Ape Cave. Here the remnants of a "lava spring" must have bubbled up from beneath the rock seal to feed the rivers of lava flowing down the tube. Climb out of the cave via a volcanic sinkhole (collapse structure) with a steel ladder, then hike the well-marked trail back to the main entrance.

Hike

37

HAMILTON MOUNTAIN

Climb past two waterfalls to a mountain top with a spectacular view of the Columbia River Gorge.

DISTANCE ■ 4 miles

ELEVATION ■ 400 feet to 2438 feet

DIFFICULTY ■ Moderate

TOPOGRAPHIC MAP ■ USGS Beacon Rock

GEOLOGIC MAP ■ DGER 87-6 Hood River

KEY REFERENCES ■ Allen (1984)

PRECAUTIONS ■ Beware of Poison Oak near the trail along the way.

About the Landscape: Hamilton Mountain overlooks the west end of the Columbia River Gorge National Scenic Area. As the Cascade Range was uplifted, the Columbia River cut down through the rocks of the ancestral Cascades. When a lava flow of the Columbia River basalts filled the channel of the ancient Columbia River, it cut a new channel just to the north or south.

Beacon Rock, about 600 feet high, is considered the largest monolith in the United States. It is a shallow basaltic intrusive body, and has been called a plug, a dome, a volcanic neck, a vent-filling, the throat of a volcano, and a dike remnant. The relatively erodible host rocks, and the volcano that was above Beacon Rock, have been removed by erosion. Beacon Rock has persisted because it is more resistant than the rocks it intruded. Beacon Rock witnessed the fast passage of the Missoula floods, and is today surrounded by slow-moving landslides. Take time to climb the steep trail and steps up Beacon Rock; it is well worth the view.

On this hike there are two waterfalls, Hardy Falls and Rodney Falls, and a splendid 360-degree view from the summit of Hamilton Mountain. The route passes early Miocene volcaniclastic rocks, Columbia River basalt, rocks associated with a late Cenozoic volcano, and late Quaternary landslide materials.

Hamilton Mountain is composed of Columbia River basalt flows.

With waterfalls, forests, and wildflowers near the trail, and Cascade volcanoes and the Columbia River Gorge as a backdrop, this is one of the most scenic hikes in the Northwest.

Trail Guide: Hamilton Mountain is in Beacon Rock State Park, which is 2 miles east of Skamania in the Columbia River Gorge. Skamania is on Washington SR 14 about halfway between Vancouver, Washington, and Hood River, Oregon. At the base of Beacon Rock, leave SR 14 and drive north (0.3 mile) to a picnic area, where there are restrooms and trail signs.

The trail to the two falls and Hamilton Mountain starts at the east end of the picnic grounds. Just northwest of the trailhead is a talus below a colonnade of Pliocene or Pleistocene volcanic rock, probably part of the volcano that had its vent at Beacon Rock.

In the first mile or so, the trail climbs 400 feet through the early Miocene (about 20 million years old) Eagle Creek Formation. This formation is dominated by conglomerates, sandstones, and tuffs, all derived from ancient Cascade andesitic volcanoes, which shed mudflows and erupted ash. Buried soils, some with petrified wood, indicate pauses in volcanism and deposition. There are a few lava flows within the Eagle Creek Formation; one is located along Hamilton Creek just east of Hamilton Mountain.

The combination of steep slopes, high precipitation, and weak rocks in the Columbia River Gorge leads to lots of mass wasting. The Eagle Creek Formation with weathered mud-rich rocks is particularly susceptible to landslides.

167

Rocks in this area dip gently south toward the Columbia River, making them even more likely to fail. There are large areas of mass wasting both east and west of Beacon Rock State Park. Along this trail, the landslides are relatively small and shallow. Evidence for the weakness of the Eagle Creek Formation and for the mass wasting includes weathered rock (oxidized), a muddy and slippery trail, hummocky (uneven) ground, and boulders of basalt which originated far above and have slid/flowed to lower elevations.

At about the 800-foot elevation, the trail reaches Hardy Falls and then Rodney Falls. Waterfalls are almost always located at resistant rocks. In this case, Hardy Creek plunges over lava flows. The potholes (here as much as 15 feet in diameter) attest to the power of a fast-moving stream armed with stones to erode the resistant rock.

From Rodney Falls descend to the bridge, cross Hardy Creek, and begin the ascent of the southwest ridge of Hamilton Mountain. Climbing the switchbacks you encounter basalt breccia with pillows. When the Grande Ronde Basalt (about 16 million years old) encountered water of a tributary of the ancient Columbia River, the hot lava broke into angular fragments (breccia) and formed rounded masses (pillows) in the cold water. The lava filled a valley cut in the Eagle Creek Formation.

At about 1600 to 1700 feet (between the two sections of switchbacks) are excellent views to the east. In the foreground is a talus of basalt fragments that have fallen from the cliffs on the southeast side of Hamilton Mountain. Just beyond the talus is a cliff of stratified volcaniclastic rocks. In the middle ground is Bonneville Dam, constructed from 1933 to 1937. The north abutment of the dam is against part of the toe of the Bonneville (or Cascade) landslide. Notice the convex-to-the-south curve of the north bank of the Columbia River just upstream of the dam. This is the toe of the giant (14 square miles) Bonneville landslide which occurred about 750 to 300 years ago. In the distance, Wind Mountain, a Pliocene diorite intrusion (on the north side of the river), is surrounded by another big landslide. Also, look southwest to Beacon Rock far below.

Beyond the viewpoint climb more switchbacks to the summit of Hamilton Mountain. This portion of the climb is on lava flows of the Grande Ronde Basalt. This lava originated in the southeast corner of Washington and flowed all the way to Willapa Bay on the coast in perhaps a week. Imagine how voluminous and fluid such a lava flow must be.

The best view is along the ridge a short distance north of the brushy summit. Forty miles to the northeast is Mount Adams (12,267 feet), which has not erupted in historic time. Across the Columbia River Gorge 25 miles to the southeast is Mount Hood (11,245 feet), which had a small eruption in 1801. The glaciers on these two volcanoes were more extensive about 15,000 years ago when you could have watched Missoula floods rush west below you.

Chapter 5
COLUMBIA BASIN

Channeled Scabland of the Columbia Basin

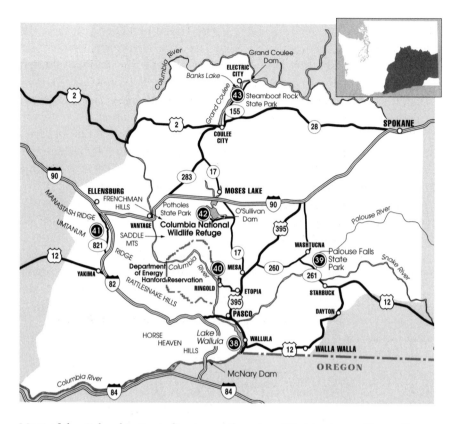

Most of the Columbia Basin lies in southeastern Washington, with small portions to the east in Idaho and to the south in Oregon. It is a basin because it is surrounded by mountains: the Cascades to the west, the Rockies to the northeast, and the Blue Mountains to the southeast.

Some call the Columbia Basin by other names: the Columbia Plateau, or the Walla Walla section of the Columbia Basin. The Native American meaning of Walla Walla is many waters, a strange description of the Columbia Basin desert with mean annual precipitation as low as 8 inches, and with plenty of sagebrush and sand dunes. But many rivers meet at the edge of the Columbia Basin: the little Walla Walla River; the bigger Yakima, Wenatchee, Okanagan, Spokane, Clearwater, Snake, John Day, and Deschutes Rivers; and the mighty Columbia River itself. So there are, indeed, many waters in this desert.

The Columbia Basin was affected by two of the best documented catastrophic events in the earth's history: enormous basaltic lava flows and giant glacier outburst floods. These events are in large part responsible for the landscape of this area, where the largest documented floods in geologic history swept the earth's youngest basalt plateau.

More than 99 percent of the basalt in the Columbia Basin erupted in a relatively short period of geologic time, between 17 and 14 million years ago (the Miocene epoch). Concurrent with volcanism were subsidence, for example, the Pasco Basin (Hike 40); deformation, for example, the Yakima Fold Belt (Hike 41); erosion by rivers (Wallula Gap, Hike 38; and Yakima Canyon, Hike 41); and sedimentation in the Ringold Formation (Hike 40).

Both folding and faulting occurred (and may still be occuring) in the Columbia Basin. North-south oriented compressional stresses created the anticlines (convex-upward folds that include the basalt flows and any interbedded sediments) of the Yakima Hills. A major fault-like feature called the Olympic-Wallowa lineament (Hike 38) stretches northwesterly from northeastern Oregon across southeastern Washington (see figure 10). There is evidence for both dip-slip (vertical) and strike-slip (horizontal) motion on the Olympic-Wallowa lineament, which may be responsible for some southeastern Washington earthquakes.

Eolian (wind deposited) sediments are common in the Columbia Basin. They accumulated during the Quaternary, and are indirectly associated with glaciation. The Columbia Basin was a major route for meltwater from the Cordilleran

figure 10. Distribution of the Columbia River Basalt Group (shaded) in the Pacific Northwest

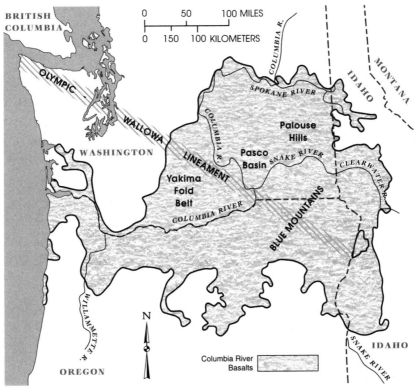

Ice Sheet to the north and smaller glaciers in the mountains to the east and west. Meltwater rivers have great variation in annual (and daily) discharge. With glaciers melting in the summer, there is a lot of meltwater carrying a lot of sediment. The high water level prevents vegetation from growing on the outwash plain (like a floodplain, but with sediment deposited by meltwater derived from a glacier). In the winter, with the glaciers frozen, discharge is low, and vast expanses of sediment are exposed. The cold weather prevents vegetation from colonizing the exposed sediment.

The prevailing southwesterly winds of the Pacific Northwest erode the exposed sediment and deposit it to the northeast. The wind is not strong enough to transport pebbles and cobbles, but moves sand short distances, producing dune fields (Hike 42). The silt is suspended by the wind, and was transported further to the northeast to become the Palouse Loess of the Palouse Hills in the eastern Columbia Basin. The loess there is as much as 300 feet thick; water has eroded it into thousands of small hills.

The grand finale in the Columbia Basin, except for our dam-building, was the Missoula floods (see figure 11). One lobe of the Cordilleran Ice Sheet advanced south from British Columbia and dammed a northwest flowing river, the Clarks Fork near Cabinet Gorge on the Idaho-Montana state line. The ice dam formed glacial Lake Missoula, which held 500 cubic miles of water (as much as one of the present-day Great Lakes). The ice dam, nearly 2000 feet high, failed repeatedly, releasing gigantic *jökulhlaups* (an Icelandic term meaning glacier outburst flood) which swept across northern Idaho and the Columbia Basin, and raced through the Columbia River Gorge en route to the Pacific Ocean. These *jökulhlaups* had discharges as great as 18 cubic miles of water per hour, velocities as great as 40 miles per hour, and depths as great as 900 feet.

The Missoula floods were studied by J Harlan Bretz in the 1920s (he had studied glaciation of the Puget Lowland a decade earlier). Bretz described the various erosional and depositional features resulting from the floods.

Let's characterize the flood velocities as fast, medium, and slow. Where the floods were fast, they eroded, as at Palouse Falls (Hike 39). The floods eroded almost all of the unconsolidated loess they encountered, and further down into the resistant basalt flows to create the Channeled Scabland. Characterized by coulees, Channeled Scabland refers to areas of mid- to southeastern Washington exemplified by deep narrow channels, for example, Grand Coulee (Hike 43), and scabs (erosion remnants of basalt) like Steamboat Rock (Hike 43).

Where the floods slowed to a medium velocity, they deposited gravel, mostly cobble-sized clasts, in giant bars. Most of the bars are perched high along flood routes (Hike 38 at Wallula Gap) or lower on the insides of bends in canyons.

Where flood velocities were slow, sand and silt settled out as Touchet Beds, named for Touchet in the Walla Walla Valley. Each Touchet Bed represents a

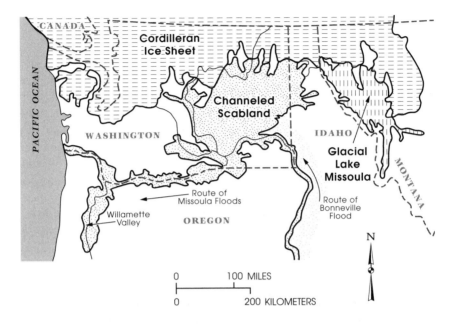

figure 11. Glacial Lake Missoula and routes of the Missoula and Bonneville Floods

separate Missoula flood; in the Walla Walla Valley there are about forty Touchet Beds, hence forty floods. Near the top of the beds is a layer of ash from Mount St. Helens that has been dated as 13,000 years old; this is part of the evidence that the most recent Missoula floods occurred between 15,300 and 12,700 years ago.

Hike
38
WALLULA GAP

This narrow rock gap served as the bottleneck for the earth's largest floods.

DISTANCE ■ 1 mile

ELEVATION ■ 390 feet to 1173 feet (top of the gap)

DIFFICULTY ■ Moderate

TOPOGRAPHIC MAP ■ USGS Wallula

GEOLOGIC MAP ■ DGER 94-3 Walla Walla

KEY REFERENCES ■ Allen and others (1986); Carson and Pogue (1996)

PRECAUTIONS ■ Do not trespass on the forty acres of private property approximately 1000 feet northeast of the route.

About the Landscape: You will walk across a layer cake of basalt flows 800 feet thick, and climb the side of a water gap that restricted and backed up the

Missoula floods. The lava flows originated to the east of here in the general vicinity of the Blue Mountains and Hells Canyon. During this Miocene volcanism, with little topography in the central part of the Columbia Basin, the lava diverted rivers and blocked drainages to form lakes. There are more than 300 individual lava flows in the Columbia Basin, and approximately 20 of them have been identified at Wallula Gap. All are between 16 and 13 million years old except one high remnant on the west side of the gap which is only 8.5 million years old.

After the lava flows were emplaced, this area underwent mild deformation. A giant east-west arch of upfolded basalt flows developed. The surface expression of this anticline is the Horse Heaven Hills, which straddle the Oregon-Washington border. Inside the anticline the lava flows dip both north to the Pasco Basin and south to Oregon's Umatilla Basin. These two basins are full of sediment overlying the basalt flows. The same lava flows that are at an elevation of more than 1000 feet at the crest of the Horse Heaven Hills anticline are close to sea level in the centers of the Pasco and Umatilla Basins.

Along the north side of the anticline is one of the most prominent structural features in Washington, the Olympic-Wallowa lineament. The lineament was recognized by Erwin Raisz in 1945; he proposed that this feature extended 400 miles from the Strait of Juan de Fuca to the north side of the Wallowa Mountains (in northeastern Oregon). In places, such as Wallula Gap, the Olympic-Wallowa lineament is a fault. There is evidence for two kinds of motion along the fault: sideways motion (such as along California's San Andreas Fault), and vertical motion (the Horse Heaven Hills up on the south and the Pasco Basin down on the north).

Wallula Gap is a spectacular water gap, a place where a stream flows through a pass in a ridge. Millions of years ago, the Columbia River was further west. Since then, growth of the Horse Heaven Hills anticline blocked the river while subsidence of the Pasco Basin caused the river to shift eastward. The Columbia River then crossed the Horse Heaven Hills at the low point, and cut this water gap.

Glacial Lake Missoula held 500 cubic miles of water dammed by a glacier. The ice dam failed perhaps 40 to 100 times between 15,300 and 12,700 years ago. Each time it failed a world-record flood swept across northern Idaho and through Spokane. From there, the floodwaters spread through dozens of channels in eastern Washington, from Palouse Falls on the east (Hike 39) to Wenatchee on the west. But all routes lead to Wallula! The floodwaters had only one place to cross the Horse Heaven Hills, which stretch from the Cascade Range on the west to the Blue Mountains on the east. That one place is here at Wallula Gap.

Lake Wallula, the reservoir, was formed when McNary Dam was built on the Columbia River at Umatilla. The normal pool elevation of Lake Wallula is 340 feet, and the Columbia River is as deep as 91 feet here. The top of the west side of Wallula Gap is 1147 feet high and was overtopped by some of the Missoula floods. These floods through Wallula Gap were more than 898 feet deep; Wallula Gap wasn't big enough! These were the largest floods on earth with glacial Lake Missoula releasing water at the rate of 18 cubic miles per hour. Wallula Gap, big as it is, could accommodate only about half that flood flow. With more water headed from Montana to the Pacific Ocean than could get through Wallula Gap, at perhaps 40 miles per hour, the water backed up into the Pasco Basin, up the Yakima Valley to Yakima, and up the Snake River to the mouth of the Salmon River. These were big floods, and they certainly modified Wallula Gap.

Trail Guide: Wallula Gap is on the Columbia River approximately midway between Walla Walla, Umatilla-Hermiston (Oregon), and Pasco-Kennewick-Richland. To drive to the beginning of this hike, start at the weigh station at Wallula Junction, at the intersection of US 12 and US 730. Go southwest on US 730, crossing the Olympic-Wallowa lineament at mile 0.8. The parking lot for the Two Sisters is on the southeast side of US 730 at mile 2. This area is called the Wallula Gap Natural Landmark; the land on the hike is owned by Walla Walla County, the Bureau of Land Management, and Whitman College.

From the parking area, go eastward over or under the fence, following a trail that leads up to the saddle just south of the Two Sisters. At the west end of the saddle, a trail leads steeply north to the east side of the Two Sisters. Scramble up to the gap between the two basalt towers, being careful of rockfall. It is not safe to climb here without a belay. The views westward across Wallula Gap and eastward to a small dune field in a Channeled Scabland are magnificent.

The Two Sisters are erosional remnants of a single lava flow that is about 15.5 million years old. You are standing at the boundary between the lower colonnade and the upper entablature. The colonnade has larger, more vertical, and more regular columns, whereas the entablature has smaller, less regular columns. The columns form as the lava shrinks during cooling. The lava shrinks into polygonal shapes just like the pattern of cracks in drying and shrinking mud.

Look to the north and east where you will see many horizontal lava flows in the cliffs. At the same elevation as you are now you can see the same lava flow, with its prominent colonnade and entablature. This lava flow once extended tens of miles in every direction, but it has been dissected, particularly by the Columbia River at Wallula Gap, and by the Missoula floods in the Channeled Scabland here and just to the northeast. The Channeled Scabland is the maze of gullies around the erosional remnants of basalts. Remember, the

Light-colored dune sand at the base of the dark Two Sisters, survivors of the Missoula floods.

highest flood was at an elevation of about 1200 feet. Let's hike to the top of the floods—but first, the dunes.

Return southeast to the trail junction in the saddle, and follow the trail east to the small dune field, or just descend eastward from the Two Sisters to the sand dunes. These are parabolic dunes, with the poorly developed convex slip faces on the northeast, indicating the prevailing wind is from the southwest.

(See Hike 42 for descriptions of types of dunes and their migration.) To the southwest is Wallula Gap; on Lake Wallula may be sailboats from the marina at Port Kelley. Wallula Gap is aligned with the prevailing winds, so we should expect the source of the sand to be from the southwest.

Note that this is a fine white sand with large flakes of muscovite mica that glitter in the sun. Yet the view to the southwest reveals only black basalt, that does not contain muscovite. Where is the source of the white sand? It has disappeared; the sand supply for the dunes has been cut off. Imagine Wallula Gap before McNary Dam was constructed in 1953: a Columbia River with channels, islands, and sand and gravel bars. The southwesterly winds deflated sand from the bars when the river was low, transported the sand to the northeast, and deposited it in the area south of the Two Sisters. With no more sand supply, the dunes are slowly becoming vegetated and inactive.

From the bare part of the dune field, walk south through the sagebrush-covered dunes or along the basalt ridge south of the Two Sisters. Keep west of CR 664 and the fences. Do not trespass on the private property to the northeast. Soon you will be able to see the grain elevators at Port Kelley. Just where the county road descends south to US 730, turn east and cross both fences and the dirt road. Continue eastward up a steep slope with taluses to the north and south. A talus is a sloping heap of angular rock fragments at the base of a cliff. The taluses accumulated due to rockfall from the cliffs of fractured basalt.

About 200 feet above the county road is a bench. There are cliffs to the west dropping down to US 730. Continue southeasterly, crossing the basalt flow to your east at any of the breaks in the cliff. Your objective is the high point to the southeast. You are now on a ridge at about the same elevation (783 feet) as the small mesa to the north. A mesa is a flat-topped hill or mountain, flat because there is a horizontal layer of resistant rock at the top. A mesa is relatively wide and low compared to a butte; the Two Sisters are buttes. Here the mesas and buttes are scabs or remnants of erosion by the Missoula floods. The mesa to the north had about 400 feet of rushing water above it.

The Pasco Basin is to the northwest beyond the dune field and the Two Sisters. You can see the petroleum tank farms near the mouth of the Snake River. To the southwest along the sides of Wallula Gap you can see huge taluses beneath high cliffs. The force of the Missoula floods removed all the loose rock at Wallula Gap, so these taluses have accumulated in the last 13,000 years.

Continue southeast along the ridge toward the hilltop. About 200 feet below the summit is a bench with witness posts along the boundary of the US Army Corps of Engineer project to build McNary Dam and create Lake Wallula. From here you can see the wheat fields on top of the Horse Heaven Hills west of Wallula Gap. Wheat doesn't grow on basalt, so there must be some other geologic material on top of the anticline. That material is a rich soil developed on a few feet of loess, or windblown silt. The wind deflated the silt from the sediments in the Umatilla Basin to the southwest, and deposited it on the Horse Heaven Hills.

Go through any break in the highest cliffs as you climb southeastward to the hilltop. The view is best from another witness post, but the summit (elevation 1173 feet) is about 100 yards southeast of the witness post. You are near the crest of the Horse Heaven Hills anticline, as are the radio towers on the mountain called Jump Off Joe to the west.

You are south of the Olympic-Wallowa lineament, which runs across the north end of Wallula Gap. Whereas the Horse Heaven Hills anticline trends east-west, the Olympic-Wallowa lineament runs more southeast-northwest. If the day is clear, you can see Rattlesnake Mountain (elevation 3565 feet) 40 miles to the northwest; the Olympic-Wallowa lineament is at the base of the steep northeast side of Rattlesnake Mountain. You are now high enough to see Oregon's Umatilla Basin to the southwest beyond Wallula Gap.

There are small alluvial fans along the edge of Lake Wallula; the fans easiest to see are sagebrush-covered gentle slopes about 3 miles to the southwest on the west side of Wallula Gap. These fans are piles of sediment deposited by intermittent streams (and mudflows) originating in the canyons cutting the margins of Wallula Gap. More difficult to see are giant gravel bars deposited by the Missoula floods.The elevation of the tops of these gravel bars is about 900 feet. Look for one gravel bar where there is a break in the basalt cliffs above the alluvial fans. Should another Missoula flood occur now, you would probably be safe. Notice that the top of this hill has a silty soil; this is old loess not stripped off by the Missoula floods, or young loess deposited later.

Nearly due north is Boise Cascade's paper mill at Wallula. Adjacent to the paper mill is a recycling plant that provides much of the fiber for making the paper. What is that large green patch just northeast of the paper mill? A forest in the desert? It's a tree farm of hybrid cottonwood trees that mature to about 75 feet tall in six years and are harvested for fiber for the paper mill. The use of fiber from the recycling plant and the tree farm greatly reduce the amount of fiber needed from the Umatilla National Forest.

Return to the Two Sisters by retracing your steps northwesterly down the ridge, or turn northeast and descend into a small dry valley. At the upper end of the valley are scattered juniper trees, and two anomalous conical basaltic hills that are further evidence of the height of the Missoula floods. Scabs or erosion remnants come in many shapes: cones, ridges, buttes, and mesas.

Descend the valley going northwesterly toward the old corral. Look for rocks that are not basalt; if you are lucky you may find a granitic or other rock transported here on an iceberg riding a Missoula flood. Most of the light-colored rocks are basalt with a white or gray coating of caliche, a calcium carbonate that accumulates during soil formation in an arid climate. The precipitation here is only about 8 inches per year.

Walk south of the corral and go west across CR 664 and the fence near the cattle guard. Turn north and retrace your steps along the ridge or through the dunes to the parking area at the base of the Two Sisters.

PALOUSE FALLS

Hike 39

During the creation of the Channeled Scabland by the Missoula floods, the Palouse River took a shortcut to the Snake River. The result was a waterfall in a desert.

DISTANCE ■ 1 mile

ELEVATION ■ Start, 910 feet; high point, 940 feet; top of falls, 765 feet

DIFFICULTY ■ Moderate

TOPOGRAPHIC MAP ■ USGS Palouse Falls

GEOLOGIC MAP ■ DGER 94-14 Connell

KEY REFERENCE ■ Carson and Pogue (1996)

PRECAUTIONS ■ There are hazards at Palouse Falls. Be on the lookout for rattlesnakes and poison oak. Do not get close to the canyon rim where there are no fences or guardrails. Be particularly careful not to slip on the route from the poison oak patch to the lip of the falls!

About the Landscape: Palouse Falls is spectacular any time of the year, but particularly in the late winter and spring. This waterfall is 184 feet high, and is in the bottom of a canyon that (downstream from the falls) is 377 feet deep. Much of the year the deep plunge pool in the enormous amphitheater receives only a small flow of clear water. In the spring, Palouse Falls turns into a giant chocolate milkshake; rain and snowmelt turn the river brown with silt from the highly erodible Palouse Hills. The falls are dirty and noisy, and make huge waves in the plunge pool.

The origin of Palouse Falls and the canyon of the Palouse River is unusual. The ancestral Palouse River traveled west from the Rocky Mountains of Idaho to the Pasco Basin of south-central Washington. Why did the Palouse River abandon the western part of this route, leaving the Washtucna and Kahlotus Coulees on the bottom of a dry valley? There is a low east-west divide between the Snake River (to the south) and the ancestral Palouse River (to the north). Much of the discharge of the Missoula floods went south from Spokane, through Cheney, and into the drainage basin of the Palouse River (this Missoula floods route is called the Cheney-Palouse Tract). The valley of the ancestral Palouse River was not big enough to accommodate the Missoula floods, which therefore jumped the divide and rushed south to the Snake River. The floods cut three deep coulees across the divide: the canyon of the Palouse River here, HU or Davin Coulee just to the west, and Devils Canyon to the north of Lower Monumental Dam.

These three coulees started as waterfalls on the north rim of the canyon of the Snake River. With each Missoula flood the waterfalls migrated upstream and the coulees got longer. Devils Canyon extends from the Snake River almost to Kahlotus Coulee; the head of Davin Coulee is at the HU Ranch, and the deep canyon of the Palouse River starts at Palouse Falls. After an unknown number of Missoula floods, the present route of the Palouse River was lowest, and the river abandoned Washtucna Coulee. Therefore, the Palouse River no longer goes to the Pasco Basin; instead, it is a tributary to the Snake River.

The route to Palouse Falls State Park gives you an opportunity to see and understand the complex history of the Missoula floods and drainage changes in this area. You'll see some valleys that are dry and others that had water flowing

Palouse Falls is part of the rectangular drainage pattern on the Columbia River basalts.

down them. These valleys are cut in the Columbia River basalts, which are well exposed in cliffs at the state park.

Trail Guide: Palouse Falls State Park is located off SR 261 between Washtucna (a town and a coulee) and Starbuck (a town and a coffee). To get there from Ritzville (on I-90), drive 27 miles south on SR 261 to the town of Washtucna. Washtucna Coulee is the ancient east-to-west valley of the Palouse River; the valley was deepened, steepened, and eventually abandoned as a result of the Missoula floods.

Continue southwest on SR 261 along Washtucna Coulee for 6 miles. Turn southeast (left) at the grain elevators (that's all that's there) at McAdam/Sperry; set your trip odometer to 0.0 here. From McAdam/Sperry to mile 4.4, SR 261 goes through the Palouse Hills, thick blankets of loess that have been (and continue to be) eroded by running water (at mile 1.1 and 1.2, roadcuts show white Mazama ash from the eruption that formed Crater Lake, Oregon).

At mile 4.4 you leave this part of the Palouse Hills and start to cross the easternmost channel of the Missoula floods. This basalt-floored channel has two coulees; the western, HU or Davin Coulee, starts just south of the low point at HU Ranch (mile 5.4), and the other is the canyon of the Palouse River.

To the south from mile 7.1 to mile 8.6 and beyond, there are ridges of loess which rise 200 feet above the basalt floor of the channel. These "islands" are erosional remnants of loess that were streamlined in a north-south direction by the rush of the Missoula floods toward the Snake River. At mile 8.6 turn northeast (left) and proceed 2.5 miles to Palouse Falls State Park.

To get to Palouse Falls from Dayton (on US 12), go 15 miles north on US 12. Set your trip odometer to mile 0.0 as you turn west (left) onto SR 261 and proceed down the valley of the Toucannon River. This valley was cut in the Columbia River basalts and then partially filled by Touchet Beds (slackwater sediments of the Missoula floods). Notice as you go downvalley these beds of sediments (each bed represents a separate Missoula flood) get coarser, indicating that the floods were rushing up the Toucannon River from the Snake River.

At mile 0.0 the Touchet Beds are sand and silt, but by mile 9 (a mile northwest of Starbuck) they include lots of gravel. From mile 10.2 (the bridge over the Toucannon River) to mile 11.7 (the mouth of the Toucannon River) there is a marsh, sediment deposited because Lower Monumental Dam (construction between 1961 and 1970) backed the Snake River up into its tributary. From mile 12 to the bridge over the Snake River (mile 14.7) you are driving on a giant gravel bar deposited by the Missoula floods which were rushing down the Palouse River and dumping into the Snake River. Up and down the Snake River, on the insides of the bends, are two more huge gravel bars deposited by the Missoula floods.

Lyons Ferry State Park (mile 15.3) and the mouth of the Palouse River are just north of the Snake River bridge. From here, SR 261 winds up onto the floor of the easternmost channel of the Missoula floods. This channel is more than 6 miles wide; the canyon of the Palouse River is incised into the channel, and loess islands (to the southwest from mile 17.9 to mile 20.1 and beyond) rise above the channel floor. At mile 8.6 turn northeast (right) and proceed 2.5 miles to Palouse Falls State Park.

Most tourists walk down the short slope southeast of the parking lot, lean on the fence, look over the cliff at Palouse Falls, and drive away. For the complete tour, however, walk southwest from the parking lot (restrooms, water) to the covered overlook at the edge of the canyon. You'll pass a big notch in the canyon wall, and on the opposite side are more big notches trending northwest-southeast. These are fractures in the basalt that have been differentially eroded. A group of parallel fractures is called a fracture set. Look up and down the zigzag canyon; this is an example of angular drainage. There are multiple fracture sets in this area; the three most prominent sets trend northeast, northwest, and north-northwest. The Palouse River follows these fracture sets because they are weaknesses in the bedrock that are more easily erodible.

From the overlook, walk northeast along the canyon rim to the tourist vista. Each lava flow may have a basal colonnade of large polygonal columns, and an upper entablature of small less regular columns; the thickness ratio of colonnade to entablature varies from one flow to another. There are two flows behind Palouse Falls, one at the lip of the falls, and a thick one above the falls (see figure 12). The two lower flows are Grande Ronde Basalt, and the two upper flows are Wanapum Basalt. The picket fence of columns above and to the left of Palouse Falls is part of the colonnade of the upper (Ginkgo) flow. The appropriately named Palouse Falls flow is just below the falls.

Walk north along the fence and then east along the canyon rim (use caution!). At the southeast corner of this plateau, you are almost 100 feet above the falls; do not descend here. Turn northwest and follow the canyon rim to the north corner of the plateau. Carefully descend to the railroad tracks, and keeping an ear out for trains, walk along the tracks to the north end of the embankment. Turn southeast and descend the crude trail that goes diagonally down the embankment. Cross the area of grass and brush (including poison oak) to the Palouse River at a small waterfall. At the base of the cliff to the southwest, where the Palouse River makes a 90-degree turn, is an interbed between the Palouse Falls flow below and the Ginkgo flow above (see figure 12). The interbed includes fine-grained sediment, microfossils (such as diatoms), and organic matter. A pond formed in a low place on the Palouse Falls flow after it was erupted. This pond filled with sediment, which was buried by the Ginkgo flow 15.5 million years ago.

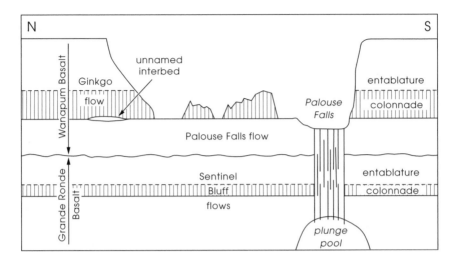

figure 12. Stratigraphy of the Columbia River basalts at Palouse Falls

Be very cautious if you continue southeast to the top of Palouse Falls. Follow the faint trail between the basalt cliff above you and the river below you. The lip of the falls is just beyond the "picket fence" part of the Ginkgo flow's colonnade. It is not safe to continue west at this level and then down to the plunge pool.

Hike

40 HANFORD REACH

At the undammed Hanford Reach, the White Bluffs record the eastward shift of the Columbia River millions of years ago.

DISTANCE ■ 3 miles

ELEVATION ■ 410 feet to 890 feet

DIFFICULTY ■ Easy

TOPOGRAPHIC MAPS ■ Hanford; Locke Island

GEOLOGIC MAP ■ DGER 94-13 Priest Rapids

KEY REFERENCE ■ Gustafson (1978)

About the Landscape: Imagine a place in the Columbia Basin with no lava flows within miles (except straight down). The Hanford Reach (51 miles long) is also the only free-flowing stretch of the Columbia River between Canada and the Pacific Ocean. Here the Columbia flows southeasterly through the Pasco Basin, a depression full of sediments. In most of the basin, the top of the basalt is below sea level. This basin is bounded by anticlines in three directions:

the Saddle Mountains to the north, the Rattlesnake Hills (and the Olympic-Wallowa lineament) to the south, and other Yakima folds to the west. To the east is the flatter part of the Columbia Basin.

On this hike you'll get a good look at the Ringold Formation of late Miocene and Pliocene age (about 8 to 4 million years old) formed during a time the Columbia River was shifting from a southerly course (toward Goldendale) to an easterly course (to Wallula Gap, Hike 38). Rising structures to the south slowed and dammed the Columbia River, resulting in deposition of sediments on floodplains and in lakes. Overall the Ringold Formation changes upward, from fluvial gravels near the base, to sandy beds in the middle, to fine-grained lake beds near the top. Many mammal fossils have been found in the Ringold Formation.

The Columbia cut down through the Ringold Formation, leaving the White Bluffs, a 500-foot bank of light-colored sediments on the northeast side of the river. Because the Columbia erodes at the base, and because of groundwater, the high and steep White Bluffs are unstable. This is the desert, yet there is plenty of water from irrigation to the north and east that seeps into the ground and reduces the friction within the Ringold sediments. Much of the White Bluffs are landsliding toward the river, and in places, actually making the channel narrower.

Most of the activity at the Department of Energy Hanford site takes place on the southwest side of the Columbia River. For more than half a century this has been a place for nuclear reactors and the storage of radioactive and chemical wastes. This hike is on the northeast side of the river in the Wahluke Wildlife Area. Even more than elsewhere on the Columbia, the Hanford Reach is prolific with salmon and birds. The future of the river is unclear: although no more dams are likely, the question is if the Hanford Reach will be managed by counties for agriculture, or protected as a national wild and scenic river?

Trail Guide: Eltopia is just west of US 395, just northeast of Pasco, and far southwest of Spokane and Ritzville. Set your trip odometer at 0.0 at the Eltopia exit on US 395 and drive west. At mile 1.3, at a roadcut in the Saddle Mountains basalt (Miocene), is the last lava flow you'll see on this excursion. At mile 5.3 (Homestead Corners, Eltopia post office) turn north on Glade N Road. At mile 7.7, turn west toward Ringold. At miles 10 and 11.9 cross irrigation ditches; the first is Potholes Canal, which flows south from Potholes Reservoir (Hike 42).

At mile 13.8 turn west and descend toward the Columbia River. Note the extensive dune field across the river. At mile 14.6 turn north on Ringold River Road, and at mile 15.8, enter the Wahluke Wildlife Area. Pause at the seasonal waterfalls on the east side of the road at mile 16.7. Some irrigation water from higher ground to the east is seeping through the sediments and moving west toward the Columbia River. Here the water issues from the bluffs as springs that are depositing tufa. Tufa is a form of limestone, a rock composed of calcium carbonate. The groundwater dissolved the calcium carbonate from caliche that soil-forming processes have deposited in the sediments of the White Bluffs.

At mile 18.1 is the start of a giant landslide complex. At mile 19.5 is an oxbow, a lake that was a former channel of the Columbia River on the east side of Savage Island. At mile 23.5 park near the gate which is just downriver from a power line crossing.

As you start north on the old paved road, look southwest across the river to the Hanford townsite (abandoned in World War II when our nuclear weapons program began). Behind the Hanford townsite is Rattlesnake Mountain, part of an anticlinal ridge on the Olympic-Wallowa lineament, and at the southwest edge of the Pasco Basin.

To the west is Gable Mountain, the east end of a plunging anticline of the Yakima Fold Belt. Far to the west, Umtanum Ridge is part of this anticline (Hike 41). A plunging anticline is an upfold of rocks with a crest that decreases in elevation; this one disappears to the east beneath the sediments of the Pasco Basin. In about 1980, when the Hanford site was a candidate for deep disposal of our nation's spent commercial nuclear fuel rods, a tunnel was excavated inside Gable Mountain to test the basalt flows. The results were not encouraging so the site was abandoned.

To the northwest are the Saddle Mountains, part of another anticline of the Yakima Fold Belt and the north edge of the Pasco Basin. The Columbia River enters the Pasco Basin through Sentinel Gap, a notch in the Saddle Mountains, and turns east when it hits Umtanum Ridge (another anticline) at Priest Rapids.

For less than 1 mile the road stays near the river and the exposures of the Ringold sediments are in the toes of landslides. As you will see later, the undisturbed Ringold Formation is nearly horizontal (just like when the sediments were deposited). Here, however, near the river the layers are broken and tilted because a slump (blocks of sediment) rotated eastward as they slid westward. Note that the strata dip as much as 30 degrees away from the river.

The road climbs gently uphill through badlands topography. This area has steep slopes and an arid climate (less than 10 inches of precipitation per year) which reduces vegetation cover. The silts and sands are poorly consolidated, and subject to erosion during rare but intense rainfall events. Running water has cut the badlands, characterized by gullies and short steep slopes.

A bench with an elevation of just over 600 feet is about 2 miles from the gate. On a clear day, the Cascade volcanoes Mount Rainier and Mount Adams are visible to the northwest and west, respectively. If the river is not high, there are many islands that provide birds protection from predators.

Ripples in sands of the Ringold Formation

From the bench to the top of the White Bluffs is a nearly continuous exposure of the Ringold Formation. Note the vertical joints (breaks) in the strata that form crude columns with a rectangular pattern. Ripple marks in the sands indicate they were deposited by currents. The thin beds of silt suggest deposition in a quiet environment like a lake. Pauses in deposition are marked by buried soils; the soils are brownish with iron oxides and whitish with calcium carbonate. A thick caliche layer is near the top of the White Bluffs. Caliche (calcium carbonate) is common in soils formed in an arid climate; the calcium is leached from the rock or sediments, and the carbonate may come from carbon dioxide in the atmosphere and soils. At the very top of the White Bluffs is loess, silt deposited by the wind, probably in the last 10 to 15 thousand years.

Walk about 100 yards beyond the gate at the top, and turn left to the edge of the White Bluffs. The hummocks are slump blocks from landsliding along the bluffs. Look up the river to abandoned reactors from nuclear weapons production. Look north across nearby dunes to the Saddle Mountains anticline. Look west across the Pasco Basin and beyond the Yakima Fold Belt to Cascade volcanoes. As you return, you might consider the future of the Hanford Reach of the Columbia River.

41 YAKIMA CANYON

How did the river incise these anticlines of resistant basalt?

DISTANCE ■ About 2.5 miles

ELEVATIONS ■ 1338 feet to 2016 feet

DIFFICULTY ■ Easy

TOPOGRAPHIC MAP ■ USGS Wymer

GEOLOGIC MAP ■ DGER 94-12 Yakima East

KEY REFERENCE ■ Reidel and Hooper (1989)

PRECAUTIONS ■ Be very careful of rattlesnakes; wear boots and long pants. Listen and watch for trains on the railroad tracks.

About the Landscape: Yakima Canyon is a world-class example of cross-axial drainage and incised meanders. Cross-axial drainage refers to the situation where a stream cuts across a prominent topographic axis. In this case, the Yakima River cuts across four ridges: from north to south, these are Manastash Ridge, Umtanum Ridge, Yakima Ridge, and Ahtanum Ridge (Yakima Canyon cuts through Manastash and Umtanum Ridges).

Each of these ridges is an anticline, a long uparch of rocks. These anticlines are part of the Yakima Fold Belt, an area where the rock layers of the Columbia Basin are wrinkled due to north-south compression. Between the anticlines are synclines, or long downfolds of the rock.

From north to south, the folds are:

GEOGRAPHIC FEATURE	ASSOCIATED FOLD
Kittitas Valley (Ellensburg)	syncline
Manastash Ridge	anticline
Umtanum Creek (start of hike)	syncline
Umtanum Ridge (end of hike)	anticline
Wenas Valley/Selaah Creek	syncline
Yakima Ridge	anticline
Naches Valley/Moxee Valley (Yakima)	syncline
Ahtanum Ridge (Union Gap)	anticline

The folded rocks are the Miocene Columbia River basalts and Ellensburg Formation. The basalts are lavas that flowed here from vents far to the southeast. Sediments, generally mudstone and sandstone of the Ellensburg Formation, interbed with and overlie the basalts. The hundreds of basalt flows are about 2.5 miles thick.

Anticlines, if they contain sedimentary rocks, are often associated with oil and gas. Hoping to find petroleum-bearing sedimentary rocks beneath the basalts, Shell Oil Company drilled a 3-mile-deep well in Yakima Canyon. Because

The Yakima River cuts across an anticline of Columbia River basalts.

the Yakima River has cut about 0.5 mile into the anticlines, there was that much less basalt to drill through; however, the Shell drilling did not find economic quantities of oil or gas.

There are four ways a stream becomes cross-axial: damming, headward erosion, superposition, and antecedence. With damming and headward erosion, the master stream had a different course. Today the Yakima River flows south across the fold belt from Ellensburg to Yakima. Suppose that the river originally flowed east from Ellensburg, through the Kittitas Valley to the Columbia River near Vantage. If this original route was dammed by a large landslide, or ice from the northeast, or a lava flow from the southeast, a lake would form. The lake would overflow at the lowest point on its perimeter, perhaps south toward Yakima, cutting across the ridges.

Or, suppose an aggressive stream was eroding headward toward the north from Yakima. (Remember, water and sediment go downstream, but a gully carves its way up a hill.) This stream might cut across the ridges and capture the original river in the Kittitas Valley.

With superposition and antedence, we assume that the river has not had a major course change. Suppose that the folds in the basalt already existed, but were covered with a plain of younger sediment. The Yakima River may have been meandering southward on the sediments. A change in geologic conditions, such as uplift of the area, might cause the river to cut down though the sediments and superpose itself into the preexisting folds (folds first, stream erosion later).

The favored theory for the cross-axial drainage at Yakima Canyon is antecedence: the river was there first and was powerful enough to cut through the rising anticlines (stream first, folds later). The basalts are about 15 million years old; the folds may have been growing simultaneously with the eruptions, and the folds may still be growing today.

If a river is meandering before it becomes cross-axial, the meandering habit may be preserved as the river incises through the rocks. A river meandering across a floodplain may be cutting tens of feet into the sediments. Here the Yakima River has cut through thousands of feet of lava flows.

This hike usually provides the opportunity to see at least a dozen bird species, and in the spring, a great profusion of wildflowers.

Trail Guide: SR 821 follows the Yakima River from Ellensburg to Yakima. The Umtanum Recreation Site (Bureau of Land Management) is between mileposts 16 and 17. From the sign on the west side of the highway, drive 0.25 mile north to a parking lot where there are outhouses.

Cross the footbridge to the west side of the Yakima River and the mouth of Umtanum Creek. Follow the trail west through high shrubs—be wary of trains when crossing the railroad tracks. In a few paces the trail splits: the northwest fork goes up Umtanum Creek (which runs along a syncline); take the southwest fork up a tributary canyon with an intermittent stream.

For about 0.5 mile the trail climbs along the east side of this tributary valley with basalt cliffs and taluses, sloping heaps of angular rock fragments that have fallen from cliffs. The vesicular lava flows have columnar joints. In some trailcuts you can see the colluvium beneath the talus surface. The colluvium here is a mixture of basalt cobbles and tan sediment; many of the cobbles are coated with white caliche (calcium carbonate).

There is a flow contact at a row of tiny caves along the trail: below is a weathered (yellow-brown) flow top with lots of vesicles (gas bubble cavities). Above is a fresh (gray-black) flow base with columnar joints. The trail reaches the canyon floor at a grove of cottonwood and willow trees just before a Y in the canyon. Take neither fork; double back to the northeast along an old road. (In a short distance up the southwest fork is an aspen grove and a spring coming out of a pipe.) As the old road flattens, the basalt gets buried by loess, tan windblown silt. There are shallow cuts in light gray mudstone of the Ellensburg Formation.

The old road circles southeasterly around the ridge. There is a good view from the northernmost point to the west up Umtanum Creek and north up Yakima Canyon. Notice the incised meanders of the Yakima River; one to the east has been abandoned. It is half of a giant smooth bowl 0.5 mile in diameter and 600 feet deep. The river has shifted to the southwest and cut down another 100 feet. On the sides of the bowl to the east, and on the slope to the northwest are stone stripes, a form of patterned ground characterized by downhill creeping bands of angular rocks separated by bands of fine-grained sediment on which vegetation grows. In the next mile, the old road will cross two draws with more stone stripes. Stone stripes are common on steep slopes beneath rock outcrops if there is not enough rockfall to form a talus.

After the two draws, the old road wraps around a ridge at just over 2000 feet, and 700 feet above the river. From here is a spectacular view of the Stuart Range to the northwest and the Yakima Fold Belt in all directions. The highest point in the glaciated Stuart Range is Mount Stuart (9415 feet), composed of Cretaceous granite. Here at 2000 feet you are just above the slightly older Grande Ronde Basalt flows and just below the slightly younger Wanapum Basalt flows. You can see three ridges from here: one to the east has I-82 on its south flank, a second to the south has a single tower on the crest, and a third farther south has four towers plus power poles. Where the Yakima River has cut more than 1900 feet into the second ridge you can see that the anticline is asymmetric: the south limb has gently dipping basalts whereas the north limb has near vertical basalts.

This is the high point on the old road; from here it zigzags southerly and downward about 2 miles to above Wymer, which used to be a tiny community (the bridge shown on old maps is no longer there). The prominent ridge in about 1 mile has prickly pear cactus in addition to the ever-present sagebrush and bunchgrass.

Hike 42 POTHOLES DUNES

No river or lake existed in the desert, only dunes. Then dams drowned the dunes.

DISTANCE ■ Minimum 3 miles round trip from Winchester Wasteway to Potholes Reservoir (there is no established trail; one can wander in the dune field all day)

ELEVATION ■ Start, 1092 feet; Potholes Reservoir, 1039 feet

DIFFICULTY ■ Moderate

TOPOGRAPHIC MAPS ■ USGS Royal Camp and Mae

GEOLOGIC MAP ■ DGER 90-1 Moses Lake

PRECAUTIONS ■ This is a hunting area. If you want to hike here during hunting season, wear bright red clothes and make noise. In summer, beware of heat exhaustion (there's plenty of water). Carry a compass and walk in a general northeasterly direction. Look back often, and try to remember your route. You can see a lot further from the top of a dune than between dunes. If you do get lost, go east to Potholes Reservoir, and follow the shore southeast to Potholes State Park.

About the Landscape: This is the largest dune field in the Pacific Northwest. It's the desert; rainfall is about 8 inches per year, yet water is everywhere. The creeks (Frenchman Hills Wasteway and Winchester Wasteway) and the trees would not exist were it not for the Columbia Basin Irrigation Project. The dam and all the irrigation have created Potholes Reservoir (our objective) and raised the water table, drowning part of the dune field and adding countless small lakes to the Columbia Basin. The water and vegetation (streams, lakes, wetlands, trees, shrubs, grasses, wildflowers) have multiplied and diversified the wildlife in this desert. You are likely to see deer, coyotes, beaver, and countless birds.

The best season for this hike is spring, with many migrating birds and wildflowers at their peak, but this area is also delightful on a winter day if there isn't too much wind. At any time of year, be careful that you don't get lost. This is a sea of sand dunes: the dune field stretches 24 miles west to east, and 9 miles south to north. The sand moves in response to the prevailing southwesterly winds, which helps to explain the shapes of the dunes, but more on this later.

Trail Guide: The sand dunes are located in the general vicinity of various state and federal lands: South Columbia Basin State Wildlife Recreation Area (with a western Desert Unit that is the site of this hike, a central Potholes Unit, and an eastern Seep Lakes Unit), Potholes Reservoir State Park, and Columbia National Wildlife Refuge. To reach the trailhead, first take SR 17 south from Moses Lake and I-90, or north from Mesa and US 395. Set your trip odometer at 0.0 at the junction of SR 17 and 262.

Go west on SR 262. On the way to O'Sullivan Dam you will pass many features of the Missoula floods. To the south is typical Channeled Scabland: erosional remnants of basalt, with channels and closed depressions between the scabs. To the north is Lind Coulee, one of the longer channels cut by the Missoula floods. The lower end of Lind Coulee is backflooded by Potholes Reservoir. A giant gravel bar deposited by the Missoula floods is to the north of the coulee.

Dunes (mostly barchans) drowned by Potholes Reservoir

Cross O'Sullivan Dam from mile 6.3 to mile 9.8. This 3.5-mile-long earthrock dam impounds Potholes Reservoir to the north. To the south is a spectacular portion of the Channeled Scabland: there is literally a maze of scabs and buttes, channels and lakes. One could hike in this area for days.

The entrance to Potholes Reservoir State Park is on the north at mile 11.3. To the south is the east end of the Frenchman Hills anticline, an elongated structure of stratified rocks; in this case, the rocks are the Miocene Columbia River basalts. This anticlinal ridge extends west to the Cascades; the Columbia River has cut a water gap through this anticline at Vantage.

Continue west to mile 15.3 and turn north on a dirt road, "C SE." There are signs for public fishing and public hunting. At mile 16.5 cross the Frenchman Hills Wasteway and enter the Potholes dune field. Continue north, passing a road that enters from the west. At mile 17.4 the road bends east and then north around a sand dune, enters a grove of trees, and then curves west just before the parking area at mile 18.1. The hike begins at the bridge across Winchester Wasteway, on the north side of the parking lot (outhouses here). Start the hike by crossing the bridge over Winchester Wasteway; this is the only easy way back to the parking lot. As you walk north, the trees gradually become fewer and smaller, and the trail becomes fainter. Soon there are no main trails, just game trails, and faint trails made by hunters and hikers (most of the fisherfolk get to the reservoir by boat).

If you're really looking for a trail, try the north-northeast side of some of the dunes. This is the steep side of the dunes, fun to run, roll, and slide down. Foot traffic moves so much sand that a sort of trail is obvious. The steep side of a dune is called the slip face; although it looks steeper, the slip face of a dune is always about 35 degrees, the angle of repose of dry sand. The angle of repose is the steepest slope a material can hold without failing and is dependent on grain size, angularity of the particles, and moisture content.

The slip face of a dune is on the downwind side (the prevailing wind in the Pacific Northwest is the westerlies). The slip faces of these dunes are on the east, toward the Potholes Reservoir. When wind of sufficient velocity blows, grains of sand creep, roll, and bounce up the gentle western side of the dune, mostly staying within a few feet of the ground. The sand grains continue over the top of the dune, and fall into the wind shadow above the slip face. The sand piles up at the top of the slip face until the angle of repose is exceeded. Then the slip face fails, and sand flows down toward the base of the dune. In this way, the base of the dune very slowly migrates downwind, and therefore the whole dune slowly moves easterly. We will return to this principle.

As you walk over the dunes, note the color of the sand grains. Geologists are curious about sources of sediments. To the south and southwest note the Frenchman Hills anticline. This anticline is composed of black basalt flows

192

with the dominant minerals of dark-colored pyroxene and calcium-rich pla-gioclase. So there is a local source for the dark sand grains—the dark miner-als and tiny rock fragments of the basalt flows.

The light-colored grains are derived from light-colored rocks, which are ex-posed far away, to the west in the Cascade Range, to the north in the Okanogan Highlands, and to the east in the Rocky Mountains. After this bedrock was weath-ered and eroded, it was transported to the Columbia Basin by the Columbia River and its tributaries, and by the Missoula floods. Wind blew these grains off sand-bars along the Columbia River as well as sediments deposited by the Missoula floods and deposited the sand in dunes. The dunes are slowly migrating to the east-northeast; the leading edge of the dune field is southeast of Moses Lake, about 10 miles east-northeast of here.

Look on the northeast side of a group of particularly large dunes less than 0.5 mile from the southwest shore of the reservoir. Between the dunes is a straight fence aligned almost exactly northwest-southeast. Yet the fence dis-appears where it is nearest the dunes. Careful inspection reveals that the dunes are on top of the fence, that the dunes have migrated northeasterly across the fence. You can crudely estimate how fast the dunes moved. If, for example, the fence was built in the 1920s, and if the base of the slip face is about 70 feet northeast of the fence, then the dune has migrated about 1 foot a year.

Humans have cut off much of the sand supply, and have slowed the rate of dune migration. The building of dams along the Columbia River created reservoirs that covered sandbars which supplied dune sand. Irrigated land has crops that reduce wind erosion. The construction of O'Sullivan Dam to make Potholes Reservoir drowned much of the dune field. The reservoir and irriga-tion raised the water table that greatly increased the vegetation here. The vegetation reduced the area of bare sand, anchored the dunes, and reduced the rates of sand transport and dune migration.

As you stand at the shore of Potholes Reservoir, realize that this is only a small part of the Columbia Basin Irrigation Project. Water is pumped from Roosevelt Lake behind Grand Coulee Dam up into Banks Lake in the Upper Grand Coulee (Hike 43). From Banks Lake (elevation 1570 feet) the water flows south by gravity into Lower Grand Coulee (on the west) and Billy Clapp Lake (on the east). Further south the irrigation water reaches Moses Lake (eleva-tion 1046 feet) and Potholes Reservoir (elevation 1039 feet). From here canals lead south to the vicinity of Othello, Connell, Mesa, Basin City, and Eltopia. The water eventually reaches the Pasco Basin and Lake Wallula, a reservoir on the Columbia River with an elevation of 340 feet.

Before this century's irrigation project, the last time the Columbia desert was really wet was about 15,000 years ago. For a couple of thousand years there were floods every few decades. The failure of glacial Lake Missoula's ice dam released 500 cubic miles of water to sweep across eastern Washington. The Potholes area was a sort of flood crossroads. Huge quantities of water followed today's irrigation routes from Grand Coulee Dam southward toward the Pasco Basin. But other channels, such as upper Crab Creek and Lind Coulee, led flood waters westward toward the Potholes.

Other flood routes diverted water away from the Potholes. For example, when the floods reached this area, part of the water flowed west through the Quincy Basin to three cataracts, dropping the water about 700 feet to the Columbia River. The other portion of the water rushed south across the east end of the Frenchman Hills, carving the spectacular Channeled Scabland south of O'Sullivan Dam, and then drained west along Lower Crab Creek, as well as south toward the Pasco Basin.

The Missoula floods swept away any dunes that had existed here before 15,000 years ago. Therefore, the present dunes have formed and migrated here in the past 13,000 years.

All of these dunes have the same general cross section in a west to east direction. To the west (or southwest) is the gentle upwind slope. The top is flat, rounded, bumpy, or crested. The east (or northeast) slope is the steep downwind slip face. Inside the dunes there are giant cross-beds dipping easterly at about 35 degrees; each cross-bed was once a flow of sand down the slip face. Sand moves up the gentle west slope and across the top of the dune, then cascades down the slip face. One flow of sand buries the previous bed of sand; as more cross-beds are deposited, the dune marches on. In places where the dunes are being eroded by the wind, you may be able to see the dipping cross-beds.

Although the dunes all have the same east-west profile, there is considerable variation in the plane views of the individual dunes. Some are much longer than they are wide and the slip faces are more or less straight: these are called transverse dunes. Transverse dunes are oriented perpendicular to the dominant wind. With the prevailing winds from the southwest, the crests of these dunes trend northwest-southeast.

Other dunes here are more or less equidimensional, and are curved, with ends, or horns, pointing upwind: these are parabolic dunes, convex in a downwind direction. The low horns have the most vegetation; the horns and the high part of dune partly surround a bowl (sometimes called a blowout) that is open to the southwest (upwind).

Elsewhere in this dune field (particularly to the east of Potholes Reservoir and south of Moses Lake), there is a third dune type, a barchan. Barchans are also curved and more or less equidimensional, but the horns point downwind, so the dune is concave downwind. Also, there are transitional dune types. Barchans may link in chains perpendicular to the wind and therefore be somewhat like transverse dunes. In this area, some of the dunes are transitional between transverse and parabolic.

Dunes come in different shapes with three of the most important factors being sand supply (scarce or abundant), wind (one or more prevailing directions and the angle between them), and vegetation. These factors can change through time; for example, there is more vegetation here now due to the Columbia Basin Irrigation Project. More vegetation promotes parabolic dunes: the vegetation anchors the horns while the higher, drier, less-vegetated center of the dune migrates downwind. Sand abundance is particularly important in determining transverse dunes versus barchans: with more sand there are big transverse dunes; with less sand there are small barchans.

A sand dune is a waveform. As you walk easterly or westerly crossing many dunes and interdune depressions, imagine that this is the ocean. The dunes are big waves, with a wave height of about 40 feet and a wavelength of about 1000 feet. These waves are asymmetrical, with the steep side downwind. Considering the slip faces, one could imagine these as breaking waves. The wind makes water waves and sand dunes.

There are smaller waveforms here: ripples. The ripples have wavelengths of a few inches and wave heights of less than an inch. The orientation of dunes reflects long-term wind patterns. The orientation of the much smaller ripples is a response to the most recent strong wind. Notice that the ripple orientations are not all parallel because the topography of the dunes influences the direction of the wind. The ripples are on the dunes. Perhaps you have noticed ripples on waves during a storm on a lake or the ocean.

The size of both the dunes and the ripples is influenced by the size of the sand grains. With larger grains the dunes and ripples are slightly larger. However, normal winds cannot move grains larger than sand. Pebbles, cobbles, and boulders are left behind by the wind. What about grains smaller than sand? Particles of silt and clay rise high in the air column; the wind carries the finest sediment in suspension. The silt and clay is deposited far downwind as a blanket. The thick silt (or loess) in the Palouse Hills to the east of here was deposited by wind over the past 2 million years. During the Dust Bowl of the 1930s, the wind eroded soil in the Great Plains, and some of this dust covered skyscrapers on the East Coast and ships on the Atlantic Ocean!

Notice almost all of the particles here are dark or light, and sand-sized. There are three exceptions. The first consists of larger, white, irregularly shaped particles; most of these are fragments of vertebrate bones, particularly rodents and birds. Imagine an owl eating a mouse, or a coyote eating a rabbit. The pellets will lose their coherence, and the bone fragments will be scattered across the desert.

A second exception to sand-sized particles is the gray band of silt-sized particles visible near the top of most of the dunes (and visible along the side of the dirt entrance road). If you get close to this less than 1-inch-thick silt layer you will notice that the bottom is more speckled, whereas the rest is a uniform battleship gray. This ash was deposited on May 18, 1980, from Mount St. Helens.

This volcano in Washington's southern Cascade Range exploded at 8:32 A.M., and the debris was carried northeast toward Spokane by the prevailing winds. This morning ash was a composite of old volcanic rocks at Mount St. Helens that were fragmented by the violence of the eruption. At about noon, the character of the eruption changed; new magma (molten rock) turned to ash, and pumice was carried high in the eruptive column until about 5:30 P.M. The afternoon ash drifted downwind and was deposited as the gray blanket.

The final exception to the sand-sized particles is the occasional pebble or cobble. What is their source? They are too big to have been transported here by the wind. They are not meteorites. Animals? Birds? Humans? Nobody knows.

Hike
43

STEAMBOAT ROCK

Island in the sky: a scab of the earth's youngest flood basalts carved by the earth's greatest floods.

DISTANCE ■ 1 to 2 miles

ELEVATION ■ Start, 1600 feet; high point, 2312 feet

DIFFICULTY ■ Moderate

TOPOGRAPHIC MAPS ■ USGS Steamboat Rock SW (southwest), Steamboat Rock SE (southeast), Electric City (northeast), and Barker Canyon (northwest)

GEOLOGIC MAP ■ DGER 90-6 Banks Lake

KEY REFERENCE ■ Crosby and Carson (1999)

About the Landscape: One of the most spectacular places from which to experience the effects of the Missoula floods is a mesa in the middle of upper Grand Coulee. Steamboat Rock, an erosion remnant of lava flows, rises 742 feet above Banks Lake.

This area is dominated by three geologic units: late Mesozoic granitic rock characteristic of the Okanogan Highlands to the north, Miocene basalt flows which originated far to the southeast, and Pleistocene glacial and flood deposits.

About 100 million years ago, large bodies of granitic magma rose into the earth's crust in the area now known as the Okanogan Highlands. The magma cooled slowly within the earth's crust, allowing time for the growth of large crystals of light-colored feldspar and quartz and dark-colored mica and hornblende.

As this area was uplifted and eroded, the granitic plutons or batholiths became exposed at the earth's surface.

About 16 million years ago, fissures opened in southeastern Washington and adjacent states. Fluid basaltic lava flowed in all directions, but particularly to the west where they ponded against the ancestral Cascade Range. To the north these lava rivers/lakes lapped against the Okanogan Highlands, burying the southernmost portions of the granitic plutons with hundreds of feet of basalt.

It took millions of years for the granitic batholiths to cool, and the erosion that brought the granite to the surface lasted for tens of millions of years. But all the lava flows revealed at Steamboat Rock were probably erupted in less than a million years.

The boundary, or geologic contact, between the underlying Mesozoic granitic rock and the overlying Cenozoic basalt is called an unconformity, a break in the geologic record. At this place, we don't know what happened between the intrusion of the granite and the extrusion of the basalt. This particular type of unconformity is a nonconformity. Nonconformities have plutonic rocks (this includes granitic and many metamorphic rocks) beneath strata (this includes sedimentary as well as volcanic rocks). Nonconformities almost always indicate long time periods about which we know little, except that there were millions of years of erosion.

The elevation of the nonconformity is approximately at the surface of Banks Lake. Small islands of granite are present northeast of Steamboat Rock, but most of the granite is hidden beneath the lava flows and the reservoir.

Steamboat Rock is very dark because it is a layer cake of dark lava flows. Once these flows were continuous with the walls of Grand Coulee, but erosion has carved the coulee and left Steamboat Rock in the middle. The erosion started with ancient streams. This drainage system likely included the ancestors to canyons in four directions from Steamboat Rock: Foster Coulee to the west, Barker Canyon to the north, Northrup Canyon to the east, and Whitney Canyon to the south. The main stem of this drainage system was the present Grand Coulee, which stretches south-southwest from Grand Coulee Dam to Soap Lake and Ephrata.

Grand Coulee is one of the most spectacular canyons on earth, yet it has no river. J Harlen Bretz determined the origin of Grand Coulee in the 1920s. A gigantic glacier called the Cordilleran Ice Sheet formed over British Columbia and adjacent provinces and states. This glacier advanced and retreated many times during the Pleistocene (last 2 million years of earth's history) Ice Age. One lobe (the Okanogan Lobe) of the ice sheet advanced southward in the general vicinity of the Okanogan River, reaching the northwestern Columbia Basin about 15,000 years ago.

Although the general course of the Columbia River is north to south across

197

Washington, the river flows north from the present location of Grand Coulee Dam. As the Okanogan Lobe of the Cordilleran Ice Sheet advanced southward, it blocked the Columbia River, creating a huge lake that extended upriver toward Spokane. The southeastern limit of the Okanogan Lobe was south of the site of Grand Coulee Dam. Glacial Lake Columbia was created, and sat where Franklin D. Roosevelt Lake (reservoir) is located today. The lowest point on the rim of glacial Lake Columbia was between the present towns of Grand Coulee and Electric City.

Glacial Lake Columbia overflowed toward the southwest and began to turn a minor drainage system into the Grand Coulee. A glacier diverted one of the largest rivers in North America across a portion of the Columbia Basin. The river slowly cut through the basalt flows, but later the river's discharge was greatly magnified by a series of catastrophic events.

The Cordilleran Ice Sheet blocked another river, the Clarks Fork. (Clarks Fork flows northwest from Montana toward the Columbia River; Clarks Fork of the Yellowstone River is on the other side of the Continental Divide.) The lobe of ice near the Idaho-Montana border dammed a lake about 2000 feet deep and 500 cubic miles in volume. Glacial Lake Missoula flooded, eroded, and escaped its ice dam, sending the world's largest-ever flood westward toward the Pacific Ocean. The ice readvanced, and in a few decades, glacial Lake Missoula reformed, and another catastrophic flood ensued. These gigantic floods occurred 40 to 100 times between 15,300 and 12,700 years ago.

Much of the discharge of each flood rushed from Spokane toward the Grand Coulee Dam. The fast deep floodwaters caused erosion on a scale the Columbia River could not possibly have accomplished alone. The Grand Coulee is about 25 miles long, more than 2 miles wide in most places, and about 700 feet deep, with near-vertical walls.

The top of Steamboat Rock is a good place from which to look up and down the Grand Coulee. From here you can view the glaciated Waterville Plateau to the northwest, and the unglaciated remainder of the Columbia Basin to the southeast.

The torrents of water sweeping down the Grand Coulee left scabs of basalt (by far the largest is Steamboat Rock) and scoured basins on the coulee floor (such as Sun Lakes). Banks Lake doesn't count, it is artificial.

The Columbia Basin Irrigation Project begins with Grand Coulee Dam on the Columbia River. Water from Roosevelt Lake is pumped up and southwest into Banks Lake (a reservoir). From Dry Falls Dam at the southwest end of Banks Lake, near Coulee City, irrigation water flows (by gravity) south to the Potholes Reservoir (Hike 42) and further south to the Pasco Basin. This route is one of the many paths the Missoula floods took in a southerly direction across Washington.

Trail Guide: Steamboat Rock State Park lies on the west side of SR 155, which runs aong the east shore of Banks Lake between Electric City (near Grand Coulee Dam) and Coulee City (near Dry Falls Dam). From SR 155 go north into the state park approximately 3 miles to a parking area. From the parking area look northwest at the cliffs of the mesa. There is only one break in the cliffs. The trail rises about 200 feet in the short distance to the base of the cliffs. The trail steepens from the base of the cliffs to a saddle about 100 feet below the top of the mesa. This saddle was likely carved by floodwaters sweeping west across the southern end of Steamboat Rock. Imagine such a flood, 700 feet above modern Banks Lake, and 1300 feet above the Columbia River before it was dammed, first by a glacier and then by humans.

The crude trail goes in several directions from this saddle. Go south for a short (about 1 mile) loop around the edge of the smaller (and slightly lower) southern mesa top of Steamboat Rock. The view southwest along the giant Grand Coulee from the southwestern end of Steamboat Rock is spectacular! Be careful not to get too close to the edge. Please don't throw rocks from the mesa; it's hard to tell if someone might be right below.

Off to the west is the Waterville Plateau portion of the Columbia Basin. The

Columbia River basalts unconformably overlie older crystalline rocks.

northern portion of the Waterville Plateau was covered by ice from British Columbia that blocked the Columbia River. To the east is the rest of the Columbia Basin. The Missoula floods filled the Grand Coulee to the brim, and the floodwaters spilled over the slightly lower southeast wall in places.

One cannot help but notice the huge granitic boulders all over the top of the mesa. Their light color is in sharp contrast to the black basalt. The granite is older than the basalt by about 100 million years, so how did the granite boulders get on top of the basalts of Steamboat Rock? There are two possibilities: glacier and iceberg.

The glacier that covered the northern Waterville Plateau extended far enough southeast to dump boulders on top of Steamboat Rock. In addition, the Missoula floods, which scoured at least part of the top of Steamboat Rock, were carrying large icebergs that may have been stranded on top of the mesa. As the icebergs melted, their loads of sediment, including granitic boulders, would have been deposited.

For a longer hike, go northeasterly across the saddle and make a circuit of the edge of the larger (and slightly higher) northern mesa top. Here are even more granitic boulders, some of which have been broken by weathering since they were deposited. Also, on the northern mesa top are moraines, ridges of till deposited by ice.

As you make the circuit, be aware of places where large portions of the edge could fall to the floor of the coulee below (particularly if there is an earthquake). In places, there are large cracks many feet back from the edge—someday these blocks will fall. At the base of Steamboat Rock taluses of basaltic blocks have accumulated since the last Missoula flood swept the Grand Coulee clean about 13,000 years ago.

From the northeast end of the mesa top you can see white granite poking up above the surface of Banks Lake. From the southeast side, view sand dunes on the low part of the peninsula. There is no source for the sand today, but before Banks Lake was created, Grand Coulee had more dry floor covered in part by sediment from Missoula floods. The prevailing southwesterly winds transported sand from down the coulee to this location.

The top of Steamboat Rock is a fascinating small ecosystem, with deer and smaller mammals, and many species of birds and plants. The birds can fly here, of course, but the deer must go all the way down to Banks Lake to drink.

Chapter 6
OKANOGAN HIGHLANDS AND ROCKY MOUNTAINS

Terraces south of Cave Mountain

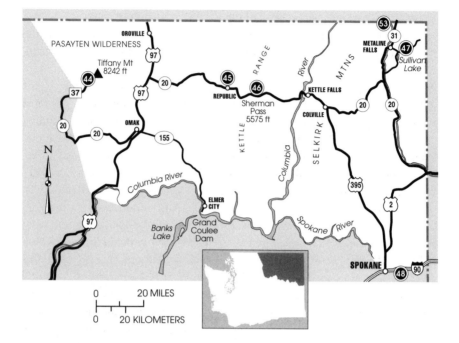

This geologic province extends east from the Pasayten fault to beyond the Idaho border and is bounded on the south by the Columbia River basalts (see figure 13). Two distinct groups of rocks occur, separated roughly by the Columbia River as it flows south from Canada. To the west are the accreted Okanogan Highlands terranes composed mostly of Mesozoic and Tertiary igneous and metamorphic rocks. The Rocky Mountains, constructed chiefly of Precambrian and Paleozoic sedimentary and metasedimentary rocks of ancient North America, lie to the east.

During the latest part of the Precambrian period, North America was part of a supercontinent called Rodinia. The rocks of Rodinia included the 1.7 billion to 900 million year old rocks of the Belt-Purcell Supergroup, such as those seen in the Dishman Hills (Hike 48). The 800 to 680 million year old Windemere Supergroup consists of sediments deposited along the western margin of Rodinia as it split apart. The rocks to the west of this rift can now be found in Siberia!

The geologic problem is how to fit the pieces of Rodinia back together when several of the necessary pieces are missing. Some reconstructionists believe that Antarctica and Washington were once joined. Others prefer a connection between Washington and Australia. Near Metaline Falls are sedimentary rocks deposited on a continental shelf during Cambrian and Ordovician time (570 to 440 million years ago) on the continental margin that developed when ancestral North America split apart. The limestones make up Gardner Cave (Hike 53), while slightly metamorphosed shales and quartzites of the same age can be seen along the Elk Creek Trail (Hike 47).

West of the Columbia River is the "new" part of North America, consisting of accreted terranes. As in the North Cascades, there is confusion about terminology and terrane definitions. Most geologists agree on the definition of the Intermontane Superterrane (or Domain, in the North Cascades terminology). Part of the Intermontane is Quesnellia or the Quesnel terrane, which makes up most of the Okanogan Highlands. Quesnellia is composed of subterranes, including a 230-million-year-old island arc developed on a 360-million-year-old seafloor. When Quesnellia accreted 170 to 190 million years ago, the intense smashup folded and faulted rocks along the edge of North America and generated plutons of granite and diorite like those along the Freezeout Ridge Trail (Hike 44).

The Eocene Extensional Event also made its mark in northeast Washington. As in the North Cascades, great elongate slabs of crust dropped down and were filled with sediment. The most notable of these is the Republic graben, which includes lake sediments containing some of the world's most remarkable fossils (Hike 45). At the same time that the grabens were dropping, metamorphic core complexes were upwelling and big slabs were sliding off the top. At least five of these structures have been recognized in northeast Washington, including the Okanogan Dome, the Kettle Dome (Hike 46), the Vulcan Mountain Dome, the Lincoln Dome, and the Spokane Dome (see figure 13). All are of Paleocene to Eocene age (roughly 60 to 45 million years ago) and are composed mainly of gneiss and of mylonites warped up into structural domes. Closely associated with these metamorphic core complexes are batholiths of plutonic rock like the Colville batholith, which contain mainly granites that crystallized between 60 and 45 million years ago. There are also volcanic rocks of similar age and probably of the same origin as the plutonic rocks except that these magmas were able to make it all the way to the surface of the earth. One example is the Tom Thumb Tuff that contains many of the best fossils in the Republic graben.

Since the Eocene, not much happened in this province except slow uplift and erosion, which exposed rocks once buried deeply within the earth. There were also some extensive lake deposits formed when the Columbia River basalts blocked rivers flowing south.

The final chapter in the geologic history of the region was the invasion of the Purcell Trench Lobe of the Cordilleran Ice Sheet from Canada about 17,000 years ago. At its maximum it covered most of the Okanogan Highlands. Between 15,000 and 13,000 years ago, the ice was thick enough to create a series of ice dammed lakes, including glacial Lake Missoula, Lake Clark, and Lake Kootenay. Glacial Lake Missoula was the largest of these, containing as much water as the combined volume of Lake Erie and Lake Ontario at the present time.

Periodically, the water level got so high the ice dam burst sending colossal floods across northeast Washington (Hike 48). This happened at least dozens

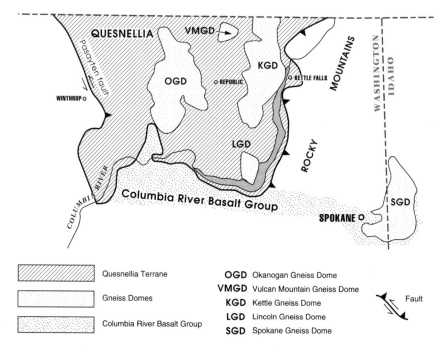

Quesnellia Terrane

Gneiss Domes

Columbia River Basalt Group

OGD — Okanogan Gneiss Dome
VMGD — Vulcan Mountain Gneiss Dome
KGD — Kettle Gneiss Dome
LGD — Lincoln Gneiss Dome
SGD — Spokane Gneiss Dome

Fault

figure 13. Gneiss Domes in the Quesnellia Terrane

of times and fundamentally changed the landscape (see Columbia Basin chapter for more details).

Hike

44

FREEZEOUT RIDGE

This hike is a Sierra Nevada look-alike with granitic rocks galore and almost gentle rolling hills above timberline.

DISTANCE ■ 2 miles

ELEVATION ■ 6580 feet to 7600 feet (Whistler Pass)

DIFFICULTY ■ Moderate

TOPOGRAPHIC MAPS ■ USGS Tiffany Mountain; Green Trails No. 53 Tiffany Mountain

GEOLOGIC MAPS ■ DGER 90-11 Oroville; DGER 90-12 Omak

KEY REFERENCE ■ Hurlow and Nelson (1993)

About the Landscape: The Okanogan Range batholith of north-central Washington is a huge mass of plutonic rock that crystallized during the Cretaceous period (114 to 111 million years ago) when numerous terranes were

204

being added to the western margin of North America. At that time there was at least one and possibly two subduction zones operating. The subduction zone that formed the Freezeout Ridge magmas is called the Okanogan-Spences Bridge arc and it once extended about 200 miles from here north into central British Columbia. Like the present day Cascadia subduction zone, the arc consisted of numerous volcanoes and immense volumes of molten rock injected into the earth beneath them.

Along the Freezeout Ridge Trail, you can see evidence for at least a half dozen different magmas. Some were large oozing masses that formed plutons. Others were injected into fractures to form dikes, sills, and veins. It is a little like nachos with melted cheese, except that here all we see is the cheesy part.

Trail Guide: Take the Pearrygin Lake/East Chewuch River Road north from Winthrop. At about 7 miles, bear right onto FR 5010/37 and in another mile, bear right again on FR 37. Continue about 6 miles to the junction of FR 37 with another right fork. Follow the fork and cross a bridge over Boulder Creek. This gravel road has some nasty washboards by late summer. The trailhead at Freezeout Pass is another 3.2 miles.

The trail begins just beyond the cattleguard on the east side of the road. The trail climbs moderately and is a bit rough in places, with lots of rocks, braids, and branches to negotiate. Stay on the best-beaten path and you will get to Whistler Pass with no problem. From there to the summit of Tiffany Mountain (8242 feet), there is no trail so just use your best judgement. After the snow melts in July there is no source of water, so come prepared. You can supplement your view of the rocks with views of fantastic wildflowers in late July and early August.

The trail begins at 6500 feet and follows the ragged path of a long-abandoned roadbed through a thin forest of lodgepole pine and subalpine fir until it breaks out into meadows at about 1.5 miles. Scattered along the trail are numerous outcrops and erratic boulders of plutonic rocks. A granodiorite containing both biotite and hornblende is the most common rock type, but also look for darker patches of diorite and gabbro. Some of the granodiorite contains abundant inclusions of a dark, porphyritic basalt with big bright white phenocrysts of plagioclase feldspar.

One side trail worth taking is at about 0.75 mile and leads out to the right to a fine view of jewel-like Roger Lake, which owes its existence to the steadfast effort of beavers in the valley below.

Upon reaching the alpine meadows there are excellent views in every direction out over the gentle summits of the Okanogan and Pasyaten Wilderness. Although this area is actually higher than the Cascade Crest, it is too dry to support the extensive alpine glaciers that carved the more rugged peaks and valleys to the west. So a topography smoothed by the Cordilleran Ice Sheet persists in the high country here.

A panorama of peaks in the Pasayten Wilderness can be seen from the alpine meadows of Freezeout Ridge on Tiffany Mountain.

At about 2 miles, a faint trail branches off toward Tiffany Mountain rising toward the northeast. A large outcrop of granodiorite has been sliced into big vertical slabs by expansion joints in the meadow to the southeast. This outcrop is worth a side trip for a closer view, because it shows evidence of magma mixing. The main rock is a light-colored granodiorite, but parts of it contain swirls of a darker porphyritic diorite or gabbro. Most likely the molten diorite/gabbro was injected into a cooler pool of granodiorite where it crystallized almost immediately.

At Whistler Pass (elevation 7600 feet), wander amidst numerous boulders, rounded by a combination of mechanical and chemical weathering, to view some of the varieties of plutonic rock found here. See more of the same if you decide to scramble up the ridge to the summit of Tiffany Mountain, including the predominant biotite granodiorite, diorite, gabbro, and a pink, potassium-feldspar-rich pegmatite. Do not mistake the abundant dark lichen for some dark mineral in the rock. Do look carefully at the map lichen *(Rhizocarpon geographicum)*, in distinctive colors of chartreuse bordered by black. Because these lichen grow at a well defined rate of about 10 millimeters in the first 25 years and a constant 15 millimeters per century thereafter, their diameter can be used to estimate how long rock surfaces have been exposed. If you measure the diameter of the largest lichen colony on the rock, you will know how long ago the rock surface was exposed. This is one of those nice marriages of geology and botany that makes communication among scientists really useful.

STONEROSE FOSSIL BEDS

Hike **45**

Walk a couple of city blocks, climb a hill, cross a road, and discover the nature of life in the Eocene.

DISTANCE ■ 0.25 mile

ELEVATION ■ 3500 feet to 3550 feet

DIFFICULTY ■ Easy

TOPOGRAPHIC MAP ■ USGS Republic

GEOLOGIC MAP ■ DGER 90-10 Republic

KEY REFERENCES ■ Washington Geology Vol. 24, No. 2; Wehr and Barksdale (1995); Wehr and Hopkins (1994); Wolfe and Wehr (1987); visit the Stonerose website at *www.stonerosefossil.org*

About the Landscape: If you were time-traveling through Washington between 50 and 45 million years ago, you would not recognize this place. Neither the Cascades nor the Olympics would have existed. The Republic area would have consisted of a lush subtropical forest with a lake about 20 miles long and 3 miles wide filling a slowly sinking fault basin called a graben. As streams flowed into the lake, they deposited sediments containing bits and pieces of the plants and animals living in the forest and in the lake itself. These formed fossils, mostly of leaves and fern fronds, but also of insects, fish, flowers, fruits, and seeds.

This hot and humid climate was part of a natural global warming process during the Eocene epoch. We are not sure what caused the global warming, but it may have been huge amounts of carbon dioxide released into the atmosphere by immense eruptions of basalt along the Oregon-Washington coast. At the same time, equally huge basalt flows erupted in a belt that extended from Greenland to Scotland. The clay-rich lake sediments deposited in the Republic area were eventually buried deep within the earth and lithified into shales and sandstones of the Klondike Mountain Formation.

The most fossil-rich part of this unit is the Tom Thumb Tuff, which is composed mainly of volcanic ash in which abundant fossils have been preserved. Discovery of these fossils is significant for paleontologists who have learned much about the evolution of ancient plants and animals. A wealth of information has also been provided for paleoclimatologists, who seek to reconstruct natural variations in the climate to assess the impacts that humans might have on present-day conditions.

Shales of the Klondike Mountain Formation contain 50-million-year-old plant, animal, and insect fossils.

Trail Guide: Entering the town of Republic on SR 20, turn left on Kean Street. The Stonerose Interpretive Center is in the same building as the visitor information center on the corner; it is open May 1 to October 31 from 10 A.M. to 5 P.M. Tuesday through Saturday and 10 A.M. to 4 P.M. Sunday.

A map is available at the Stonerose Interpretive Center where, for a small fee, you can get a collecting permit plus equipment, including a hammer, chisel, and bag. After you return, they will identify your fossils and, if you have made a significant find, ask you to contribute your rocks to their research collection. You don't have to do this, but if you do your discovery could be of genuine scientific value. Be aware that although geologists consider fossils to be abundant at this site, they are not easy to find.

After getting your permit and collecting equipment from the interpretive center, walk west on Kean Street to Eureka and turn left. Head uphill to a flat terrace, which has an outcrop of shale highly altered by the circulation of hot fluids in the earth. In other words, this outcrop is a fossil hot spring. Continue another few hundred feet uphill and cross a road leading to the abandoned Knob Hill mine and look for a sign indicating the Boot Hill fossil site.

Do not be deceived, it is hard work to find fossils here. In the summertime, you may swelter in the sun for an hour before you find anything more than a tiny leaf fragment or an unidentifiable stem. A fish fossil might take days of looking, although fish scales are fairly common. The best strategy is to look for rocks of fine mud and silt with distinct layers thinner than about a quarter inch. You can chisel these from the outcrops or sort through blocks in the talus piles. If it is a typical hot summer day in Republic, it is a good idea to gather an armload of rocks and take them back to the shade of the shelter. Here the technique is to use a chisel to split the layers into sheets. Splitting reveals most of the best fossils, although fine specimens can be found by digging into the depths of the talus.

If you do find fossils, be sure to take them back to the Stonerose Center for identification. Some very significant finds have been made at this site by amateur fossils hunters. Finds have included fossil feathers that have helped clarify the role of birds in these ancient forests. Note that some of the dark brown to black features that look like feathers are dendrites formed by the precipitation of manganese oxide from water circulating along bedding planes and through fractures after the sedimentary rocks were formed.

KETTLE CREST

Hike 46

This is your chance to look at the heart of a metamorphic core complex. These enigmatic structures occur in a swath extending more than 1000 miles through the mountains of the western United States and Canada.

DISTANCE ■ 3.75 miles

ELEVATION ■ 5510 to 6780 feet

DIFFICULTY ■ Moderate

TOPOGRAPHIC MAP ■ USGS Sherman Peak

GEOLOGIC MAP ■ DGER 75-3 Sherman Peak; DGER 10-10 Republic

KEY REFERENCES ■ Campbell and Thorsen (1975); Fox (1994); Fox and Wilson (1989)

PRECAUTIONS ■ This is open range country, so disinfect any water you find along the way, or bring your own.

About the Landscape: The rocks in the vicinity of Sherman Pass are part of the Kettle Gneiss Dome, one of several metamorphic core complexes found between the Okanogan River and the Kettle River in northeastern Washington.

As core complexes go, this is a big one—about 80 miles in length, extending from well south of Sherman Pass to well north of the Canadian border. It consists mainly of metamorphic rocks (schists and gneisses) that have been warped up into a huge dome-like structure (the gneiss dome).

For reasons not fully understood, the process of formation began about 60 million years ago when a huge batch of rock in the crust was pressure-cooked into a partially molten mass with a consistency something like a slushy beverage. Being hot and buoyant, the core rocks began to rise, pushing the overlying rocks into a dome. In places, rocks near the surface detached and slid off the top of the dome along low-angle faults. Within the dome, almost everything was stretched and bent and intruded by molten rock. The molten material in some places made it to the surface producing thick layers of ash and lava.

By about 48 million years ago the metamorphic core complex was complete. The construction of the core complexes was the main event in the geologic history of the Okanogan—as metamorphic and igneous rocks churned underground, volcanoes burst forth at the surface, earthquakes rumbled around fault zones, and this part of the state was stretched out to double its original width.

Trail Guide: At Sherman Pass, 17 miles east of Republic on SR 20, turn north on FR 495 and go 0.1 mile to a large parking lot. Walk about 50 yards back up the road to the trailhead on the right. This is a hike with panoramic views in all directions out over the Kettle Range on excellent trails to an old Forest Service lookout on top of Columbia Mountain. The elevation gain is about 1200 feet, with the steepest section the last 0.5 mile to the lookout.

The trail begins with a gentle climb through a lodgepole pine, subalpine fir, and larch forest littered with granitic boulders. The first outcrops, found in an open area beneath some power lines, are part of the 45- to 48-million-year-old Kettle Crest pluton. These rocks show a mineral alignment probably due to the fact that the magma of the pluton was being stretched out like taffy when crystallization occurred. Look closely at this outcrop and you will see a quartz-feldspar dike that cuts through the pluton but shows no mineral alignment. Apparently, the stretching ended before the dike was formed.

About 100 yards up the trail the outcrops are quite different. A diorite containing dark hornblende crystals shows no evidence of stretching. Either this pluton is younger than the granodiorite or it was outside the zone where stretch-marks were developed. Clearly the Kettle Crest pluton is not a single batch of igneous rock, and multiple intrusion is typical of core complexes. About 0.6 mile out, look to your right to see a pit dug by some prospector looking for precious minerals, probably gold or silver. Looking up at the cliff on your left you can see a yellow orange gossan, which is why the diggings are here. Gossans are zones where hot fluids have circulated through the earth; you could call them fossil hot springs. As the hot water oxidizes the rock it also sometimes deposits metals. Iron oxides in shades of yellow, orange, and red are common. Gold and silver are rare, but where you find a gossan you have a much better chance of striking it rich.

The twisted and contorted rocks in the heart of the core complex lie another 100 yards beyond the gossan. These are schists and gneisses, once clay and lime oozes on an ancient seafloor, transformed to metamorphic rocks by microplate collisions and burial deep within the earth.

At a little over 1 mile, the trail begins a long traverse along the west side of Columbia Mountain. From here, there is a good view south toward the granodiorite summit of Sherman Peak, which is framed by snags from a 1988 forest fire. Walking along the trail you also get panoramic westward views into the Republic graben, another big rip in the heart of Washington during Eocene time, like the Chiwaukum graben (Hike 28).

At about 2 miles, take a hard right and begin a 660-foot climb to the summit of Columbia Mountain. There is a spring in about 0.25 mile that was developed as a stock watering station. When the water table is high, this is a gusher; in the late summer it barely trickles or goes completely dry. The rocks from here to the summit are part of the Tenas Mary Creek assemblage. These particular rocks are orthogneisses, which means they are part of a pluton that has been metamorphosed. The age is unknown. These rocks could be as old as Precambrian, or as young as Tertiary. The most distinctive feature is phenocrysts (big crystals) of feldspar that can be up to 2 inches in length.

At the summit, wander around for views in every direction across the high rolling uplands of the Okanogan Highlands and picture the scene 15,000 years ago when the Cordilleran Ice Sheet covered this entire landscape.

Contorted schists of the Kettle Metamorphic Core Complex are seen along the Kettle Crest trail.

Hike

ELK CREEK FALLS

Unlike the exotic terranes to the west, this is bona fide Yankee crust that has been part of North America for at least 500 million years.

DISTANCE ▪ 1 mile

ELEVATION ▪ 2615 feet to 3300 feet

DIFFICULTY ▪ Moderate

TOPOGRAPHIC MAP ▪ USGS Metalline Falls

GEOLOGIC MAP ▪ DGER 90-13 Colville

KEY REFERENCES ▪ Dutro and others (1989); Watkinson and Ellis (1987)

About the Landscape: The rocks seen on this hike are part of the Maitlen Formation, low-grade metamorphic rocks, consisting mainly of phyllite and quartzite with some marble here and there. The phyllite consists of the minerals quartz, muscovite (sericite), plagioclase, chlorite, and pyrite. Phyllites with a lot of chlorite are greenish; those with a lot of muscovite are tan or silvery. The quartzites show a similar range of colors, but are composed almost entirely of quartz, as the name implies. The difference between the two is that phyllites form crinkly sheets of rock, whereas quartzites are blocky. These rocks were originally deposited as marine sediments during the early Cambrian period (575 to 545 million years ago) making them some of the oldest rocks found in Washington.

The early Cambrian was a time when an ancient continent that included the core of North America was rifting into separate terranes. A similar setting can now be found in the rift valleys of East Africa.

This hike also displays the effects of human intervention in geologic processes. Mill Pond was created in 1910 when a dam was built to provide power for a cement plant in Metalline Falls. Since then, a delta has built out into the east end of the lake impounded by the dam.

Trail Guide: From the town of Metalline Falls, take SR 31 north for 2 miles to CR 9345. Turn right (east) and drive 4 miles to a parking lot at the Mill Pond Historic Site. The trailhead (trail 560) is at the northwest end of the parking area; the trail goes north across the road to begin. This is a loop with a moderate ascent for the first 0.5 mile and a moderate descent in the last 0.5 mile with ups and downs in between. A recommended extension (or alternative) is trail 520, a nearly level, barrier free, loop of 0.6 mile.

As you make a gentle climb up through the pine, maple, and alder forest, note that most of the bits and pieces of rock along the trail are composed of phyllite, a metamorphic rock that breaks in wavy sheets. After about 1 mile

The placid waters of Mill Pond are seen from an open ridge made up of 500-million-year-old quarzites and phyllites of the Maitlen Formation.

of hiking, the trail breaks out into an open ridge with a great view down to Mill Pond and the delta with distributary channels built out from its eastern end since 1910 when the lake was created by a dam. Just past some switchbacks as the trail continues eastward along the ridge, are outcrops of a quartz-chlorite-feldspar phyllite with very distinct foliation. Another 100 yards to the east, blocks of white to pink quartzite can be seen.

As the trail descends to Elk Creek Falls, slabs of quartzite with big patches of massive white quartz form outcrops over which the falls descend. Notice a dike of white massive quartz cutting up through the quartzite in the bed of Elk Creek. As the trail crosses to the east side of the bridge over the falls, the quartzite is replaced by outcrops of mica-rich phyllite.

Returning to the trailhead, it is worthwhile to continue 0.5 mile down the road to the dam which impounds Mill Pond. The north buttress of the spillway is an excellent exposure of the Maitlen Formation, with a display of fold structures and a spectacular view of foliation in the phyllite dipping into the canyon below.

DISHMAN HILLS

Hike 48

This is Spokane's wilderness version of Central Park in New York City, with rocks, landforms, and vegetation the way they were before buildings, roadways, parking lots, and lawns changed the landscape for human habitation.

DISTANCE ■ 1.5 miles

ELEVATION ■ 1980 feet to 2100 feet

DIFFICULTY ■ Easy

TOPOGRAPHIC MAP ■ USGS Spokane NE

GEOLOGIC MAP ■ DGER 90-17 Spokane; USGS 98-115 (digital)

PRECAUTIONS ■ There is no potable water available en route.

About the Landscape: The geologic history of the Spokane Valley began more than 1.5 billion years ago, toward the end of the Precambrian era. About this time, the sediments of the Pritchard Formation were deposited in the first layer of an immense pile of sedimentary rocks we now call the Belt-Purcell Supergroup.

About 800,000 years ago the western edge of ancestral North America was rifted off to eventually become pieces of Siberia, Australia, or Antarctica. One of the games geologists play is trying to identify the origin of the jigsaw puzzle pieces of microplates, but so far there is not much agreement as to what went where, or what came from where. But in the hills south and east of Spokane, we can see some of the rocks of ancient North America that were left behind. These are now mostly bent, broken, and metamorphosed.

Then for more than a billion years we know nothing about what went on around Spokane because all the rocks that could tell the story have been removed by erosion.

The next chapter available for rock reading is at the end of the Cretaceous period when huge masses of molten rock pushed up into the earth and crystallized into granite that can be found in hills surrounding Spokane on all sides. The oldest of these plutonic rocks is about 100 million years with the youngest intruded about 50 million years ago during the Eocene epoch. Most of these older rocks have been buried by the vast outpouring of Columbia River basalts in the Miocene epoch, beginning about 16 million years ago. Nearly all of the Spokane Valley is covered by this lava, which extends from here to the Washington coast (see Hikes 37 and 43 for more details). At the same time, sedimentary rocks of the Latah Creek Formation were deposited in lakes formed when lava dammed streams flowing into the Columbia Basin.

The last major episode in Spokane geology was the Missoula floods. Actually there was not one flood, but as many as forty to one hundred. These great walls of water burst forth from glacial Lake Missoula as dams of ice disintegrated,

Outcrops of granite in the Enchanted Ravine in the Dishman Hills.

releasing huge amounts of water that had backed up into a lake as much as 2000 feet deep (see also Hikes 38, 39, and 42). The floodwaters ripped through the Spokane Valley, stripping the landscape down to bare bedrock and cutting channels large and small. For further details about this area, visit the Dishman Hills website at *www.sd81.k12.wa.us/Regal/DishmanHills/Map.htm*

Trail Guide: Travelling east on I-90 through Spokane, take the East Sprague exit (Exit 285) and drive east on Sprague Avenue about 0.75 mile to Sargent Road. Turn right and proceed about three blocks to a big parking lot and grassy area at Camp Caro. The trail begins just behind the Environmental Education Center building to the south. An easy trail, especially suitable for families, rambles over hill and dale through a remarkable wilderness park created in the midst of suburban development on the outskirts of Spokane. The route, as described, is a loop with numerous possible side routes that could make this an all-day excursion.

A short distance up the trail, the ruins of a building foundation are built into an outcrop of the dominant rock type in the area. This is a porphyritic granodiorite that consists of quartz, plagioclase feldspar, some biotite mica, and very large phenocrysts of potassium feldspar. Some of these phenocrysts are as much as an inch or more in length. Although this rock shows little evidence of metamorphism, it has been mapped as part of the Precambrian Pritchard Formation. It is possible that this is actually a Cretaceous to Tertiary pluton, because they have been found elsewhere in this area.

A little less than 0.5 mile from the trailhead, Caro Cliff rises on your left. This is also composed of porphyritic granodiorite broken into large blocks by several sets of expansion joints. Along the trail are large blocks of rock that have broken off the cliff and fallen to the ground below. This would not be a good campsite location!

Just beyond Caro Cliff, take the trail junction to the right toward the Enchanted Ravine. This is probably a channel carved by the Missoula floods that may follow along a fault or closely spaced set of joints that made the rock here more susceptible to erosion than the surrounding area. Because it is deep enough to be relatively protected from sunlight, there exists a moist microclimate allowing thicker vegetation to develop. Thus a lot more birds and other animals can be seen and heard if you walk quietly.

As you ascend the far end of the ravine, look for rounded holes eroded in the granite walls on the left. This is differential weathering that might have been due to the presence of inclusions in the granite that were more easily broken down by reactions with surface and ground water. The granite cliff on the right shows that weathering is also concentrated along the joint planes because ground water more easily flows through these fractures in the rock.

From the Enchanted Ravine the trail rises to a high plateau covered by Douglas fir and ponderosa pine. Here and there you get a good view out toward the Spokane Valley, one of the main channels for the Missoula floods. Along the trail there are scattered outcrops of granite, some of which are cut by light-colored pegmatite dikes composed of large quartz and feldspar crystals. There are also a few inclusions of biotite schist in the granitic rock.

At the next junction turn right again, and head gradually downslope back toward Camp Caro. In about 0.25 mile, there is another junction. If you turn left you can make a short side trip to East and West Ponds—possibly giant potholes scoured out of the bedrock by the Missoula floods. Because they are filled only by rain water (and snowmelt), they dry out toward the end of the summer, but wetland vegetation, including cattails and ferns, is still maintained. From here you can walk another mile looping around the west end of the park or return to Camp Caro.

Chapter 7
BLUE MOUNTAINS

A view into the Blue Mountains

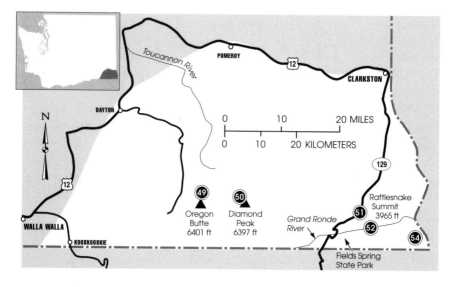

The Blue Mountains are an uplifted portion of the Columbia Basin–Snake River Plain. The basin-plain stretches from the Cascades on the west to Yellowstone National Park on the east, and is characterized by young volcanics, particularly basalt flows younger than 16 million years. In general the basin-plain is arid and covered by sagebrush, grasses, weeds, and wheat.

The Blue Mountains are an exception: their height allows enough precipitation for forests. The term Blue Mountains has two geographic meanings. The term is applied to all the mountain ranges in northeastern Oregon, including the Wallowas, Elkhorns, and Strawberries, which rise to nearly 10,000 feet and experienced alpine glaciation (see *Hiking Oregon's Geology* by Ellen Bishop and John Allen). This meaning includes lower mountainous areas, including a long ridge that extends southwest into Oregon from the general vicinity of Lewiston (Idaho), Clarkston (Washington), and where the Grande Ronde River enters the Snake River at the mouth of Hells Canyon (Hike 54).

The more restricted geographic meaning of the term Blue Mountains applies to this long northeast-trending ridge. These Blue Mountains straddle the Oregon-Washington line, and in this guide we deal with only the Washington portion of "the Blues."

At Oregon Butte, which is in Washington (Hike 49), the Blues rise to their greatest elevation, 6401 feet, not high enough for glaciers to have formed during the Pleistocene Ice Age.

The Blue Mountains are a huge anticline, or uparch of rock, cut across at the extreme northeastern end by the Snake River. The Grande Ronde River (Hike 52) meanders northeasterly along the southeast flank of the Blues. Smaller rivers flow northwest or southeast down the limbs (sides) of the anticline.

Because there has been no glaciation, the crest of the Blue Mountains has very low relief. The flanks of the Blues have been deeply dissected by streams like the Walla Walla, Touchet, Toucannon (Hike 50), and Wenaha. Many of these canyons are nearly 0.5 mile deep, and expose the rocks inside the anticline.

Almost all the bedrock of the Blue Mountains is Miocene lava of the Columbia River basalts. Vents for some of the lava flows are located near Puffer Butte (Hike 51). The same lava flows that are more or less at sea level in the Columbia Basin to the northwest are about a mile high along the crest of the Blues.

Geologic circumstances allow us to look beneath the basalts to the underlying rocks of the Blue Mountains in only two places in Washington. One of these is on the northwest flank of the Blues where the Toucannon River has cut through the basalts into exotic terrane rocks (Hike 50). The other is along the Snake River near the mouth of Hells Canyon (Hike 54).

In almost all the Blue Mountains, the basalt near the surface is covered by a few feet of fine-grained material. Some of this material is from the weathering of basalt, but most is loess (wind blown silt) and volcanic ash. Most of the ash appears to be from a volcano more than 300 miles to the southwest—Mazama ash—from the formation of Crater Lake about 7000 years ago. Soil has formed on the loess and ash and, except on dry south-facing slopes, forests have grown.

Hike 49

OREGON BUTTE

A basalt flow containing stream cobbles is at the top of the Blues.

DISTANCE ■ About 2.5 miles

ELEVATION ■ 5500 feet to 6401 feet

DIFFICULTY ■ Easy

TOPOGRAPHIC MAPS ■ USGS Oregon Butte; USGS Wenaha-Tucannon Wilderness, Umatilla National Forest

GEOLOGIC MAP ■ DGER 93-4 Clarkston

KEY REFERENCE ■ Swanson and Wright (1983)

About the Landscape: Oregon Butte is in Washington, so how did it get its name? Maybe because at 6401 feet it offers a great view of Oregon to the south, but the views of Washington and Idaho are just as good. These mountains are volcanic, and experienced uplift, but they are also mountains of erosion. There are a few relatively level upland areas, but most of the Blue Mountains is a combination of steep-sided valleys and sharp ridges. The Blue Mountains in Washington were not high enough to be glaciated.

Streams have cut deep canyons in the basalts of the Blue Mountains anticline.

All the lava flows on this hike are a part of the Columbia River basalts (with two exceptions at Oregon Butte). More specifically, the bedrock here is all Grande Ronde Basalt (by volume about three quarters of all of the Columbia River basalts) which erupted about 16 million years ago.

Most south-facing slopes on this hike get a lot of sun, so grasses, wildflowers, and shrubs abound. The shady north-facing slopes have coniferous forests dominated by Douglas fir, true firs, larch, lodgepole pine, and Englemann spruce. **Trail Guide:** Set your trip odometer at 0.0 in Dayton at the intersection of US 12 and Fourth Street. Go southeast on Fourth Street, which becomes CR 9115. At mile 5 turn left up Hatley Gulch. In the mid-1970s, this intersection is where the Bureau of Reclamation proposed an earth-rock dam on the Touchet River. (For an alternative route to the Oregon Butte trailhead, continue on CR 9115 and FR 64 past the Bluewood ski area and then turn east on FR 46 to Godman Spring.)

At the top of Hatley Gulch (mile 9.4), turn right (east) on CR 9124. At about mile 13.5 turn right (south) on CR 1424. Turn right (south) again at the Kendall Monument (mile 15.4). CR 1424 becomes FR 46 where you enter the Umatilla National Forest (mile 16.3). At mile 26.8 turn left (east) onto FR 4608 at Godman Spring (this route meets the alternative route via the Bluewood ski area here). Park at the end of the road (mile 33.1), the edge of the Wenaha-Toucannon Wilderness Area.

Take some time to explore the variety of the Grande Ronde Basalt near the parking area. There are multiple lava flows, each with a basalt colonnade of large polygonal columns (the steepest parts of the slopes). The distribution and size of the vesicles varies considerably, with most vesicles near flow tops. The gentler part of the slopes are the upper parts of the lava flows, the tops of which are commonly weathered. Most of the weathering took place in the warm humid climate of the Miocene. Dark iron silicate minerals weathered to reddish iron oxides and hydroxides.

The trail starts at the east end of the parking area; the thick soil is dominantly loess (wind-deposited silt) and ash (mostly from the eruption at Crater Lake about 7000 years ago). Below the trail an alder patch has curved trunks due to soil and/or snow creeping downhill.

There are some trails not shown on the map. After going east for a little less than a mile, the main trail turns south and ascends West Butte Ridge. This trail turns east again and passes just south of the summit of West Butte (6292 feet). From West Butte there is a good view southeast to the lookout at Oregon Butte. Continue east, down the switchbacks to a saddle: to the south is King Creek which flows to Butte Creek, the Wenaha River, and the Grande Ronde River; to the north is Panjab Creek which flows to the Toucannon River (Hike 50).

From the saddle, contour east on the north slope of Oregon Butte to Oregon Butte Spring. This is probably the highest spring in the Blue Mountains, and there isn't much rock mass above to store water to supply the spring during the long dry summer and early fall. But snow banks persist late on the north slope of Oregon Butte; much of the meltwater percolates through the soil and into the permeable parts of the basalt: the vesicular zones, the breccia, and the joints between the columns. The Columbia River basalts are one of the great aquifers of North America.

There are two trail junctions on the ridge just east of Oregon Butte Spring. Head south up the west side of the ridge (don't cross the ridge if your objective is Oregon Butte). The lava flow on the summit of Oregon Butte is most unusual! The dark basalt contains light-colored clasts of sandstone, quartzite, and chert. Such clasts within an igneous rock like basalt are called xenoliths (strange rocks). Evidently, a stream rounded the cobbles, then the lava flowed over and incorporated them. The clasts may be related to those on Lime Hill (Hike 54).

The north end of a dike swarm is just down the west slope below the summit of Oregon Butte. A dike swarm is a group of dikes of about the same age; in this case, the vertical dikes fed the basalt of Dodge (about 15.5 million years old), a member of the Wanapum Basalt. The dike swarm cuts the flows of the older Grande Ronde Basalt. There are five segments of this dike swarm (average dike thickness is 65 feet) trending south-southeast 9 miles from Oregon Butte to the Wenaha River.

The lookout is on the National Historic Lookout Register. On a clear day it's a spectacular view from the "top of the Blues." Nearby are dozens of flows of the Grande Ronde Basalt exposed in the sides of ridges and canyons. In the distance are the Seven Devils Range (southeast) of Idaho, and the Wallowa (south-southeast) and Elkhorn (south-southwest) Mountains of Oregon.

On the return there are two possible shortcuts. The first is to descend northwest on a very faint trail through the forest from the summit area to the saddle between Oregon Butte and West Butte (you bypass Oregon Butte Spring). The second is a trail that contours along the north side of West Butte; it begins at the first switchback ascending the east ridge of West Butte and contours along the north slope of West Butte Ridge.

Hike 50

DIAMOND PEAK VIA THE TOUCANNON RIVER

Best view in the Blues.

DISTANCE ■ 9 miles

ELEVATION ■ 3500 feet to 6379 feet

DIFFICULTY ■ Moderate

TOPOGRAPHIC MAPS ■ USGS Stentz Spring, Diamond Peak; USGS Wenaha-Toucannon Wilderness, Umatilla National Forest

GEOLOGIC MAP ■ DGER 93-4

KEY REFERENCE ■ Swanson and Wright (1983)

About the Landscape: At the edge of the Wenaha-Toucannon Wilderness of Umatilla National Forest we see the contrast between the relatively level and undissected top of the Blue Mountains anticlinal ridge, and the deep, steep-sided canyons cut by streams dissecting this uplift. The rocks are all the same type, basalt, and the same age, about 16 million years old, but the landforms vary as do the soils and vegetation.

The forests along this route are as spectacular and varied as anywhere in the Blues. On the floodplain and canyon sides of the Toucannon River, there are large grand fir, Douglas fir, Englemann spruce, ponderosa pine, and larch. There are yew trees galore, one of the greatest concentrations of yews anywhere. Red alder is the only significant deciduous tree along the river.

A grass-tree mosaic tops the Blues: patches of forest interspersed with meadows. In places, the meadows have so little soil over the basalt bedrock they are barren of vegetation. Elsewhere, the meadows have wildflowers in great profusion, including cone flower, coyote mint, everlasting flower, heartleaf arnica, Indian paintbrush, lupine, Nuttall's linanthastrum, penstemon, pale agoseris, scarlet gilia, sulphur flower, and yarrow. Mountain mahogany trees grow at the edge of the meadow at the top of the Toucannon canyon. The upland forests have soils composed of ash (mostly from Mount Mazama) and loess; these forests include true firs and lodgepole pine. There is even one western juniper just south of the summit of Diamond Peak!

Trail Guide: Thirteen miles north of Dayton and 23 miles west of Pomeroy, the Toucannon River goes under US 12. Drive up the Toucannon River road toward Camp Wooten; this becomes FR 47. (There are shortcuts from the southwest near Dayton and from the northeast near Pomeroy; the roads on the shortcuts are part paved and part gravel.)

As you drive southeasterly up the Toucannon River, note the basalt flows in the canyon walls. The Miocene lava flows from here to Diamond Peak are all part of the Grande Ronde Basalt.

Four miles south of the entrance to Camp Wooten (east side of road) is Panjab Campground and a bridge over the Toucannon River. Before or after the hike take a look at the rocks along the lower mile of Panjab Creek. You'll see rocks very different from the monotonous basalt which stretches for tens of miles in every direction and lies exposed in a quarry, in roadcuts, and in gullies (west side of FR 4713).

One hundred or so million years ago, the Wallowa terrane moved across the ancestral Pacific Ocean and slammed into the west edge of North America. Although there are many minor rocks (chert, argillite, and sandstone), the dominant lithologies are (or were) volcanic and volcaniclastic (sedimentary, derived from volcanoes) rocks metamorphosed to greenstone and green schist. These rocks were part of a volcanic island arc near the equator more than 200 million years ago.

Why is there this island of ancient rocks surrounded by young basalt flows?

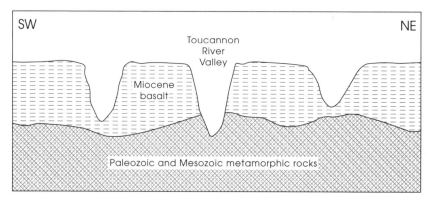

figure 14. Diagramatic cross section of the Blue Mountains near the upper Toucanon River.

The ancient rocks were eroded into a landscape with hundreds of feet of relief. This landscape was buried by lava flows during the Miocene, but as the Blue Mountains have been uplifted, streams like the Toucannon River have cut deep canyons into the basalts (see figure 14). Here a canyon just happens to be located across a hill in the landscape of the old rocks.

The trailhead is 5 miles up the Toucannon River along FR 4712, near the mouth of Sheep Creek (the old rocks were along FR 4713 up Panjab Creek).

The trail follows an old road for about 0.5 mile before gradually dropping down to the north edge of the narrow flood plain of the Toucannon River. There are occasional exposures of columnar basalt. Every mile or so the trail crosses a small alluvial fan deposited by a tributary stream where the canyon side meets the valley floor. Through time, the Toucannon River has cut a canyon in places almost 2000 feet deep; the river also moves slowly back and forth across its floodplain, cutting into the valley side, eroding the toes of taluses and alluvial fans, and depositing gravel bars.

About midway between Sheep Creek and Bear Creek is a large terrace on the north side of the Toucannon River. The top (or tread) of the terrace, high above the river, is part of an ancient floodplain; the Toucannon River was at this level perhaps a million years ago, and has since then cut down to its present position.

About 1 mile before Bear Creek the trail passes along the base of a talus slope. A talus is loose rocks that have fallen from the cliffs above and formed a sloping heap. Rockfall is one of the processes of mass wasting, the downslope movement of material (without streams or glaciers). The river is a "sewer" for mass wasting; that is, the river cuts into the toe of the slope, erodes material, and transports it down the valley.

At Bear Creek (which enters the Toucannon River from the south), the trail

The crest of the Blue Mountains anticlinal ridge is behind the canyon of the Toucannon River.

jogs southwest up the valley side and then splits (no sign). To the left, the Bear Creek Trail goes up to Hunter Spring. Follow the Bear Creek Trail to the right; it crosses a tributary stream and descends to a crossing of the Toucannon River (sign).

In the next mile or so, the Bear Creek Trail ascends from 4100 feet to 5500 feet by way of switchbacks. There are basalt cliffs near the bottom and the top, but mostly there is colluvium, the loose material creeping down the hill. The components of the colluvium are chunks of basalt (derived from the lava flows) and a fine-grained matrix that originally was mostly loess and ash.

The first of many meadows at the top of the canyon is the one just south of Jelly Spring. The meadows have very thin soils; in fact, in the next few miles there are places where the trail through meadows is on bedrock, with cross-sections of basalt columns visible. The trail almost disappears at Jelly Spring Meadow. Proceed south along the west edge of the ridge. The view west reveals the deep dissection of the Blue Mountains: steep canyon sides with nearly horizontal basalt flows visible in the grass portions of this grass-tree mosaic.

The trail wanders south and a little east through meadows and forests; once you pass the second meadow at 5800 feet, the trail has little slope for miles. This broad ridge is an undissected remnant of the top of the Blue Mountain anticline. The trail passes just east of one grassy hilltop (elevation 6193 feet) and over the next (elevation 6325 feet), both with a great variety of wildflowers. Between these two hilltops is a forested saddle with a basalt flow exposed on the east side.

Just south of the hilltop at 6325 feet is a T in the trail: to the west is Diamond Spring and (eventually) Oregon Butte; to the east, it is less than 1 mile to the trailhead at the end of FR 4030 (at the saddle between Diamond Peak and Mount Misery). From the T go about 20 yards east along the trail and look south for a gap in the trees. Here an old trail goes south through the forest and up onto the northwest-trending ridge of Diamond Peak. Follow the trail about 0.5 mile southeast to the end of the ridge, which is the summit of Diamond Peak (elevation 6379 feet)

The panorama from the summit is spectacular. A mile to the east is Mount Misery. To the southeast are Idaho's Seven Devils Mountains (70 miles away) on the far side of Hells Canyon of the Snake River (Hike 54). To the south-southeast are Oregon's Wallowa Mountains (60 miles away) on the other side of the canyon of the Grande Ronde River (Hike 52). To the south-southwest, are Oregon's Elkhorn Mountains (90 miles away). Seven miles to the west is Oregon Butte (Hike 49). Below the summit, a cliff of resistant basalt wraps around the ridge and below is a maze of canyons and ridges, with a relief of about 2000 feet. Almost no uneroded uplands remain south of Diamond Peak: streams are dissecting the Blues.

Hike
51

PUFFER BUTTE

Look down from a Miocene volcano into a twisting canyon more than a half mile deep.

DISTANCE ■ About 0.75 mile
ELEVATION ■ 4020 feet to 4485 feet
DIFFICULTY ■ Easy
TOPOGRAPHIC MAP ■ Field Springs
GEOLOGIC MAP ■ DGER 93-4 Clarkston
KEY REFERENCE ■ Reidel and others (1992)

About the Landscape: Landforms are ephemeral. Most of the earth's landscape is very young. In the last 20,000 years, glaciers have retreated, dunes

Column in a Saddle Mountains basalt flow

have advanced, streams have cut canyons in some places and built floodplains in others, and sea level has risen hundreds of feet. Over a thousand volcanoes have erupted. Here, as we walk on the skeleton of a Miocene volcano, we see ghosts of the past.

Most of the volume of the Columbia River basalts was erupted quickly as hundreds of lava flows; dikes are the chief bits of evidence for where these flows originated. This surprises many, for when we think of lava flows, we think of volcanoes. There are a few buried Miocene vents, like at Ice Harbor Dam on the Snake River. But, in the vicinity of Field Springs State Park are three volcanoes that were not buried by late lava flows, and survived 14 million years of erosion adjacent to a river that cut a canyon more than half a mile deep.

Puffer Butte is in Field Springs State Park, an area with more than volcanoes to offer. From the park brochure: "The park has a mile-long trail to the top of the butte from which one can enjoy an excellent vista into three states, along with a view 3,000 feet down into the Grand Ronde Canyon. Field Springs is a naturalist's paradise with wildflowers blooming from late spring through summer. The park is forested with ponderosa pine, western larch, Douglas fir and grand fir. It supports wildlife such as deer, elk, black bear, coyote and porcupine." The park's extensive trails are excellent for cross-country skiing. Pick up a trail map and a bird list before you start your hike.

Trail Guide: From Clarkston follow SR 129 for 6 miles up the west bank of the Snake River to Asotin. In Asotin SR 129 turns west, and exposes many Miocene gravels and lava flows as it ascends the hill. Follow SR 129 for 19 miles to Anatone.

Anatone lies on the plateau at the east end of the Blue Mountains anticline. Beneath the plateau are basalt flows. Visible to the southwest, are two volcanoes associated with the Columbia River basalts. To the left is Puffer Butte (4485 feet), a volcanic vent for the basalt of Sillusi, a member of the Saddle Mountains Basalt. To the right is Big Butte (5010 feet), a vent for the slightly older Roza Member, part of the Wanapum Basalt.

Continue southwest for 2.5 miles on SR 129 to Rattlesnake Pass (3965 feet) and another 0.7 mile to the first entrance to Field Springs State Park. Turn left and drive 1.1 miles south on a county road to a parking area with an outhouse. To the east is a borrow pit or quarry with poor exposures of the basalt of Umatilla.

From the parking lot walk about 0.5 mile south on Corral Trail (see park map) to a picnic table near a fence, gate, and spring. You can recognize the spring by the moist depression filled with large deciduous thorny shrubs.

The view to the south and east is spectacular. A little of the Grande Ronde

River shows 2900 feet below (Hike 52). To the south the Wallowa Mountains of Oregon rise above the Joseph Upland. To the west, Idaho is visible on the far side of Hells Canyon (Hike 54). The north and south sides of the canyon of the Grande Ronde show horizontal bands resulting from differences in rocks, soils, moisture, and vegetation. There are ledges from differential erosion of dozens of lava flows and the erodible contacts between them.

Water seeping from between some flows allows different species and densities of vegetation to grow at these moist horizons. Intermittent streams that are tributaries to the Grande Ronde River have cut north-south trending V-shaped valleys separated by sharp ridges. To the east, the mass-wasting scars on some valley sides are from extreme precipitation events (perhaps during the heavy rain on deep snow in February 1996).

Look closely; the Grande Ronde River is very curved (that's how it got its name). But these meanders are not on a floodplain as at La Grande, Oregon. These meanders are cut deeply into the lava flows and are called incised meanders. As the Blue Mountains were uplifted (more than a mile), the Grande Ronde River cut down into the bedrock (more than half a mile). In places, the intermittent tributaries have deposited large alluvial fans in the bottom of the canyon of the Grande Ronde River, which itself cuts into the toes of the alluvial fans.

The view is even better from the hill 0.5 mile to the south, but don't walk due south across private property (note the no trespassing signs on the fence at the south boundary of the state park). Instead, walk west through the gate along the Grande Ronde Trail and then south across the saddle and up the hill. Due south, on the far side of the river, is a cutoff incised meander; this is a place where there was a meander cut off after river incision. Cutoff meanders are common on the erodible alluvium of floodplains, but rare once a river has incised. There's a slightly higher and older cutoff incised meander to the south-southeast on this side of the river.

This hill is a remnant of a volcano the same age as Puffer Butte. If you look very closely to the south-southeast on the far side of the river, you may be able to see two dikes cutting cliffs and crossing ridges. One of these dikes fed Puffer Butte volcano; the other fed a slightly younger lava flow. Look north at Puffer Butte, the Miocene volcano that is the high elevation of this hike. Look 5 miles to the northwest to Big Butte (elevation 5010 feet), another Miocene volcano that was one of the vents for the Roza Member of the Wanapum Basalt.

Return to the gate near the spring just south of the park boundary. From the gate follow a faint, unnamed trail northwest along the south edge of the forest. The trail switchbacks south below and then north between two outcrops of basalt. The lower outcrop has large columns of massive basalt; the upper basalt is partly vesicular and partly brecciated. This faint trail ends at a cairn at the top of the forested east-facing slope. Ascend north-northwest through a meadow of bunchgrass. At the south edge of the forested, gently rounded top of Puffer Butte is a picnic table. The true summit of the volcano is in the woods about 100 yards to the north, but the best view is from the picnic table at the top of the meadow.

Now you're on a Miocene volcano, a vent for the basalt of Sillusi, part of the Umatilla Member of the Saddle Mountains Basalt. From here the lava flowed many tens of miles to the west at a time when there was not much relief. If a volcano erupted here now, the lava would flow east along the canyon of the Grande Ronde River. You have a 180-degree view to the south of this deep canyon and the Wallowa Mountains in the distance.

From the picnic table, an old road called Overlook Butte Climb goes north and then east to the parking area. However, we recommend Puffer Butte Trail, which starts out going south through the meadow, then switchbacks northeast and enters the woods. Just before the forest is a small outcrop of basalt with tiny plagioclase phenocrysts—a porphyritic volcanic rock. The plagioclase crystals grew during the slow initial cooling when the magma was in a chamber under the volcano. Then the rest of the magma cooled too fast for crystal growth when the lava was extruded at the earth's surface.

Descend southeast through the forest about half a mile until Puffer Butte Trail meets a gravel road. Turn right (downhill) on the road and join Corral Trail just to the west of the parking area.

Hike

52 GRANDE RONDE

A meandering river incises its floodplain and cuts a half mile into basalt flows.

DISTANCE ■ About 2.5 miles

ELEVATIONS ■ 1073 feet to 1248 feet

DIFFICULTY ■ Easy

TOPOGRAPHIC MAP ■ USGS Black Butte

GEOLOGIC MAP ■ DGER 93-4 Clarkston

KEY REFERENCES ■ Reidel and others (1992)

About the Landscape: Streams with low gradients and a load of relatively fine sediment wander (or meander) in big loops back and forth across flood plains (see Hike 8), occasionally eroding the valley sides. Erosion is on the outside of the bend (the cut bank) where the stream is deepest and fastest.

The channel on the far side of the Grande Ronde River was abandoned when the incised meander was cut off.

Deposition is on the inside of the meander loop (the point bar) where the stream is relatively shallow and slow. A meandering stream may cut (or incise) through the flood plain sediment (alluvium) and into the bedrock. This incision may be due to several causes, but is most commonly associated with uplift of an area. That's what happened here: as the Blue Mountains anticline grew (more than a mile of uplift), the Grande Ronde River cut down (more than half a mile of incision).

To give you an idea of how much the Grande Ronde meanders, La Grande, Oregon, is 70 miles to the southwest (as the crow flies), but 150 river miles upstream. At La Grande a graben (a downfaulted area) is filling with erodible sediment across which the Grande Ronde River meanders freely. Here, however, the river is incised 2900 feet into the Columbia River basalts, and the meanders can't migrate much because of the resistant bedrock. There may be only one river on earth with more spectacular incised meanders than these: the Goosenecks of the San Juan River in southeastern Utah.

Here we see not only a deep canyon with incised meanders, but also Miocene lava flows and dikes which fed them. This is a desert landscape with grasses, wildflowers, sagebrush, and cactus; small trees survive only next to the river and at springs.

Trail Guide: From Clarkston follow SR 129 for 6 miles up the west bank of the Snake River to Asotin. In Asotin SR 129 turns west uphill, and exposes many Miocene gravels and lava flows in roadcuts. Follow SR 129 for 19 miles to Anatone.

As you leave Anatone, set your trip odometer to 0.0; continue southwest on SR 129. At mile 1.6 turn left onto Montgomery Road, which heads east, then curves south, then curves east again. At mile 2.5 turn right on Shumaker Road, which leads south over the edge of the plateau and down Shumaker Creek into the canyon of the Grande Ronde River. Drive slowly down the long steep dirt road; you are traveling through time. The lava flow at the canyon rim is part of the Weissenfels Ridge Member of the Saddle Mountains Basalt, perhaps 12.5 million years old. Most of the rocks exposed in this canyon are flows of the Grande Ronde Basalt, about 3 million years older. This is a layer cake of many lava flows, with the oldest at the bottom and the youngest at the top. You are descending through more than 0.5 mile of Columbia River basalts, and this is only a fraction of their total thickness.

As you descend the grade, look at the landscape to the south-southwest across the Grande Ronde River (elevation 1082 feet at the mouth of Shumaker Creek). A small hill with an elevation of about 1460 feet is the core of an ancient incised meander. This meander was cut off to give the twisting canyon of the Grande Ronde River a rare mile-long straight reach.

At mile 7.9, just 1000 feet before reaching the Grande Ronde River, turn left across a cattle guard and cross Shumaker Creek. In this vicinity are relatively fine-grained slackwater sediments deposited by the Missoula floods, and younger, relatively coarse-grained alluvium deposited by Schumaker Creek. In a half mile there is a basalt cliff next to the road, and then more alluvium and Missoula flood sediments. At mile 9.8 is the end of the road and the parking area for the Shumaker Unit of the Joseph Creek Wildlife Area (cooperatively managed by the Washington Department of Fish and Wildlife and the US Army Corps of Engineers).

Before following the path downriver, look at the map on the sign at the east end of the parking lot. There are some basalt columns on the left before you cross an unnamed creek (usually dry) and then Myers Creek (sometimes dry). This part of the path near the river may be overgrown in places, but most of the hike is along an old road 50 to 250 feet above the river.

As the trail ascends, look at the alluvial fan across the Grande Ronde River. It was deposited by an intermittent creek; its toe is now being eroded by the river. Just before the sharp bend (uphill) in the old road, there are two interesting exposures. The first is red volcanic breccia (Miocene) that appears to be cut by a dike. The second is gravel (Miocene or younger) with a wide variety of lithologies including basalt, greenstone, and quartzite. The gravel was probably deposited by the Grande Ronde River long ago.

From the bend in the old road look south across the river. Note that this part of the canyon has a wide, curved, gentle slope below the steep cliffs above. This is the outside of a former meander loop of the Grande Ronde River, part of which was cut when the river was about 400 feet above its present elevation. Also look east to where the river winds around a high, narrow meander core.

The old road rises to the north for a short distance. If you look due north you'll see a vertical basalt dike cutting the horizontal lava flows. This Miocene dike is part of the Grande Ronde Basalt and was feeding a lava flow now high on the canyon wall.

The old road descends gently toward the mouth of Hackberry Gulch, then turns north and ascends along the west bank of the intermittent stream for 300 yards. Cross Hackberry Gulch and contour southeasterly along the old road. There are roadcuts of lava and colluvium, and an excellent view of the meander core to the south. From top to bottom, the core of the incised meander has basalt cliffs, old Grande Ronde River gravels (the gentle slope at the north end), and modern alluvium. Note, where the current slows enough to deposit sediment, how the modern alluvium is concentrated in gravel bars on the inside of the bend of the meander. On the meander core and elsewhere along this hike you can see terracettes (little terraces), perhaps eroded by the hooves of livestock and game animals.

As you walk southeasterly you encounter small talus slopes and basalt cliffs. At depth in the talus slopes there is silt (originally deposited by the wind); some coatings of caliche (calcium carbonate) are evident on the rocks.

A few feet above the road is a contact between two basalt flows. Above the contact are large columns of basalt (the bottom of a flow). There are three features to observe at the contact: vesicles (gas cavities at the top of a flow), breccia (rock broken from flow movement), and red soil (from weathering between eruptions and baking by the overlying flow). The lateritic soil is characteristic of tropical weathering, so the climate here must have been hot and humid during the Miocene. This interpretation of paleoclimate is substantiated by the subtropical species of petrified wood found elsewhere in the Columbia River basalts (e.g., at Ginkgo State Park at Vantage).

The old road becomes faint at the core of the next meander. There is a good view of most of two wavelengths of incised meanders. From the saddle or hill (elevation 1248 feet) one can descend west, south, or east to the river. The nearly level ground by the river is a beautiful and peaceful place to rest or camp. From this vicinity you can look west-northwest to Puffer Butte (Hike 51), almost 3500 feet above you.

Chapter 8
THE FOUR CORNERS

The Four Corners: Jurassic sandstone, Tertiary igneous rocks, and Quaternary dunes

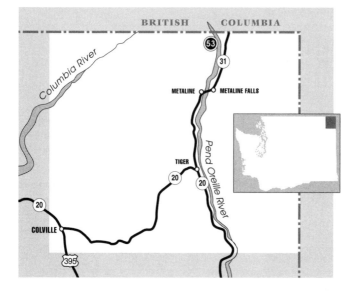

We conclude this book with hikes close to the four corners of Washington (the hikes' mean distance from any one of Washington's geographic corners is less than 5 miles). These hikes illustrate the great variety of Washington's landscapes: a cavern, a canyon, and sea cliffs. Together, the four corners of the state have Paleozoic, Mesozoic, and Cenozoic volcanic and/or sedimentary rocks. All four have seen dramatic geomorphic changes in the past few million years, if not the past 20,000 years.

In the last two million years, groundwater has dissolved early Paleozoic limestone to create Gardner Cave (Hike 53), and started to fill it with stalactites and stalagmites. When the northeastern corner of Washington was under ice repeatedly, in the last million years or so, solution of limestone was probably enhanced by cold temperature, high pressure subglacial meltwater.

Meanwhile, in the southeastern corner of the state, the Snake River was finding its way from southern Idaho to the Lewiston Basin. In the past few million years, a tributary of Idaho's Salmon River captured the Snake River, and Hells Canyon was the result (Hike 54). The mean annual temperature at Hells Canyon during the cold glacial climate of 20,000 years ago was 10 to 20 degrees Fahrenheit lower; the Bonneville flood roared down Hells Canyon about 14,500 years ago (between Missoula floods, traveling in the opposite direction).

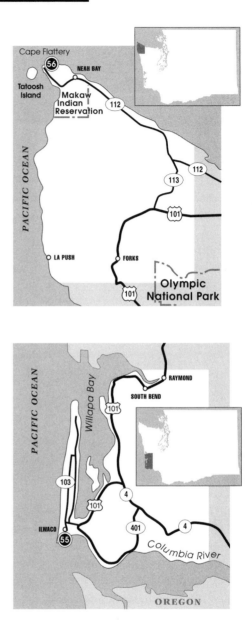

Twenty thousand years ago. sea level was almost 400 feet lower (the source of water in ice sheets was the ocean), so the Pacific coast was much farther west. Cape Disappointment (Hike 55) was high and dry except for the passage of an occasional Missoula flood. Sea level did not reach its present height until about 5000 years ago. Since then, waves at Cape Flattery (Hike 56) have cut (or at least modified) sea cliffs, arches, and sea caves.

In these four hikes alone, you'll see two of the mightiest rivers in North America (the Snake and the Columbia), waves (the Pacific is rarely calm), fragments of the earth's greatest temperate rain forest, and a great variety of rocks in terms of age and composition. You'll walk in a cavern, and on a ridge above the mouth of the deepest canyon in the United States. You'll stand at the top of a cliff of Tertiary rocks, hearing surf and sea birds, and perhaps watch the sun set across the Pacific.

237

Hike 53

GARDNER CAVE

Take a walk through this geologic treasure, one of the longest and the only easily accessible limestone cave in Washington.

DISTANCE ■ 5 miles

ELEVATION ■ 2690 feet to 2750 feet

DIFFICULTY ■ Easy

TOPOGRAPHIC MAP ■ USGS Boundary Dam

GEOLOGIC MAP ■ DGER 93-13 Colville

KEY REFERENCES ■ Bush and others (1992); Martin (1990)

About the Landscape: The story of Gardner Cave began about 500 million years ago when, in a setting very similar to the rift valleys of East Africa today, the margin of ancestral North America was ripped apart to form a new ocean. Apparently the seas were warm and bio-productive, because layers of calcium carbonate sediment at least 5000 feet thick were deposited on the seafloor where these sediments were eventually buried and hardened into limestone rock now called the Metaline Limestone. Considering the geologic history of the western margin of North America, it is miraculous that nothing happened to this limestone for nearly half a billion years. It just sat there undisturbed, except for a few hydrothermal events that created large deposits of lead and zinc in some of the limestone.

The formation of Gardner Cave probably began about 2 million years ago when glaciers began to advance and retreat across the landscape of northeastern Washington. There were at least six advances of ice across the United States-Canadian border; as these ice sheets melted they released huge torrents of meltwater. At least some of this meltwater infiltrated the limestone and began to dissolve great cavities in the rock underground. By the beginning of the most recent ice advance about 20,000 years ago, there was a well-developed cave system here and part of the near surface portions collapsed under the weight of the advancing ice.

Right now the cave is in a period of transition. There is not enough water for active erosion, so as ground water trickles down from above, deposition dominates, creating stalactites and stalagmites and other unusual cave deposits that you will see on this hike.

According to local legend, the cave was discovered in 1899 by Ed Gardner, a bootlegger, who lost it in a card game in 1921 to Bill Crawford, who in turn donated the land to the state park system.

Trail Guide: Turn left off SR 31 just north of Metaline and follow the Boundary Road 11 miles north to a parking area in Crawford State Park. You can only

This flowstone in Gardner Cave is called "The Christmas Tree."

visit Garnder Cave as part of a guided tour. Park rangers offer free tours every 2 hours, 10 A.M. to 4 P.M., Thursday through Monday from May through September. You might also want to take the side road to Boundary Dam on the way in or out. Tours of an underground powerhouse are offered here on about the same schedule as the tours of Gardner Cave.

The trail to the cave begins at the northeast end of the parking lot. The route to the cave entrance is barrier free. There is a paved walkway through the cave, but the route underground involves several stairways.

From the parking lot, follow the paved trail climbing a moderate slope to a sinkhole that allows access to the cave. The entrance consists of a set of stairs that winds down about 30 feet to the beginning of a long traverse underground. Although Gardner Cave is small by Carlsbad Cavern standards, it is claimed to be the second longest cavern in Washington and, in less than 500 feet, it displays most of the features found in much larger caves.

As you enter the cave, you will go down a set of stairs into the Grotto. As you descend, notice the Waterfall, a formation of flowstone and dripstone that is active in the spring, but dries out in the late summer. At the base of the stairs on the right is a somewhat bizarre Christmas Tree, which has an age date of 90,000 years. Nearby is the Pipe Organ that consists of stalactites colored orange and brown by iron oxides. Before becoming a state park, Gardner Cave was repeatedly vandalized by visitors who had no concept of its value. Nature will eventually repair the damage, but it will take hundreds or even thousands of years to complete the job.

The next major feature is the Beehives consisting of bulbous stalactites on the ceiling and stalagmites on the ground underneath. Below on the right, just beyond a bridge, are the Fried Eggs. These are small circular stalagmites colored by iron oxides. To the left of the second bridge is dark flowstone known as the Polar Bear Foot that reaches out toward the trail from a small side passage. There are also columns called the Calcite Castle and Cave Bacon, a reddish striped flowstone. Further down on the right is the Buddha, a formation stained blue-gray by innumerable handprints patting the "stomach" for luck.

At the second set of stairs, look to the right to see one of the biological components of the cave, a packrat nest made of twigs and abundant guano droppings left by the inhabitants. Just ahead is the Cave Frog which hangs upside down from the ceiling, and a series of terraced pools called gours. One hypothesis for their origin is that as calcite-saturated cave water flows over rapids it is agitated, causing carbon dioxide to be given off, which results in calcite deposition creating the lip of a dam. The dam increases the agitation so that even more deposition occurs until a pool is eventually formed.

As you descend the third set of stairs look up to see Soda Straws, also known as tubular stalactites, on the ceiling. These begin when the surface of a drop of ground water is in contact with the ceiling rock. The calcite there is deposited as a tiny ring around the outer surface of the drop. The next drop also precipitates around the surface of the ring and eventually a hollow tube is formed. Also note the white stripes on the floor of the cave where soda straws have broken off and fallen to the ground.

Just before the fourth set of stairs leading to a platform at the end of the cave, there is a huge column where a stalactite has grown down from the ceiling to meet a stalagmite growing up from the floor. Look carefully to see cave bugs encapsulated by the precipitated calcite. Within the heart of this column, there may be bugs as much as a million years old preserved—almost like the mosquitoes of Jurassic Park.

Hike 54

HELLS CANYON

Hike up to a ridge between the Grande Ronde and Snake Rivers to see an exotic terrane in Washington's southeast corner.

DISTANCE ■ 5 miles

ELEVATION ■ Start, 858 feet; high point (Lime Hill), 2922 feet; destination, 2400 feet

DIFFICULTY ■ Difficult

TOPOGRAPHIC MAP ■ USGS Limekiln Rapids (ID-WA)

GEOLOGIC MAP ■ DGER GM-40 Southeast Asotin County

KEY REFERENCES ■ Reidel and others (1992); Vallier (1998)

PRECAUTIONS ■ The first part of this hike is steep. There is unlikely to be shade or water anywhere along the route. Look out for poison oak and rattlesnakes. A topographic map is highly recommended.

About the Landscape: Hells Canyon of the Snake River is famous for its whitewater and for being the deepest canyon in North America. From the summit of He Devil (9393 feet) in Idaho's Seven Devils Mountains, it is more than 8000 feet down to the Snake River (in a horizontal distance of just over 5 miles). This hike begins 1 mile from the mouth of the Grande Ronde River; you ascend to the ridge between the Grande Ronde River to the west and the lower part of Hells Canyon to the east.

Most of the visible rock is Miocene basalt flows typical of the Blue Mountains, including the Imnaha Basalt, the oldest unit of the Columbia River basalts. But you will also walk on an exotic terrane—a bunch of rocks that formed far away in the ancestral Pacific Ocean and were later accreted to North America. These rocks have fossils indicating that they originated near the equator. This is confirmed by paleomagnetic evidence.

This particular exotic terrane, the Wallowa terrane, is one of many in the Blue Mountains region of northeastern Oregon. These exotic terranes are exposed in two places in the southeasternmost part of Washington: here in lower Hells Canyon, and on the approach to Hike 50. The Wallowa terrane is composed of volcanic and sedimentary rocks that were part of an island arc like those in today's western Pacific Ocean. The island arc existed more than 200 million years ago, and plate tectonic forces added it to North America more than 100 million years ago.

Trail Guide: Set your trip odometer at 0.0 in Clarkston at the intersection of US 12 and SR 129. Follow SR 129 up the west bank of the Snake River to the stop sign in Anatone at mile 6.2. Between Clarkston and Asotin the prominent rock (Swallow Rock) above the highway is an intracanyon basalt, lava that flowed down an ancient canyon; it is thick and narrow in contrast with the generally thin widespread lava flows of the Columbia Basin. On the opposite side of the river is a giant gravel bar with huge gravel pits; this is Tammany Bar, deposited by the flood from Lake Bonneville (a much larger version of Utah's Great Salt Lake) about 14,500 years ago.

After the stop sign in Asotin, continue south on Snake River Road. The fine-grained white material in scattered roadcuts is Mazama ash from the explosive eruption that formed Crater Lake in southwestern Oregon about 7000 years ago. At mile 20.6, the pavement turns to gravel, and mile 20.9 is an excellent stop for geology and archeology. The rock here is the Wild Sheep Creek Formation which is Triassic in age (about 230 million years old). This part of the Wild Sheep Creek Formation is weakly metamorphosed basalt. The outcrop was sandblasted by the Snake River in flood during pre-dam times. Also, there is desert varnish (a coating of clays and iron and manganese oxides). Native Americans drew petroglyphs on the rock by chipping off the desert varnish.

At mile 29, pass the Heller Bar Recreation Site parking lot. Ahead is the mouth of the Grande Ronde River and the community of Rogersburg, which is built on gravels of the Bonneville flood. Continue along the dirt road that lies on the northwest side of the curves of the Grande Ronde River. These are incised meanders; the river has kept its meandering pattern while cutting more than 2800 feet into the lava flows (see Hike 52).

Cross the bridge over the Grande Ronde River at mile 31.8. Due west is the type locality of the Miocene Grande Ronde Basalt which forms the bulk of the Columbia River basalts. A type locality is a place where there is good exposure of a rock unit for a detailed description. Large volumes of lava of this formation (the Grande Ronde Basalt) were erupted in a relatively short time period about 16 million years ago.

On the south side of the bridge, the road climbs the narrow core of an incised meander. At mile 32.1, turn left toward Rogersburg and follow the road along the south side of the Grande Ronde River. At mile 33.2 there is an exposure at an intermittent stream and an old road. From youngest (top) to oldest (bottom) there are Mazama ash, loess, slackwater sediments of the floods from glacial Lake Missoula, and ancient gravels of the Grande Ronde River. From here the road leads north past two red towers (left, mile 33.7) toward a cliff and a locked gate at mile 34.1. Find a parking place in the last 0.5 mile before the gate.

Walk east across modern alluvium of the Grande Ronde River and fine-grained sediments deposited by the Missoula floods. Ascend northeast up the largest gully (cut in the Imnaha Basalt) to the crest of an asymmetric ridge (the ridge trends northwest and is steep on the gully side and gentle on the Rogersburg side). Climb southeast up the crest of the ridge through lava flows of the Imnaha Basalt. The Imnaha Basalt, having erupted about 17 million years ago, is older than the Grande Ronde Basalt.

At about 1500 feet elevation (helpful to have a map or an altimeter), you can continue southeast up the ridge (Grande Ronde Basalt), but we recommend contouring east along an old road near the contact between the older Imnaha Basalt and the overlying Grande Ronde Basalt. The road swings southeast into a gulch along the Limekiln fault, which strikes south and is near vertical. To the east, the older (Triassic) Martin Bridge Limestone has been upthrown; to the west, the younger (Miocene) Columbia River basalts have been down-dropped (in a relative sense). Considering the thickness of the different geologic units, the fault offset is more than a thousand feet, so that at the same level there are rocks with an age difference of about 200 million years.

As you climb, the old road crosses the gulch (and the fault) six times. On the east there is steeply dipping limestone with different characteristics in different places: massive or bedded, pure or shaly, cavernous or not. On the west there is nearly horizontal Grande Ronde Basalt. The old road leads to a

Lime Hill is between the Snake River (right) and the incised meanders of the Grande Ronde River.

saddle at 2300 feet. The gulch and the saddle are a topographic expression of the erodible zone along the Limekiln fault. (If you're not in a hurry, walk northwest about 100 yards to the top of a small northeast-trending ridge. There is a good view of the mouth of the Grande Ronde River to the north and of incised meanders to the west.)

From the saddle, ascend southeasterly up Lime Hill (2922 feet), composed of Triassic Martin Bridge Limestone. The Snake and Grande Ronde Rivers are more than 2000 feet below you. One mile east is Idaho, and 4 miles south is Oregon. Did you notice the quartzite cobbles and boulders on Lime Hill? Many are stained pink or brown by iron oxides. There are rare other lithologies. Similar quartzites are scattered across northeastern Oregon, including some just below the summit of the highest peak in the Wallowa Mountains (Sacajawea Peak, 9833 feet). The source and age of these gravels is unknown, but they overlie the exotic terrane rocks and underlie the Columbia River basalts. They may be alluvium from an early Tertiary stream system that headed west toward the Pacific Ocean from the ancient Rockies.

Speaking of exotic terranes, what's so exotic about the Martin Bridge Limestone? Limestones (composed of calcium carbonate) are generally deposited within 30 degrees of the equator (e.g., Great Barrier Reef of Australia, Bahama Islands carbonate bank). What's limestone doing at 46 degrees latitude? The answer is plate tectonics. This limestone was deposited in an island arc, probably in the western Pacific within 15 degrees of the equator. It has come a long way, and is mostly deformed (not horizontal as first deposited) and partly metamorphosed to marble.

Descend Lime Hill toward a saddle about 0.5 mile to the south-southwest. You'll encounter an old road that goes south for many miles, contouring around ridges and across draws at about 2600 feet. From the saddle going south there is an unnamed east-flowing intermittent stream, then a ridge, then east-flowing intermittent Anaconda Creek, then another ridge. On the topographic map this second ridge starts at 3273 feet and has elevation points of 2715 feet and 2510 feet as it descends eastward toward Wild Goose Rapids on the Snake River (Birch Creek is to the south of this ridge).

To the east-northeast of the saddle (wrapping around the eastern base of Lime Hill) is the Triassic Doyle Creek Formation, but you're not likely to see the volcaniclastics and metabasalt unless you descend to the cliffs below. The old road stays in the Miocene Imnaha Basalt to past the second ridge; along the way you'll encounter columnar basalt, in places spheroidally weathered. Because corners and edges have more surface area, they weather faster than faces; in time angular joint blocks become rounded.

Leave the road where it crosses the second ridge (the one between Anaconda and Birch Creeks). Follow the ridge east-southeast toward elevation points 2715 feet and 2510 feet. About halfway between these elevation points, you'll drop from the younger basalts to the Wallowa terrane, which here is made up of the Triassic Wild Sheep Creek Formation. This formation includes lots of metabasalt, plus unmetamorphosed basalt, breccia, sandstone, argillite, tuff, and limestone. Follow the ridge past the 2510 feet elevation point; you'll walk on red argillite, purple sandstone, greenstone (metabasalt), and limestone. The Triassic island arc had a variety of volcanic and sedimentary environments.

The end of this hike is at about 2400 feet on the ridge between Anaconda and Birch Creeks. Here is an excellent view up (south) and down (north) Hells Canyon of the Snake River, 1600 feet below you. The unconformity to the east is a textbook example: Columbia River basalts overlying the Wild Sheep Creek Formation, with more than 200 million years of missing history.

To return, when you get to the 2600-foot saddle you can contour along the west side of Lime Hill, gently descending to the 2300-foot saddle at the Limekiln fault. From the 2300-foot saddle you can go northeast, descending into the gulch which you came up; or you can go northwest and descend the ridge west of the gulch, regaining your original route at about 1500 feet.

FIGURE 15

Stratigraphy of the lower Hells Canyon Area

CENOZOIC	Quaternary	Holocene	alluvium, loess, Mazama ash	
		Pleistocene	Touchet Beds (Missoula floods slackwater sediments)	
			Bonneville gravel	
		?	Grande Ronde alluvium	
	Tertiary	Miocene	Columbia River Basalt Group	Grande Ronde Basalt
				Imnaha Basalt
		?	Sediments of Lime Hill	
MESOZOIC	Triassic		Martin Bridge Limestone	
			Doyle Creek Formation	
			Wild Sheep Creek Formation	

Hike 55

CAPE DISAPPOINTMENT

Washington's southwest corner: where the river meets the sea.

DISTANCE ■ South hike, about 0.75 mile; north hike, about 0.75 mile
ELEVATION ■ sea level to 210 feet
DIFFICULTY ■ Easy
TOPOGRAPHIC MAP ■ USGS Cape Disappointment
GEOLOGIC MAP ■ DGER 87-2 Ilwaco
KEY REFERENCE ■ Wells (1989)

About the Landscape: With the possible exception of the Cascade volcanoes, this may be Washington's most dynamic area in terms of geomorphology. Two agents change the landscape with every storm and season: first, the Columbia River, one of the largest entering the Pacific Ocean, transports sediment to the coast and deposits giant sandbars; also, from time to time, the river erodes its banks and bottom. Second, waves travel far across the Pacific Ocean, gently adding sand to beaches, or violently eroding beaches and (over time) even resistant headlands.

The bedrock here is the Eocene Crescent Formation. Mostly it is pillowed and massive basalt that was erupted on the seafloor or oceanic islands. In places there are silty interbeds with marine microfossils.

Cape Disappointment, part of Fort Canby State Park, is rich in history. Pick up a park brochure, which reads:

> In 1788, English explorer Captain John Meares, in seeking the Columbia River, recorded missing the passage over the bar, and in his discouragement named the nearby headland Cape Disappointment.
>
> In 1792, American Captain Robert Gray successfully crossed the river bar and named the river after his ship, the Columbia Rediviva.
>
> To secure America's claim to the area and find overland trade routes, the Lewis and Clark Expedition traveled west, arriving at Cape Disappointment in November 1805.

Trail Guide: Ilwaco is the town farthest southwest in Washington. It can be reached via US 101 from Grays Harbor or Willapa Bay (to the north) or from Astoria, Oregon (to the southeast across the Columbia River). From the west end of Ilwaco, drive 2 miles south along the west side of Baker Bay (a mudflat at low tide). Drive straight at the crossroads near the Fort Canby State Park entrance, then turn right to the parking area for the Lewis and Clark Interpretive Center. The large coniferous trees here and along the trails are Sitka spruce.

Walk uphill to the Lewis and Clark Interpretive Center (restrooms). In front of the interpretive center you're at the top of a sea cliff of the Crescent Formation with a good view to the west and south. To the west is the North Jetty at the mouth of the Columbia River; this jetty, almost 2 miles long, was built about 1916. To the south, across the mouth of the Columbia River (3 miles wide) you may be able to see the South Jetty or surf breaking on it. Funds for the South Jetty, 7 miles long, were appropriated in 1885, but it was not completed until 1936.

There are two important questions to be asked. Why no delta? Why the jetties? Generally, at the mouth of a river sediment is deposited as the water slows, and a delta is built out into the lake or the ocean. Even though there are more than a hundred dams trapping the Columbia River's sediments, tributaries like the Cowlitz and Willamette Rivers supply abundant sediment to the lower Columbia. The simple explanation for the lack of a delta here is waves. The high wave energy of this part of the Pacific Ocean redistributes the sediment carried to the mouth of the Columbia. Some of the sediment is trapped in the estuary (at low tide giant sandbars are visible between here and the Astoria-Megler bridge). And some of the sediment (particularly mud) is transported further west, out onto the continental shelf, down the Astoria (submarine) canyon, and onto the deep ocean floor. But much of the sediment (particularly sand) is (or was) transported north and south by the waves, adding to beaches.

The giant spit just west of Willapa Bay was formed by north-flowing winter currents, and the Clatsop Plains just south of the Columbia's mouth were deposited by south-flowing summer currents. The wave-built beach ridges and wind-deposited dunes in these two places are 5000 years old and younger, and attest to the great amount of sediment the Columbia River has delivered to the coast.

Why the jetties? The shifting sandbars made the river's entrance shallow and unpredictable. Add waves, tides, and currents to understand why there were hundreds of shipwrecks in this area. The intent of the jetties was to narrow the river's mouth, thereby increasing the current velocity, and therefore transporting the sediment further west into deeper water. Also, the east-west oriented jetties greatly reduced the north-south movement of sand. The jetties may have helped shipping, but channel maintenance requires dredging.

The jetties have significantly changed the sediment budgets of the northern Oregon and southern Washington coasts. The prevailing winds are from the southwest, so waves and longshore currents move north most of the time (summer is the exception). The South Jetty acts as a dam to longshore drift to the north; therefore, during the last century beach accretion has increased on the Clatsop Plains. The North Jetty prevents most Columbia River sediment

Behind jetty riprap are sea cliffs of Eocene pillow basalt (topped by Cape Disappointment Lighthouse).

from reaching the Washington coast, which is (overall) suffering beach erosion from here to Gray's Harbor.

South hike (to Cape Disappointment Lighthouse): The trailhead is at the east end of the Lewis and Clark Interpretive Center (or, you can start from the east end of the parking lot). After the trails from the interpretive center and the parking lot join, continue southeast to the northeast end of Deadman Cove, passing southeast of the Coast Guard station. The cove is here because of wave action on erodible rocks, erodible because there are sedimentary rocks and/or a fault here. The sides of the cove are resistant basalt of the Eocene Crescent Formation.

Walk westward down to the pocket beach of sand and driftwood. A pocket beach is small, with bedrock on each side (in contrast with beaches many miles long west of Willapa Bay and along the Clatsop Plain). Look at the basalt on the sides of the cove; fractures in the dark basalt contain veins of minerals such as calcite (calcium carbonate) and zeolites (various silicates). The small island in the cove is a sea stack; the rock (in this case, basalt) is particularly resistant to wave erosion. It's probably calm in the cove now, but with storms out of the southwest, waves enter here, slowly eroding the basalt and depositing the beach.

Climb up from the beach and turn south to the narrow concrete road. Walk up the hill to the Cape Disappointment Lighthouse, the oldest lighthouse still in use on the West Coast. It began operating in 1856.

North hike (to Waikiki Beach): The trailhead for the Discovery Trail is just west of the Lewis and Clark Interpretive Center. This hike goes northwest along the top of the basalt sea cliff. Walk straight at the first junction (the road is to the right), but take the short side trail (left) at the second junction. Go up the concrete steps for a panoramic view (weather permitting). To the south are the South Jetty and northwestern Oregon. To the west is the North Jetty with a sand plain on the far side. McKenzie Head is the resistant basalt hill to the northwest; it appears to be a former sea stack (shaped by erosion) surrounded by sand deposited by waves and wind. To the north of McKenzie Head is another basalt hill, and further northwest is North Head (with a lighthouse built in 1898). All of these high areas of basalt (including the place where you're standing) have southwest-facing cliffs cut by waves. This former coastline has been abandoned as the sandy plain has grown westward. According to local people, all of this sand has accumulated since the North Jetty was constructed, and the beach is currently undergoing erosion.

Return to the Discovery Trail and continue northwest. Eventually the trail descends northeastward from the ridge toward the park office and entrance. Go west from the trail and carefully climb down the cliff toward a picnic ground. This old quarry face is worth looking at carefully. It has rounded basalt masses about 2 feet in diameter; each pillow has a glassy rind about a half inch thick. This is pillow basalt of the Eocene Crescent Formation. Pillows indicate a basaltic magma that has erupted under water: the glassy rind is lava that cooled instantly when it contacted sea water; the pillow cracked, more lava squirted from the crack, and another pillow formed, etc.

From the old quarry walk south to the east end of Waikiki Beach. This sea cliff is a good place to study the Crescent Formation. Marine basalts (some with pillows) and sedimentary rocks were deposited on a horizontal seafloor about 50 million years ago. The strata were steeply tilted as plate tectonic forces shoved them against the western edge of North America.

From the west end of Waikiki Beach (near the riprap forming the east end of the North Jetty) is a view southeast along the coast toward Cape Disappointment Lighthouse. Notice several big holes in the sea cliff; these are sea caves formed where waves crash against the more erodible parts of the cliff.

CAPE FLATTERY

Hike

56

Walk through an old growth forest to one of the most spectacular seascapes in the world. Soaring cliffs, an offshore lighthouse, sea caves that you could drive a boat through—with a lot of courage—all of this and remarkable rocks as well.

DISTANCE ■ 1 mile

ELEVATION ■ 300 feet to 200 feet

DIFFICULTY ■ Easy

TOPOGRAPHIC MAPS ■ USGS Cape Flattery Quadrangle; Custom Correct North Olympic Coast

GEOLOGIC MAP ■ USGS I-1946

KEY REFERENCES ■ Shilhanek (1992); Snavely and others (1989); Snavely and others (1993)

PRECAUTIONS ■ Be careful on the sea cliffs. Stay within the guardrails.

About the Landscape: After the immense outpouring of Crescent basalts (Hikes 3, 5, and 55) ended, this volcanic terrane was driven northward by plate tectonic forces and jammed underneath the southern margin of what is now Vancouver Island. One result of this underthrusting was a deep depression, known to geologists as the Tofino-Fuca Basin. During late Eocene to Miocene time, the basin was gradually filled with sediments delivered by rivers flowing mainly from source areas to the north and northeast in British Columbia. About 44 to 42 million years ago, the Tofino-Fuca Basin consisted of a narrow area of shallow water terminated by submarine cliffs dropping off almost vertically for a thousand feet or more. The Cape Flattery breccia consists of angular blocks of sedimentary, igneous, and metamorphic rock that tumbled off these cliffs onto a sandy shoreline, and then were carried by great submarine avalanches down into the depths of the basin.

Clearly the Cape Flattery area has been lifted out of the sea to form the dramatic cliffs that dominate the landscape today. This could be due to rebound as the Cordilleran Ice Sheet retreated or to tectonic uplift related to the Cascadia subduction zone. But eventually the persistent erosion of the waves crashing on shore will straighten the shoreline so that the wild headlands and bays of the North Coast will be transformed into the subdued sandy beaches of Ocean Shores. The only hope for topographic salvation is continued subduction of the Juan de Fuca Plate.

Trail Guide: Take SR 112 to Neah Bay. At the west end of town, turn left and follow the signs to Cape Flattery. At about 3.3 miles the pavement turns into a rough dirt road. Continue 4.6 miles and turn left into a large parking area at the trailhead. This very well maintained trail is all downhill on the way in, and a moderate climb on the way back out. Boardwalks take you across the bogs and recently added guardrails will be appreciated by those prone to vertigo.

The beginning of the hike gives no clue to what you will see at the end. After driving more than 5 miles over an unpaved, seriously potholed road you end up in this unattractive potholed parking lot. If this is your first hike, you are now seriously questioning your investment in this field guide. Have faith and start walking down an old overgrown roadbed that was created when this tip of Washington was part of a strategic defense network intended to provide an early warning of enemy attack on the United States.

Hopefully you will appreciate the outstanding trail construction, with board-walks through the bogs and cedar stairs down the steep slopes. For the first 0.5 mile, the only geology to be seen is the soil developed on a thin veneer of glacial drift deposited during the last glatiation. About 0.5 mile from the trailhead a huge blowdown proves that the veneer is indeed quite thin because the roots of this tree have been ripped right out of bedrock. This is a good place to examine the Cape Flattery breccia, which is the bedrock in this area. A breccia is a rock type that looks a lot like concrete; big pebbles surrounded by sand. In a breccia the pebbles are angular rather than rounded. To be geologically correct, you should call these blocks of rock clasts, rather than pebbles. Careful examination reveals that the clasts consist of a variety of igneous, sedimentary,

Cliffs perforated by sea caves and sea arches form the dramatic shoreline of Cape Flattery at the northwest corner of Washington state.

and metamorphic rocks that probably came mostly from Vancouver Island.

Continuing along the trail through giant cedars and Douglas fir, you finally reach a point of land that projects out into the sea toward Tatoosh Island. If you fear heights do not go any further, because the trail now threads its way out onto a very steep, very narrow headland that drops precipitously off into the ocean below. As the trail comes onto the headland, there is an overlook to the north where you can get a spectacular view of sea caves that have been eroded into the cliffs along fractures which cut through the Cape Flattery breccia. Some of these caves are connected and are big enough that only the daring can take a kayak into one and out the other. At the end of the trail a platform provides a view toward the lighthouse at Tatoosh Island. The sea cliffs cut into the breccia reveal that some of the clasts are huge—up to the size of small automobiles. This indicates that these rocks were probably deposited in exactly the same setting that exists today—steep sea cliffs dropping off rapidly into deep water.

Glossary

ablation. All processes by which snow and ice are lost from a glacier, including melting, evaporation, and calving of icebergs.

allochthonous. Refers to something formed elsewhere than its present location. Antonym of *autochthonous.*

alluvial fan. A low, fan-shaped deposit of stream sediment.

alluvium. Sediments deposited by streams.

amphibolite. A metamorphic rock containing mostly hornblende and calcium feldspar.

amygdaloidal. A rock containing numerous gas cavities that have been filled with secondary minerals such as calcite or zeolites.

andesite. Igneous volcanic rock, intermediate between basalt and dacite; volcanic equivalent of diorite.

angle of repose. The maximum slope that loose sediment can sustain without sliding.

antecedent stream. A stream that existed prior to local uplift.

anticline. A fold of rock layers that is arch-shaped. Antonym of *syncline.*

arête. A sharp-edged ridge forming the boundary between two glacial valleys.

argillite. A compact rock that shows evidence of recrystallization but no development of foliation—formed by very weak metamorphism of shale or siltstone.

autochthonous. Refers to something formed in its present location. Antonym of *allochthonous.*

basalt. Mafic igneous volcanic rock, typically fine-grained and dark in color; volcanic equivalent of gabbro.

batholith. A mass of plutonic rock that is exposed over an area of more than 40 square miles.

bedrock. General term referring to the rock underlying unconsolidated material.

blueschist. Metamorphic rock formed under great pressures, but not so great temperatures.

bread-crust bomb. A type of volcanic bomb (molten ejecta) characterized by a network of shrinkage fractures on the surface that resemble bread crust.

breccia. A rock consisting of large, angular rock fragments embedded in a finer-grained matrix.

calcareous. Containing or composed of calcium carbonate.

caliche. A crust of calcium carbonate commonly found in soils of arid regions.

carbonate. Sediment, or rocks formed by sediment, derived from the precipitation of calcium, magnesium, or iron carbonates ($CaCO_3$, $MgCO_3$, or $FeCO_3$), either from inorganic or organic sources. For example, limestone or dolomite.

chert. Hard, dense cryptocrystalline sedimentary rock, composed of interlocking quartz crystals and possibly amorphous silica (opal). The origin of the silica is normally biological, from diatoms, radiolaria, or sponge spicules. Synonymous with *flint.*

cirque. The head of a glacial valley, commonly shaped like a half-bowl with steep walls.

clast. An individual grain or constituent of a rock.

col. A high, narrow pass in a mountain range due to glacial erosion.

colonnade. A row of large prismatic columns generally in the lower part of a lava flow.

columnar joints. Parallel prismatic columns in lava flows formed by contraction during cooling.

compression. Forces that decrease the volume, thickness, or length of a rock or fossil.

conglomerate. A coarse-grained sedimentary rock, with rounded clasts larger than 2 millimeters.

contact. The boundary between two different rock types.

cross-bedding. Beds deposited at an angle to the horizontal—usually in sand dunes or stream deltas.

crust. The outermost layer of the earth, typically 3 to 45 miles thick, representing less than 1 percent of the earth's volume.

dacite. Igneous volcanic rock, intermediate between rhyolite and andesite, typically fine-grained and light in color; rough volcanic equivalent of granodiorite.

deflation. The removal of clay, silt, or sand particles by wind erosion.

deposition. Any accumulation of material, by mechanical settling from ice, water, or air; chemical precipitation; evaporation from solution; etc.

dextral transpression. A kind of fault movement where blocks are moving side-by-side and towards the right of each other.

differential weathering. When some minerals are more susceptible to weathering than those surrounding them, pits or channels are created in rock where the susceptible minerals occur.

dike. A sheet of igneous rock that cross-cuts layers of surrounding rock.

diorite. Igneous plutonic rock containing about half dark minerals and half light minerals; plutonic equivalent of andesite.

dip. The angle that a bedding plane or fault makes with the horizontal when measured perpendicular to the strike of the bedding plane or fault.

discharge. The rate of flow of a stream—or—a place where groundwater flows out at the surface.

drift. Sediment transported and deposited either by a glacier or by glacial meltwater.

entablature. The upper part of a lava flow consisting of relatively thin columnar joints compared to the colonnade below.

eolian. Pertaining to the wind or deposits by the wind.

epicenter. Point on the earth's surface directly above the focus of an earthquake.

erosion. Processes by water, ice, and wind responsible for the removal of materials of the earth's crust.

erratic. A rock carried by a glacier far enough from its source to be deposited on a different rock type.

exfoliation. A type of weathering that involves sheets of rock peeling off like layers of an onion.

exotic terrane. A terrane that has generally been moved hundreds or thousands of miles from its origin.

fault. A fracture in rocks along which there has been movement of one side relative to the other.

fjord. A long, deep, narrow arm of the sea, carved by a glacier and drowned by rising sea level.

fold. Bent rock strata.

foliation. The parallel alignment of mineral grains in metamorphic rocks.

fossil. Any evidence of past life, including remains, traces, imprints as well as life history artifacts. Examples of artifacts include fossilized bird's nests, bee hives, etc.

gabbro. Mafic igneous plutonic rock, typically dark in color; rough plutonic equivalent of basalt.

glaciomarine drift. Sediment deposited in the sea by a tidewater glacier and/or icebergs.

glass. A noncrystalline rock that results from very rapid cooling of magma.

gneiss. A metamorphic rock with alternating bands of light and dark minerals.

graben. An elongate block of crust that has been dropped down along faults on either side.

graded bedding. A type of bedding in which each layer shows a progressive change upward from coarse to fine sediment.

granite. Felsic igneous plutonic rock, typically light in color; plutonic equivalent of rhyolite. The term is commonly applied to any quartz-bearing plutonic rock.

granodiorite. A plutonic rock intermediate between granite and diorite.

graywacke. Dark-colored sandstone composed of poorly sorted rock fragments mixed wth clay.

greenschist. A foliated metamorphic rock consisting mostly of chlorite, epidote, and actinolite.

greenstone. A metamorphosed basalt with no distinct foliation.

horn. A high pointed peak bounded by three or more cirques formed by glacial erosion.

hornfels. A compact rock without foliation formed by thermal metamorphism.

ice age. Period of extensive glacial activity (i.e. the Pleistocene epoch).

ice sheet. A glacier with an area of more than 20,000 square miles that is thick enough to spread in all directions, regardless of the underlying topography.

igneous rock. Any rock solidified from molten or partly molten material.

interglacial. A period of relatively warm climate between two glacial epochs or stages.

intrusive breccia. Blocks of wallrock found along the margin of a plutonic rock.

joint. A planar fracture generally formed by expansion of rock masses, but due to contraction in lavas.

jökulhlaup. An Icelandic word for a large flood of meltwater that bursts out from a glacier.

kettle. A bowl shaped depression in till or outwash formed by melting of a block of stagnant ice.

lahar. An Indonesian word for a debris flow originating on the flanks of a volcano.

lava. Molten rock at the surface of the earth.

lava cast. A hole formed by vaporization of vegetation (i.e. tree trunks) engulfed by lava.

lava tube. A tunnel formed when lava solidifies except for a molten interior that continues to flow.

limestone. A chemical sedimentary rock composed of more than 50 percent of calcium carbonate ($CaCO_3$).

lineament. A linear topographic feature of regional extent that indicates an underlying structure such as a fault.

liquefaction. Transformation of loosely packed sediments into a liquid, generally due to shaking during an earthquake.

loess. A blanket deposit of wind-blown silt.

longshore current. A current parallel to the shore caused by waves breaking at an angle to the shoreline.

magma. Molten rock below the surface of the earth.

mantle. That portion of the interior of the earth that lies between the crust and the core.

mass wasting. A general term for the downslope movement of soil and rock due to gravity.

melange. A body of rocks consisting of large blocks of different rocks jumbled together with little continuity and surrounded by a fine matrix.

metamorphic rock. Any rock derived from other rocks by chemical, mineralogical, and structural changes resulting from pressure, temperature, or shearing stress.

microfossils. Fossil forms so small that a microscope is required for identification.

migmatite. A complex mixture of light and dark rock. Commonly the light rock is igneous or hydrothermal and the dark rock is metamorphic.

monolith. A large upstanding mass of rock.

moraine. A ridge of till deposited by a glacier.

oceanic crust. The earth's crust which is formed at mid-oceanic ridges, typically 3 to 5 miles thick.

olistostrome. A lens-like sedimentary deposit consisting of a chaotic mass of blocks embedded in a fine-grained matrix.

orthogneiss. A gneiss formed by recrystallization of a plutonic rock.

outcrop. Any place where bedrock is visible on the surface of the earth.

outwash. Sediments deposited by glacial meltwater.

pahoehoe. A Hawaiian name for lava flows with a smooth or ropelike surface.

paleosol. Soil horizon from the geologic past.

pegmatite. An igneous or hydrothermal rock with a grain size greater than about 1 inch.

phenocryst. A large crystal in a fine-grained matrix found in an igneous rock.

pillow lava. Lava extruded beneath water characterized by pillowlike shapes.

plagiogranite. A group of rocks with low potassium content, ranging from granites with only plagioclase feldspar to diorite.

plates. Rigid parts of the earth's crust and part of the earth's upper mantle that move and adjoin each other along zones of seismic activity.

plate techtonics. The history of plate movements in a region and the geologic consequences.

plug. A pipe-like body of volcanic rock that represents the path of magma to a volcanic vent now destroyed by erosion.

pluton. A large mass of plutonic rock.

plutonic. Applies to igneous rocks formed beneath the surface of the earth, typically with large crystals due to the slowness of cooling.

pothole. A bowl or cylinder-shaped hole in the bedrock of a streambed or intertidal zone formed by the erosive action of sand or gravel being swirled by currents.

pumice. A volcanic rock so full of gas bubbles that it will float on water.

pyroclastic. Fragments of volcanic rock formed by explosive eruptions.

quartz-monzonite. A light-colored plutonic rock intermediate between granite and granodiorite.

regolith. Loose rock material or soil at the surface of the earth.

rhyolite. Felsic igneous volcanic rock, typically light in color; rough volcanic equivalent of granite.

sandstone. Sedimentary rock composed of sand-sized clasts.

schist. A metamorphic rock with distinct foliation and visible mineral grains.

sea stack. A pillar of rock rising offshore that remains after wave erosion of less resistant surrounding rock.

sediment. Any solid material that has settled out of a state of suspension in liquid.

sedimentary rock. Any rock resulting from the hardening of sediment.

shield volcano. A large volcano with gentle slopes consisting predominantly of basalt flows.

shore drift. Sediment, such as sand and shells, that is moved by currents parallel to the shoreline.

skarn. A thermal metamorphic rock consisting of carbonates and calcium silicates.

slickensides. A polished fault surface, commonly with slickenlines—which are grooves or scratches showing the direction of fault movement.

slump. A type of landslide involving rotational movement on a curved slip surface.

soil. Loose materials above bedrock.

spit. Small point or finger-like extension of sand or gravel deposited by waves and longshore currents and having one end attached to the mainland.

stade. A readvance of a glacier during a stage of glaciation.

stratovolcano. A volcano consisting of alternating lava flows and pyroclastic layers.

strata. A layer of sedimentary rock.

stratified. Consisting of layers of rock or sediment.

strike. The direction or trend of a bedding plane or fault, as it intersects the horizontal.

subduction. The process of one plate descending beneath another.

subsidence. The slow to sudden settling of the earth's surface with little or no horizontal motion.

syncline. A fold of rock layers that is bent downwards into a trough shape.

talus. Rock fragments derived from and accumulated at the base of a cliff or steep rocky slope.

tarn. A high mountain cirque lake gouged out of bedrock by glacial erosion.

tectonics. Processes, such as folding or faulting, that tend to build up the surface of the earth, as opposed to erosion, which tends to tear it down.

terrane. A fault-bounded body of rock of regional extent that has a different geologic history than adjacent rocks. Terranes are generally considered to be allocthonous fragments of continental or oceanic crust that may have been transported tens to thousands of miles by plate tectonic processes.

thermoluminescence. A method of dating recent sediments by heating the material and measuring the light emitted.

till. Unlayered and unsorted sediments deposited directly by a glacier.

tombolo. A sand or gravel bar that connects an island with the mainland or another island.

trimline. A sharp line of vegetation or rock weathering in a glacial valley showing the depth of ice during a recent glacial maximum.

tsunami. A wave produced by sudden undersea displacement, generally related to earthquakes.

tufa. A hot or cold spring deposit consisting of porous calcium carbonate.

tuff. Volcanic rock formed from ash hardened into solid rock.

turbidite. Sediment or rock deposited by a turbidity current associated with a submarine avalanche.

unconformity. A gap in the geologic record where nondeposition and/or erosion occurred between the accumulation of two rock units.

ultramafic. Rocks that consist of at least 90 percent of olivine, pyroxene, or hornblende—or any combination of these minerals.

vent. The opening at the earth's surface through which volcanic materials are extruded.

vesicle. A cavity in a volcanic rock formed by entrapment of a gas bubble during solidification.

volcanic. Applies to igneous rocks that cool on the surface of the earth, including beneath water; typically with small crystals due to the rapidity of cooling. Synonym of *extrusive.*

volcaniclastic. Sediment derived from the weathering and erosion of volcanic rocks.

volcanic neck. The eroded remnants of a volcanic vent.

water gap. A deep pass in a mountain ridge through which a stream flows.

welded tuff. Ash that is extruded at such a high temperature that it is fused together into a solid rock mass.

Appendix A: General References

GENERAL GEOLOGY

Alt, D. D., and D. W. Hyndman. 1984. *Roadside geology of Washington.* Missoula, MT: Mountain Press.

Ashbaugh, J. G., ed. 1994. *The Pacific Northwest: Geographical perspectives.* Dubuque, Iowa: Kendall/Hunt Publishing Co.

———. 1995. *Northwest exposures: A geologic story of the Northwest.* Missoula, MT: Mountain Press.

Bates, R. L., and J. A. Jackson. 1984. *Dictionary of geologic terms.* Alexandria, VA.: American Geological Institute.

Dietrich, William. 1995. *Northwest passage: The great Columbia River.* New York: Simon & Schuster.

Galster, R. W., ed. 1989. *Engineering geology in Washington.* 2 vols. Washington Division of Geology and Earth Resources.

Halliday, W. R. 1963. *Caves of Washington.* Washington Division of Mines and Geology Information Circular 40.

Harris, S. L. 1980. *Fire and ice: The Cascade volcanoes.* Seattle, Wash.: The Mountaineers Books.

Hartman, W. K., and Ron Miller. 1991. *The history of earth: An illustrated chronicle of an evolving planet.* New York: Workman Publishing.

Joseph, N. L, ed. 1989. *Geologic guidebook for Washington and adjacent areas.* Washington Division of Geology and Earth Resources Information Circular 86.

Lasmanis, Raymond, and E. S. Cheney, eds. 1994. *Regional geology of Washington State.* Washington Division of Geology and Earth Resources Bulletin 80.

Majors, H. M. 1975. *Exploring Washington.* Holland, Mich.: Van Winkle Publishing Co.

Easterbrook, D. J., and D. A. Rahm. 1970. *Landforms of Washington: The geologic environment.* Bellingham, Wash.: Union Printing Co.

McKee, Bates. 1972. *Cascadia: The geologic evolution of the Pacific Northwest.* New York: McGraw-Hill.

Orr, E. L., and W. N. Orr. 1996. *Geology of the Pacific Northwest.* New York: McGraw-Hill.

Schuster, J. E., ed. 1987. *Selected papers on the geology of Washington.* Washington Division of Geology and Earth Resources Bulletin 77.

Washington Division of Geology and Earth Resources. *Washington Geology.* Published quarterly. (P.O. Box 47007, Olympia, WA 98504-7007).

GENERAL MAPS

Huntting, M. T., W. A. G. Bennett, V. E. Livingston, and W. S. Moen. 1961. *Geologic map of Washington* (scale 1:500,000). Washington Division of Mines and Geology.

Schuster, J. E., C. W. Gulick, S. P. Reidel, K. R. Fecht, and Stephanie Zurenko. 1997. *Geologic map of Washington—southeast quadrant* (scale 1:250,000). Washington

Division of Geology and Earth Resources Geologic Map GM-45.

Stoeffel, K. L., N. L. Joseph, S. Z. Waggoner, C. W. Gulick, M. A. Korosec, and B. B. Bunning. 1991. *Geologic map of Washington—northeast quadrant* (scale 1:250,000). Washington Division of Geology and Earth Resources Geologic Map GM-39.

Walsh, T. J., M. A. Korosec, W. M. Phillips, R. L. Logan, and H. W. Schasse. 1987. *Geologic map of Washington—southwest quadrant* (scale 1:250,000). Washington Division of Geology and Earth Resources Geologic Map GM-34.

ONLINE TOPOGRAPHIC AND GEOLOGIC MAP SOURCES

Division of Geology and Earth Resources (DGER)
P.O. Box 47007
Olympia, Washington 98504-7007
www.wa.gov/dnr/htdocs/ger/publist.htm

U.S. Geological Survey
Spokane Earth Science Information Center U.S. Post Office Building, Room 135
904 West Riverside Avenue
Spokane, WA 99201
www-nmd.usgs.gov/esic/to_order.htm

MAP LISTS

mapping.usgs.gov/mac/map/maplist/index.htm
ngmdb.usgs.gov/ngmdb/ngm_catalog.ora.htm

DIGITAL ELEVATION MODELS (DEMS)

duff.geology.washington.edu/data/raster/tenmeter/ asciidemzip/index.html
edc.usgs/gov/glis/hyper/guide/1_dgr_demfig/ index1m.html

Appendix B: Key References

COAST RANGES

Atwater, B. W., and E. Hemphill-Haley. 1997. *Recurrence intervals for great earthquakes of the past 3500 years at northeastern Willapa Bay, Washington.* U.S. Geological Survey Professional Paper 1576.

Babcock, R. S., R. F. Burmester, D. C. Engebretson, A. C. Warnock, and K. P. Clark. 1992. A rifted margin origin for the Crescent Basalts and related rocks in the northern Coast Range volcanic province, Washington and British Columbia. *Journal of Geophysical Research* 97:6799–821.

Babcock, R. S., C. A. Suczek, and D. C. Engebretson. 1994. *The Crescent "terrane," Olympic Peninsula and southern Vancouver Island.* Washington Department of Natural Resources, Division of Geology and Earth Resources Bulletin 80.

Danner, W. R. 1955. *Geology of Olympic National Park.* Seattle, Wash.: University of Washington Press.

Gelfenbaum, G., G. Kaminsky, R. Sherwood, and C. Peterson. 1997. *Southwest Washington coastal erosion workshop report.* U.S. Geological Survey Open File Report 97-471.

Orange, D. L., D. S. Geddes, and J.C. Moore. 1993. Structural and fluid evolution of a young accretionary complex: The Hoh rock assemblage of the western Olympic Peninsula, Washington. *Geological Society of America Bulletin* 105:1053–75.

Rau, W.W. 1979. *Geologic map in the vicinity of the lower Bogachiel and Hoh River valleys, and the Washington coast* (scale 1:62,500). Washington Division of Geology and Earth Resources Geologic Map GM-24.

———. 1980. *Washington coastal geology between the Hoh and Quillayute Rivers.* Washington Division of Geology and Earth Resources Bulletin 72.

Scharf, J. W., and J. G. Wilkerson. n.d. *Geologic guide to the Hurricane Ridge area.* Seattle, Wash.: Pacific Northwest National Parks and Forests Association.

Schwartz, M. L., P. Fabbri, and R. S. Wallace. 1987. Geomorphology of Dungeness Spit, Washington, USA. *Journal of Coastal Research* 3:451–5.

Suczek, C. A., R. S. Babcock, and D. C. Engebretson. 1994. Tectonostratigraphy of the Crescent Terrane and related rocks, Olympic Peninsula, Washington. In *Geologic field trips in the Pacific Northwest.* Seattle, Wash: Geological Society of America Annual Meeting.

Tabor, R. W. 1987. *Guide to the geology of Olympic National Park.* Seattle, Wash.: University of Washington Press.

Tabor, R. W., and W. M. Cady. 1978. *Geologic map of the Olympic Peninsula, Washington* (scale 1:125,000). U.S. Geological Survey Miscellaneous Investigation Series Map I-994.

PUGET LOWLAND AND THE SAN JUAN ISLANDS

Berg, A. W. 1990. Formation of Mima mounds: A seismic hypothesis. *Geology* 18:281–4.

Brandon, M., D. S. Cowan, and J. G. Feehan. 1994. Fault-zone structures and solution mass-transfer cleavage in Late Cretaceous nappes, San Juan Islands, Washington. In *Geologic field trips in the Pacific Northwest.* Seattle, Wash: Geological Society of America Annual Meeting.

Brandon, M. T., D. S. Cowan, and J. A. Vance. 1988. *The Late Cretaceous San Juan thrust system, San Juan Islands, Washington.* Geological Society of America Special Paper 221. Geological Society of America.

Brown, E. H., J. Y. Bradshaw, and G. E. Mustoe. 1979. Plagiogranite and keratophyre in ophiolite on Fidalgo Island, Washington. *Geological Society of America Bulletin* 90:1493–507.

Easterbrook, D. J. 1994. Chronology of pre-late Wisconsin Pleistocene sediments in the Puget Lowland, Washington. In *Regional geology of Washington State.* Washington Division of Geology and Earth Resources Bulletin 80: 191–206.

Galster, R. W., W. T. LaPrade, and B. R. Beaman. 1994. Engineering geology of Seattle and vicinity. In *Geologic field trips in the Pacific Northwest.* Seattle, Wash: Geological Society of America Annual Meeting.

Gusey, D. L., and E. H. Brown. 1989. The Fidalgo ophiolite, Washington. *Geological Society of America Centennial Field Guide* 1 (Cordilleran Section):389–92.

Johnson, S. Y., C. M. Potter, and others. 1996. The southern Whidbey Island fault: An active structure in the Puget Lowland, Washington. *Geological Society of America Bulletin* 108:334–54.

Mullineaux, D. R. 1965. *Geologic map of the Black Diamond quadrangle, King County, Washington* (scale 1:100,000). U.S. Geological Survey Geologic Quadrangle Map GQ-407.

Mullineaux, D. R., H. H. Waldron, and M. Rubin. 1965. *Stratigraphy and chronology of late interglacial and early Vashon time in the Seattle area.* U.S. Geological Survey Bulletin 1194-O.

Nelson, R. E. 1997. Implications of subfossil Coleoptera for the evolution of the Mima Mounds of southwestern Puget Lowland, Washington. *Quaternary Research* 47:356–8.

Washburn, A. L. 1988. *Mima mounds, an evaluation of proposed origins with special reference to the Puget Lowland.* Washington Division of Geology and Earth Resources Report of Investigations 29.

Yount, J. C., J. P. Minard, and G. R. Dembroff. 1993. *Geologic map of surficial deposits in the Seattle 30 x 60 quadrangle, Washington* (scale 1:100,000). U.S. Geological Survey Open File Report 93-233.

NORTH CASCADES

Babcock, R. S., and P. Misch. 1989. Origin of the Skagit migmatites, North Cascades Range, Washington State. *Mineralogy and Petrology* 101:485–95.

Barksdale, J. D. 1975. *Geology of the Methow Valley, Okanogan County, Washington.* Washington Division of Geology and Earth Resources Bulletin 68.

Beget, J. E. 1982. Recent volcanic activity at Glacier Peak. *Science* 215:1389–90.

———. 1984. Tephrochronology of Late Wisconsin deglaciation and Holocene glacier fluctuations near Glacier Peak, North Cascade Range, Washington. *Quaternary Research* 21:304–16.

Crowder, D. F., and R. W. Tabor. 1965. *Routes and Rocks.* Seattle, Wash.: The Mountaineers Books.

Erikson, E. H. Jr. 1969. Petrology of the composite Snoqualmie batholith, central Cascade Mountains, Washington. *Geological Society of America Bulletin* 80:2213–36.

———. 1977. Structure, stratigraphy, plutonism and volcanism of the central Cascades,

Washington. In *Geological excursions in the Pacific Northwest.* Seattle, Wash. Geological Society of America Annual Meeting.

Evans, J. E. 1994. Depositional history of the Eocene Chumstick Formation Implications of tectonic partitioning for the history of the Leavenworth and Entiat-Eagle Creek fault systems, Washington. *Tectonics* 13:1425–44.

Gallagher, M. P., E. H. Brown, and N. W. Walker. 1988. A new structural and tectonic interpretation of the western part of the Shuksan blueschist terrane, northwestern Washington. *Geological Society of America Bulletin* 100:1415–22.

Gardner, C., K. M. Scott, C. M. Miller, and others. 1995. *Potential volcanic hazards from future activity of Mount Baker, Washington.* U.S. Geological Survey Open File Report 95-498.

Gresens, R. L., C. W. Naeser, and J. T. Whetten. 1981. Stratigraphy and age of the Chumstick and Wenatchee Formations: Tertiary fluvial and lacustrine rocks, Chiwaukum graben, Washington. *Geological Society of America Bulletin* 92 (Part II):841–6.

Hildreth, W. 1996. Kulshan caldera—A Quaternary subglacial caldera in the North Cascades, Washington. *Geological Society of America Bulletin* 108:786–93.

Johnson, S. Y. 1991. Sedimentation and tectonic setting of the Chuckanut Formation, northwest Washington. *Washington Geology* 19:12–13.

Macloughlin, J. F. 1994. Migmatite to fault gouge: Fault rocks and the structural and tectonic evolution of the Nason terrane, North Cascade Mountains, Washington. In *Geologic field trips in the Pacific Northwest.* Edited by D. A. Swanson and R. A. Haugerud. Seattle, Wash.: Geological Society of America Annual Meeting. 2B1–17.

Mastin, L. G., and R. B. Waitt. 1995. *Is Glacier Peak a Dangerous Volcano?.* U.S. Geological Survey Open File Report 95-413.

McGroder, M. F., J. L. Garver, and V. S. Mallory. 1990. *Bedrock geologic maps, biostratigraphy and structure sections of the Methow Basin, Washington and British Columbia.* Washington Division of Geology and Earth Resources Open File Report 90-19.

Mustoe, G. E., and W. L. Gannaway. 1997. Paleogeography and paleontology of the Early Tertiary Chuckanut Formation, northwest Washington. *Washington Geology* 23:3–18.

Tepper, J. H. 1996. Petrology of mafic plutons associated with calc-alkaline granitoids, Chilliwack Batholith, North Cascades. Washington Journal of Petrology 37:1409–36.

SOUTH CASCADES

Allen, J. E. 1984. *The magnificent gateway: Geology of the Columbia River Gorge.* Forest Grove, Ore.: Timber Press.

Campbell, N. P. 1975. *A geologic road log over Chinook, White Pass, and Ellensburg to Yakima Highways.* Washington Division of Geology and Earth Resources Information Circular 54.

Crandell, D. R. 1983. *The geologic story of Mount Rainier.* Seattle, Wash.: Pacific Northwest National Parks and Forests Association.

Crandell, D.R., and R.K Fahnestock. 1965. *Rockfalls and avalanches from Little Tahoma Peak on Mount Rainier, Washington.* U.S. Geological Survey Bulletin 1221-A.

Crandell, D.R.. 1969. *Surficial geology of Mount Rainier National Park, Washington.* U.S. Geological Survey Bulletin 1288.

Crandell, D.R. 1973. *Potential hazards from future eruptions of Mount Rainier, Washington.* U.S. Geological Survey Miscellaneous Geologic Investigations Map I-836.

Decker, R., and B. Decker. 1993. *Road guide to Mount St. Helens.* Mariposa, Calif.: Double Decker Press.

———. 1996. *Road guide to Mount Rainier National Park.* Mariposa, Calif.: Double Decker Press.

Doukas, M. P. 1990. *Road guide to volcanic deposits of Mount St. Helens and vicinity, Washington.* U.S. Geological Survey Bulletin 1859.

Dragovich, J.D., Norman, D.K., Grisamer, C.L., Logan, R.L. and Anderson, G. (1998). *Geologic maps and interpreted geologic history of the Bow and Alger 7.5 minute quadrangles, western Skagit County, Washington.* Washington Division of Geology and Earth Resources Open File Report 98-530.

Driedger, C. L. 1986. *A visitor's guide to Mount Rainier glaciers.* Seattle, Wash.: Pacific Northwest National Parks and Forests Association.

Fiske, R. S., C. A. Hopson, and A. C. Water. 1963. *Geology of Mount Rainier National Park.* U.S. Geological Survey Professional Paper 444.

Halliday, W. R., and C. V. Larson. 1983. *Ape Cave.* Vancouver, Wash.: ABC Publishing.

Lescinsky, D. T., and T. W. Sisson. 1998. Ridge-forming, ice-bounded lava flows at Mount Rainier, Washington. *Geology* 26:351–4.

Krosec, M.A. 1987. *Geologic map of the Priest Rapids 1:100,000 quadrangle, Washington.* Washington Division of Geology and Earth Resources Open File Report 87-6.

Pringle, P. T. 1993. *Roadside geology of Mount St. Helens National Volcanic Monument and vicinity.* Washington Division of Geology and Earth Resources Information Circular 88.

Pringle, P. T., and others. 1994. Mount Rainier, a Decade Volcano GSA field trip. In *Geologic field trips in the Pacific Northwest,* chapter 2G. Edited by D. A. Swanson and R. A. Haugerud. Seattle, Wash.: University of Washington, Department of Geological Sciences.

Tabor, Rowland and Ralph Haugerud. 1999. *Geology of the north Cascades: a mountain mosaic.* Seattle, WA: The Mountaineers.

Schasse, H.W.. 1987. *Geologic map of the Mount Rainier 1:100,000 quadrangle, Washington.* Washington Division of Geology and Earth Resources Open File Report 87-16.

Sisson, T. W. 1995. *History and hazards of Mount Rainier Washington.* U.S. Geological Survey Open File Report 95-642.

University of Washington Department of Geological Sciences. 1963. *A geologic trip along Snoqualmie, Swauk, and Stevens Pass highways.* Revised by V. E. Livingston. Washington Division of Mines and Geology Information Circular 38.

Wolfe, E. W., and T. C. Pierson. 1995. *Volcanic hazard zonation for Mount St. Helens, 1995.* U.S. Geological Survey Open File Report 95-497.

COLUMBIA BASIN

Allen, J. E., Marjorie Burns, and S. C. Sargeant. 1986. *Cataclysms on the Columbia: a layman's guide to the features produced by the catastrophic Bretz floods in the Pacific Northwest.* Portland, Ore.: Timber Press.

Baker, V. R., and Dag Nummedal, eds. 1978. *The Channeled Scabland: A guide to the geomorphology of the Columbia Basin, Washington.* National Aeronautics and Space Administration.

Baker, V.R. 1983. *Late-Pleistocene fluvial systems,* in S.C. Porter, ed., *The Late Pleistocene,* v. 1 of *Late-Quaternary environments of the United States.* Minneapolis: University of Minnesota Press, p. 115-129.

Carson, R. J., and K. R. Pogue. 1996. *Flood basalts and glacier floods: Field trip guide to the geology of parts of Walla Walla, Franklin, and Columbia Counties, Washington.* Washington Division of Geology and Earth Resources Information Circular 90.

Crosby, C.J. and R.J. Carson. 1999. *Geology of Steamboat Rock, Grand Coulee Washington. Washington Geology,* Vol. 27 #2/3/4 p.3-8.

Mueller, Marge, and Ted Mueller. 1997. *Fire, faults and floods: A road and trail guide exploring the origins of the Columbia River Basin.* Moscow, Idaho: University of Idaho Press.

Parfit, Michael. 1995. *The floods that carved the West. Smithsonian* 26, no. 1:48–59.

Reidel, S. P., and P. R. Hooper, eds. 1989. *Volcanism and tectonism in the Columbia River flood-basalt province.* Geological Society of America Special Paper 239.

Weis, P. L., and W. L. Newman. 1989. *The Channeled Scablands of eastern Washington: The geologic story of the Spokane Flood.* Cheney, Wash.: Eastern Washington University Press.

OKANOGAN HIGHLANDS AND ROCKY MOUNTAINS

Campbell, C. D., and G. W. Thorsen. 1975. *Geology of the Sherman Peak and west half of the Kettle Falls quadrangles, Ferry County, Washington.* Revised 1980. Washington Division of Geology and Earth Resources Open File Report 75-3.

Bush, J. H., J. A. Morton, and P. W. Seward. 1992. Depositional and stratigraphic interpretations of the Cambrian and Ordovician Metaline Formation, northeastern Washington. *Washington Geology* 20:27–35.

Dutro, J. T. Jr., E. H. Gilmour, and N. L. Joseph. 1989. Paleozoic and Lower Triassic biostratigraphy of northeastern Washington. In *Geologic guidebook for Washington and adjacent areas.* Washington Division of Geology and Earth Resources Information Circular 86. 23–39.

Fox, K. F. Jr. 1994. Metamorphic core complexes within an Eocene extensional province in north-central Washington. In *The second symposium on the regional geology of the State of Washington.* Washington Division of Geology and Earth Resources Bulletin 80: 21–48.

Fox, K. F. Jr., and J. R. Wilson. 1989. Kettle gneiss dome—A metamorphic core complex in north-central Washington. In *Geologic guidebook for Washington and adjacent areas.* Information Circular 86. Olympia, Wash.: Washington Department of Natural Resources, Division of Geology and Earth Resources. 201–11.

Hurlow, H. A., and B. K. Nelson. 1993. U-Pb zircon and monazite ages for the Okanogan Range batholith, Washington: Implications for the magmatic and tectonic evolution of the southern Canadian and northern United States Cordillera. *Geological Society of America Bulletin* 105:231–40.

Martin, K. 1990. Paleomagnetism of speleothems in Gardner Cave, Washington. *National Speleological Society Bulletin* 52:87–94.

Washington Geology. Republic Centennial Issue, 1996. Various articles. *Washington Geology* 24, no. 2.

Watkinson, A. J., and M. A. Ellis. 1987. Recent structural analyses of the Kootenay Arc in northeastern Washington. In *Selected papers on the geology of Washington.* Washington Division of Geology and Earth Resources Bulletin 77: 41–53.

Wehr, W., and L. Barksdale. 1995. Implications of Middle Eocene feathers and crayfish from Republic, Washington. *Washington Geology* 23:6–10.

Wehr, W., and D. Q. Hopkins. 1994. The Eocene orchards and gardens of Republic Washington. *Washington Geology* 22:27–34.

Wolfe, J. A., and W. Wehr. 1987. *Middle Eocene dicotyledonous plants from Republic, northeastern Washington.* U.S. Geological Survey Bulletin 1597.

BLUE MOUNTAINS

Swanson, D. A., and T. L. Wright. 1983. *Geologic map of the Wenaha Toucannon Wilderness, Washington and Oregon* (scale 1:48,000). U.S. Geological Survey Miscellaneous Field Studies Map MF-1536.

THE FOUR CORNERS

Reidel, S. P., P. R. Hooper, G. D. Webster, and V. E. Camp. 1992. *Geologic map of southeastern Asotin County, Washington* (scale 1:48,000). Washington Division of Geology and Earth Resources Geologic Map GM-40.

Shilhanek, A. B. 1992. *The sedimentology, petrology and tectonic significance of the middle Eocene Flattery Breccia, Lyre Formation, northwestern Olympic Peninsula, Washington.* Masters Thesis, Western Washington University: Bellingham, Wash.

Snavely, P. D., A. R. Niem, and N. S. MacLeod. 1989. *Geology of the coastal area between Cape Flattery and Cape Alava, northwest Washington* (scale 1:24,000). U.S. Geological Survey Open File Report 89-114.

Snavely, P. D., A. R. Niem, and N. S. MacLeod. 1993. *Geologic map of the Cape Flattery, Clallam Bay, Ozette Lake and Lake Pleasant Quadrangles, northwestern Olympic Peninsula, Washington* (scale 1:48,000). U.S. Geological Survey Miscellaneous Investigations Series Map I-1946.

Vallier, Tracy. 1998. *Islands and rapids: A geologic story of Hells Canyon.* Lewiston, Idaho: Confluence Press.

Wells, R. E. 1989. *Geologic map of the Cape Disappointment–Naselle River area, Pacific and Wahkiakum Counties, Washington* [scale?]. U.S. Geological Survey Miscellaneous Investigations Series Map I-1832.

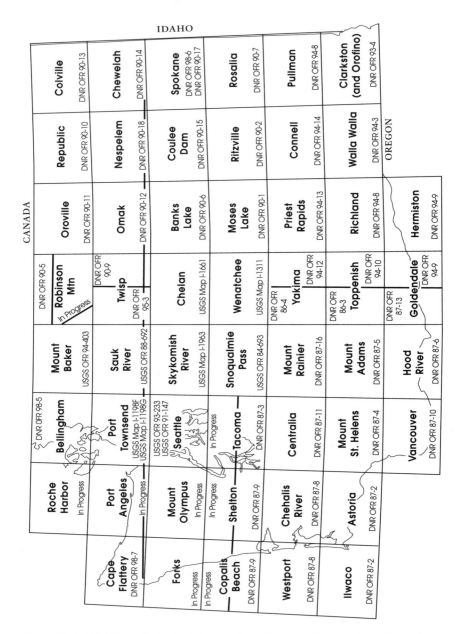

figure 16. 1:100,000-scale Geologic Maps of Washington. The numbers of completed maps by the U.S. Geological Survey (USGS) and the Division of Geology and Earth Resources (DGER) are shown within quadrangles. Maps can be ordered from USGS ESIC, Room 135, 904 West Riverside Avenue, Spokane, Washington, 99201. USGS open-file reports can be purchased from USGS Information Services, Box 25286, Denver, Colorado, 80225. DGER maps and open-file reports can be ordered from DGER, Box 47007, Olympia, Washington, 98504-7007.

Index

About the Authors

Scott Babcock (below, left) was perhaps destined to be a geologist because he was born in Butte, Montana. His birthplace was later consumed by the Berkeley Pit of the Anaconda Copper Company and is now one of the most toxic places on earth. Scott is a Professor of Geology at Western Washington University and is trying to compensate for his heritage by spending as much time as possible in toxin-free environments, such as the locations of most of the hikes described in this book. Contact Scott at babcock@cc.www.edu.

Bob Carson (below, right) is Professor of Geology and Environmental Studies at Whitman College in Walla Walla, Washington. After he earned an A.B. in geology from Cornell University, he worked for Texaco Inc. His other geology degrees are an M.S. from Tulane University and a Ph.D. from the University of Washington. His interests are in the earth and environmental sciences, and his courses deal with resources and pollution, human interaction with the biosphere, glaciers, volcanoes, water, landforms, and natural hazards. A whitewater guide and a member of the American Alpine Club, he has led field trips in Africa, Eurasia, South America, and throughout North America.

THE MOUNTAINEERS, founded in 1906, is a nonprofit outdoor activity and conservation club, whose mission is "to explore, study, preserve, and enjoy the natural beauty of the outdoors. . . . " Based in Seattle, Washington, the club is now the third-largest such organization in the United States, with 15,000 members and five branches throughout Washington State.

The Mountaineers sponsors both classes and year-round outdoor activities in the Pacific Northwest, which include hiking, mountain climbing, ski-touring, snowshoeing, bicycling, camping, kayaking and canoeing, nature study, sailing, and adventure travel. The club's conservation division supports environmental causes through educational activities, sponsoring legislation, and presenting informational programs. All club activities are led by skilled, experienced volunteers, who are dedicated to promoting safe and responsible enjoyment and preservation of the outdoors.

If you would like to participate in these organized outdoor activities or the club's programs, consider a membership in The Mountaineers. For information and an application, write or call The Mountaineers, Club Headquarters, 300 Third Avenue West, Seattle, Washington 98119; (206) 284-6310.

The Mountaineers Books, an active, nonprofit publishing program of the club, produces guidebooks, instructional texts, historical works, natural history guides, and works on environmental conservation. All books produced by The Mountaineers are aimed at fulfilling the club's mission.

Send or call for our catalog of more than 450 outdoor titles.
The Mountaineers Books
1001 SW Klickitat Way, Suite 201
Seattle, WA 98134
800-553-4453
mbooks@mountaineers.org
www.mountaineersbooks.org

Other titles you may enjoy from The Mountaineers Books:

Also included in the **HIKING GEOLOGY** series:
HIKING COLORADO'S GEOLOGY, *Ralph Hopkins & Lindy Birkel*
HIKING OREGON'S GEOLOGY, *Ellen Bishop & John Allen*

GEOLOGY OF THE NORTH CASCADES: A Mountain Mosaic, *Rowland Tabor & Ralph Haugerud*
Comprehensive geologic summary of Washington's North Cascade region. Appeals to hikers as well as amateur geologists.

PAGES OF STONE: Geology of Western National Parks and Monuments, Grand Canyon and Plateau Country, *Halka Chronic*
A fascinating geological tour through eight national parks and eleven national monuments. Perfect for hikers or car travelers.

100 CLASSIC HIKES IN™ WASHINGTON: North Cascades, Olympics, Mount Rainier & South Cascades, Alpine Lakes, Glacier Peak, *Ira Spring & Harvey Manning*
A full-color guide to Washington's finest trails. The essential classic for hiking this picturesque state including maps, photos, and full details you need to plan the perfect trip.

BEST HIKES WITH CHILDREN™ IN WESTERN WASHINGTON & THE CASCADES, 2nd Edition, Volumes 1&2, *Joan Burton*
These are the best-selling books in our **Best Hikes With Children™ Series**. Appealing to families, seniors, and anyone looking for fun and easy outings in the incomparable Cascade and Olympic mountains.

50 HIKES IN™ MOUNT RAINIER NATIONAL PARK, 4th Edition, *Ira Spring & Harvey Manning*
The complete, authoritative hiking guide to the Northwest's most popular national park with full-color photos and maps throughout. Written by the "godfathers" of Pacific Northwest hiking with more than 25 guidebooks to their credit.

WASHINGTON STATE PARKS: A Complete Recreation Guide, *Marge & Ted Mueller*
This is the most well-known, thorough, and reliable guide to all of Washington's beautiful state parks. Gives details for almost 200 state recreation areas and year-round activities to provide an outdoor lover's dream.

EXPLORING WASHINGTON'S WILD AREAS: A Guide for Hikers, Backpackers, Climbers, X-C Skiers, & Paddlers, *Marge & Ted Mueller*
A guide to Washington state's 55 federally reserved backcountry areas. Perfect for those seeking solitary, respectful recreation in spectacular natural settings.